WITHDRAWN
Monroe Coll. Library

MONROE COLLEGE LIBRARY

3 7340 01086161 2

Consumer, Homemaking, and Personal Services

5

D1364757

Editorial Advisory Board

Thelma T. Daley, Ed.D., NCC, Assistant Professor, Department of Counseling, Loyola College; former Coordinator of Guidance, Baltimore County (MD) Public Schools; Chairman, Woodstock Job Corps Center Industry/Vocational Advisory Board; former Chairman, Counseling and Human Development Foundation; former Secretary-Treasurer, National Board for Certified Counselors; former Chairman of the National Advisory Council on Career Education; former President of the American Personnel and Guidance Association; former President of the American School Counselor Association.

S. Norman Feingold, Ed.D., President, National Career and Counseling Services, Washington, DC; Honorary National Director, B'nai B'rith Career and Counseling Services; former President of the American Association of Counseling and Development; vocational expert to the Social Security Administration; listed in *Who's Who in America;* author of more than 100 books and articles on careers and counseling; licensed psychologist; former President of the National Career and Development Association; accredited by the National Board of Certified Counselors; member of The World Future Society; member of The National Press Club.

Bill Katz, Ph.D., Professor, School of Information Science and Policy, State University of New York at Albany; editor, *Magazines for Libraries* and *Magazines for Young People;* contributing editor to *Library Journal* and editor of *The Reference Librarian;* editor, *History of the Book* series; contributing editor and writer for *Encyclopaedia Britannica Yearbook;* author of *Reference Work* and other books and articles on collection development, reference services, periodicals, and related subjects.

The Career Information Center includes:

Agribusiness, Environment, and Natural Resources / 1

Communications and the Arts / 2

Computers, Business, and Office / 3

Construction / 4

Consumer, Homemaking, and Personal Services / 5

Engineering, Science, and Technology / 6

Health / 7

Hospitality and Recreation / 8

Manufacturing / 9

Marketing and Distribution / 10

Public and Community Services / 11

Transportation / 12

Employment Trends and Master Index / 13

Consumer, Homemaking, and Personal Services

5

Career Information Center

Seventh Edition

Macmillan Reference USA
New York

Editorial Staff

Project Director: Frances A. Wiser

Writers: Tom Conklin, Suzanne J. Murdico, Judith Peacock

Researchers/Bibliographers: Christopher D. Binkley, Peter Michael Gee

Editors: Jacqueline Morais, Joseph B. Pirret, Meera Vaidyanathan

Copyediting Supervisor: Maureen Ryan Pancza

Photo Editor: Sara Matthews

Production Supervisors: Devan Paine Anding, William A. Murray

Production Assistant: Jessica Swenson

Interior Design: Maxson Crandall

Electronic Preparation: Cynthia C. Feldner, Fiona Torphy

Electronic Production: Rob Ehlers, Lisa Evans-Skopas, Deirdre Sheean, Isabelle Ulsh

Acknowledgments: It would be impossible to acknowledge the many people who gave their help, their time, and their experience to this project. However, we especially want to thank all the people at unions and trade and professional associations for their help in providing information and photographs. We also wish to thank the U.S. Department of Labor, Bureau of Labor Statistics, for providing up-to-date statistics, salary information, and employment projections for all the job profiles.

Copyright © 1999, 1996 by Macmillan Reference USA

All rights reserved. No part of this book may be reproduced or transmitted in any form or by any means, electronic or mechanical, including photocopying, recording, or by any information storage and retrieval system, without permission in writing from the publisher.

Developed and produced by Visual Education Corporation,
Princeton, New Jersey

Macmillan Library Reference USA
1633 Broadway
New York, NY 10019

ISSN 1082-703X

ISBN 0-02-864915-X (set)

ISBN 0-02-864906-0 (volume 5)

Printed in the United States of America

printing number
1 2 3 4 5 6 7 8 9 10

This paper meets the requirements of ANSI/NISO Z39.48-1992 (Permanence of Paper).

Contents

Job Summary Chart

Job	Salary	Education/ Training	Employment Outlook	Page
Job Profiles—No Specialized Training				
Chauffeur	Average—$30,000 to $50,000	License	Fair	27
Child Care Worker, Private	Varies—see profile	None	Very good	28
Companion	Varies—see profile	None	Very good	30
Dry Cleaning Worker	Varies—see profile	None	Very good	32
Gardener and Groundskeeper	Average—$220 to $410 a week	None	Good	34
Home Caterer	Varies—see profile	None	Good	36
Homemaker	Varies—see profile	None	Varies—see profile	38
Housekeeper, Domestic	Average—$5.15 to $10 an hour	None	Very good	40
Laundry Worker	Average—$5.15 to $8 an hour	None	Very good	42
Personal Service Worker	Average—$5.15 to $25 an hour	Varies—see profile	Good	44
Personal Shopper	Varies—see profile	Varies—see profile	Good	45
Pest Control Worker	Starting—$5.15 to $7.50 an hour Average—$26,000 to $29,000	None	Very good	46
Pet Care Worker	Varies—see profile	None	Very good	48
Professional Organizer	Average—$25 to $125 an hour	None	Very good	50
Rug and Carpet Cleaner	Average—$240 to $500 a week	None	Good	52
Shoe Repairer	Average—$350 to $500 a week	None	Poor	54
Swimming Pool Servicer	Starting—$210 to $250 a week	High school	Good	56
Window Cleaner	Average—$5.75 to $8 an hour	None	Good	57

★ High-growth job

Job	Salary	Education/Training	Employment Outlook	Page
Job Profiles—Some Specialized Training/Experience				
Appliance Service Worker	Average—$350 to $760 a week	Varies—see profile	Fair	59
Barber and Hairstylist	Starting—$15,660	Voc/tech school; license	Good	60
Consumer Credit Counselor	Starting—$13,000 to $20,000	High school plus training	Very good	62
Cosmetologist	Starting—$200 to $250 a week Average—$20,000 to $30,000	Voc/tech school; license	Very good	64
Custom Tailor and Dressmaker	Average—$8 to $12 an hour	High school plus training	Fair	66
Custom Upholsterer	Average—$370 a week	Varies—see profile	Fair	69
Dietetic Technician	Average—$300 to $400 a week	Varies—see profile	Very good	71
Electrologist	Average—$35 to $75 an hour	Voc/tech school	Good	73
Floral Designer	Starting—$5.75 Average—$7 to $10 an hour	High school plus training	Very good	74
Home Security Consultant	Varies—see profile	High school plus training	Good	76
Jeweler	Varies—see profile	Varies—see profile	Fair	78
Locksmith	Average—$20,000 to $30,000	High school plus training	Good	81
Massage Therapist	Average—$20 to $50 an hour	Voc/tech school	Good	83
Nanny	Starting—$300 to $375 a week	Varies—see profile	Excellent	85
Piano and Organ Tuner and Technician	Average—$20,000 to $40,000	High school plus training	Varies—see profile	87
Watch Repairer	Starting—$450 to $500 a week Average—$30,000 to $35,000	Varies—see profile	Poor	90
Wedding Consultant	Varies—see profile	Varies—see profile	Fair	91

⭐ **High-growth job**

Job	Salary	Education/Training	Employment Outlook	Page
Job Profiles—Advanced Training/Experience				
Appraiser	Varies—see profile	Varies—see profile	Fair	94
Business Family and Consumer Scientist	Starting—$17,000 to $35,000	College	Good	96
Consumer Advocate	Varies—see profile	Varies—see profile	Varies—see profile	98
Dietitian and Nutritionist	Varies—see profile	College plus training	Good	100
Divorce Mediator	Varies—see profile	College	Good	102
Embalmer	$590 a week	High school plus training; license	Good	103
Family and Consumer Science Researcher	Starting—$18,000 Average—$25,000 to $37,000	College	Fair	105
Family and Consumer Science Teacher	Starting—$20,000 to $22,000	College	Fair	107
Funeral Director	Average—$590 a week	Voc/tech school; license	Excellent	110
Interior Designer	Average—$590 a week	High school plus training	Good	112
Personal Exercise Trainer	Average—$50 to $200 per session	College	Good	114

⭐ **High-growth job**

Job Summary Chart **ix**

Foreword

The seventh edition of the *Career Information Center* mirrors the ongoing changes in the job market caused by new technological and economic developments. These developments continue to change what Americans do in the workplace and how they do it. People have a critical need for up-to-date information to help them make career decisions.

The *Career Information Center* is an individualized resource for people of all ages and at all stages of career development. It has been recognized as an excellent reference for librarians, counselors, educators, and other providers of job information. It is ideally suited for use in libraries, career resource centers, and guidance offices, as well as in adult education centers and other facilities where people seek information about job opportunities, careers, and their own potential in the workforce.

This seventh edition updates many of the features that made the earlier editions so useful.

- A Job Summary Chart, a quick reference guide, appears in the front section of each volume to help readers get the basic facts and compare the jobs described in the volume. High-growth jobs are highlighted and identified with a star.

- Each volume of the *Career Information Center* begins with an overview of the job market in that field. These "Looking Into . . ." sections have been completely revised and updated. They also include new graphs, charts, and boxes providing information such as industry snapshots and the fastest-growing and top-dollar jobs in the field.

- Each volume has a section called "Getting Into . . . ," which contains useful information on entering the particular field. It offers self-evaluation tips and decision-making help; and it relates possible job choices to individual interests, abilities, and work characteristics. There is also practical information on job hunting, using the Internet and classified ads, preparing resumes, and handling interviews. "Getting Into . . ." also includes a section on employee rights.

- Each volume has a listing of all job profiles in the series and the volumes in which they appear, making access to profiles in other volumes easy.

- *Career Information Center* contains 676 job profiles in which more than 3,000 jobs are discussed. Each profile describes work characteristics, education and training requirements, getting the job, advancement and employment outlook, working conditions, and earnings and benefits.

- Job summaries, provided for each job profile, highlight the education or training required, salary range, and employment outlook.

- Volume 13 has been revised to reflect career concerns of the 1990s and employment trends through the year 2006. This volume includes updated articles on benefits, employment law, health in the workplace, job search strategies, job training, job opportunities at home, adjusting to job loss, and identifying opportunities for retraining.

- More than 560 photographs appear in the *Career Information Center,* including many new photos. Profile photos provide a visual glimpse of life on the job. Photos have been selected to give the reader a sense of what it feels like to be in a specific field or job.

- Updated bibliographies in each volume include recommended readings and World Wide Web sites in specific job areas. Additional titles for the vocational counselor are included in Volume 13.

- Each volume also contains a comprehensive directory of accredited occupational education and vocational training facilities listed by occupational area and grouped by state. Directory materials are generated from the IPEDS (Integrated Postsecondary Education Data System) database of the U.S. Department of Education.

The *Career Information Center* recognizes the importance not only of job selection, but also of job holding, coping, and applying life skills. No other career information publication deals with work attitudes so comprehensively.

Using the Career Information Center

The *Career Information Center* is designed to meet the needs of many people—students, people just entering or reentering the job market, those dissatisfied with present jobs, those without jobs—anyone of any age who is not sure what to do for a living. The *Career Information Center* is for people who want help in making career choices. It combines the comprehensiveness of an encyclopedia with the format and readability of a magazine. Many professionals, including counselors, librarians, and teachers will find it a useful guidance and reference tool.

The *Career Information Center* is organized by occupational interest area rather than in alphabetical order. Jobs that have something in common are grouped together. In that way people who do not know exactly what job they want can read about a number of related jobs. The *Career Information Center* classifies jobs that have something in common into clusters. The classification system is adapted from the cluster organization used by the U.S. Department of Labor. Each volume of the *Career Information Center* explores one of 12 occupational clusters.

To use the *Career Information Center*, first select the volume that treats the occupational area that interests you most. Because there are many ways to group occupations, you may not find a particular job in the volume in which you look for it. In that case, check the central listing of all the profiles, which is located in the front of Volumes 1 through 12. This listing provides the names of all profiles and the volume number in which they appear. Volume 13 also includes a comprehensive index of all the jobs covered in the first 12 volumes.

After selecting a volume or volumes, investigate the sections that you feel would be most helpful. It isn't necessary to read these volumes from cover to cover. They are arranged so that you can go directly to the specific information you want. Here is a description of the sections included in each volume.

- **Job Summary Chart**—This chart presents in tabular form the basic data from all profiles in the volume: salary, education and training, employment outlook, and the page on which you can find the job profile. Jobs with a high growth potential are highlighted and starred.

- **Looking Into . . .**—This overview of the occupational cluster describes the opportunities, characteristics, and trends in that particular field.

- **Getting Into . . .**—This how-to guide can help you decide what jobs may be most satisfying to you and what strategies you can use to get the right job. You will learn, for example, how to write an effective resume, how to complete an application form, what to expect in an interview, how to use networking, and what to do if someone has discriminated against you.

- **Job Summary**—These summaries, located at the beginning of each profile, highlight the most important facts about the job: education and training, salary range, and employment outlook.

Education and Training indicates whether the job requires no education, high school, college, advanced degree, voc/tech school, license, or training.

Salary Range is given as an approximate yearly wage unless "a week" or "an hour" is noted. These are average salaries that may vary significantly from region to region.

Employment Outlook is based on several factors, including the Bureau of Labor Statistics' projections through the year 2006. The ratings are defined as follows: *poor* means there is a projected employment decrease of 1 percent or more; *fair* means there is a projected employment increase of 0 to 13 percent; *good* means there is a projected employment increase of 14 to 26 percent; *very good* means there is a projected employment increase of 27 to 40 percent; and *excellent* means there is a projected employment increase of 41 percent or more. The outlook is then determined by looking at the ratings and other employment factors. For example, a job with excellent projected employment growth in which many more people are entering the field than there are jobs available will have an outlook that is good rather than excellent.

For all categories, the phrase *Varies—see profile* means the reader must consult the profile for the information, which is too extensive to include in the Job Summary.

- **Job Profiles**—The job profiles are divided into three categories based on the level of training required to get the job. Each profile explores a number of related jobs and covers seven major topics: description of the job being profiled, the education and training requirements, ways to get the job, advancement possibilities and employment outlook, the working conditions, the earnings and benefits, and places to go for more information.

Job Profiles—No Specialized Training includes jobs that require no education or previous work experience beyond high school.

Job Profiles—Some Specialized Training/Experience includes jobs that require one, two, or three years of vocational training or college, or work experience beyond high school.

Job Profiles—Advanced Training/Experience includes jobs that require a bachelor's degree or advanced degree from a college or university and/or equivalent work experience in that field.

- **Resources—General Career Information** includes a selected bibliography of the most recent books, audiovisual materials, and web sites on general career information, how-to books on such topics as resume writing and preparing for tests, and useful computer software. In addition, there are special sections of readings for the career counselor in Volume 13.

- **Resources**—Each volume also contains a bibliography of books, audiovisual materials, and web sites for specific fields covered in that volume.

- **Directory of Institutions Offering Career Training**—This listing, organized first by career area, then by state, includes the schools that offer occupational training beyond high school. For jobs requiring a bachelor's degree or an advanced degree, check a library for college catalogs and appropriate directories.

- **Index**—This index, which is located at the end of each volume, lists every job mentioned in that volume. It serves not only to cross-reference all the jobs in the volume but also to show related jobs in the field. For example, under the entry LICENSED PRACTICAL NURSE, you will find Home Health Aide, Nurse's Aide and Orderly, and Ward Clerk. In addition, the "profile includes" part of an entry lists other jobs that are mentioned in the profile, in this case Licensed Vocational Nurse and Registered Nurse.

- **Volume 13, Employment Trends and Master Index**—This volume includes several features that will help both the job seeker and the career counselor. A useful correlation guide provides the *DOT (Dictionary of Occupational Titles)* number of most of the job profiles in the *Career Information Center.* There is also a special section on career information for Canada. The updated and revised "Employment Trends" section contains articles on health in the workplace; employment projections through the year 2006; job search strategies; employment trends for women, minorities, immigrants, older workers, and the physically challenged; employment demographics; benefits programs; training; employment opportunities at home; employment law; adjusting to job loss; identifying opportunities for retraining. All articles have been written by authorities in these fields. The articles provide job seekers and career professionals with an overview of current employment issues, career opportunities, and outlooks. Finally, there is a master index to all the jobs included in all 13 volumes.

The *Career Information Center* is exactly what it says it is—a center of the most useful and pertinent information you need to explore and choose from the wide range of job and career possibilities. The *Career Information Center* provides you with a solid foundation of information for getting a satisfying job or rewarding career.

Comprehensive Job Profile List

The following list includes job profiles and the corresponding volume number.

Accountant, 3
Accountant, Public, 3
Actor, 2
Actuary, 3
Acupuncturist, 7
Administrative Assistant, 3
Admitting Clerk, 7
Adult Education Worker, 11
Advertising Account Executive, 10
Advertising Copywriter, 2
Advertising Manager, 10
Aerospace Engineer, 6
Aerospace Industry, 9
Aerospace Technician, 6
Agricultural Engineer, 1
Agricultural Supply Sales Worker, 1
Agricultural Technician, 1
Agronomist, 1
AIDS Counselor, 7
Air Pollution Control Technician, 1
Air Traffic Controller, 12
Air-Conditioning and Heating
    Technician, 4
Air-Conditioning Engineer, 6
Air-Conditioning, Heating, and
    Refrigeration Mechanic, 4
Aircraft Mechanic, 12
Airline Baggage and Freight Handler, 12
Airline Dispatcher, 12
Airline Flight Attendant, 12
Airline Reservations Agent, 12
Airline Ticket Agent, 12
Airplane Pilot, 12
Airport Manager, 12
Airport Utility Worker, 12
All-Round Machinist, 9
Alternative Fuels Vehicle Technician, 6
Aluminum and Copper Industry, 9
Ambulance Driver, 7
Amusement and Recreation
    Attendant, 8
Anatomist, 6
Anesthesiologist, 7
Animal Caretaker, 8
Announcer, 2
Anthropologist, 6
Apparel Industry, 9
Appliance Service Worker, 5
Appraiser, 5
Archaeologist, 6
Architect, 4
Architectural Drafter, 4
Architectural Model Maker, 4
Armed Services Career, 11
Art Director, 2
Art and Music Therapist, 7
Artificial Intelligence Specialist, 6
Artist, 2

Assembler, 9
Astronomer, 6
Athletic Coach, 8
Athletic Trainer, 8
Auctioneer, 10
Auditor, 3
Auto Body Repairer, 12
Auto Parts Counter Worker, 10
Auto Sales Worker, 10
Automated Manufacturing Manager, 9
Automobile Driving Instructor, 12
Automotive Exhaust Emissions
    Technician, 12
Automotive Industry, 9
Automotive Mechanic, 12
Avionics Technician, 12

Bank Clerk, 3
Bank Officer, 3
Bank Teller, 3
Barber and Hairstylist, 5
Bartender, 8
Bicycle Mechanic, 12
Biochemist, 6
Biological Technician, 6
Biologist, 6
Biomedical Engineer, 6
Biomedical Equipment Technician, 7
Blacksmith and Forge Shop Worker, 9
Blood Bank Technologist, 7
Boat Motor Mechanic, 12
Boiler Tender, 9
Boilermaking Worker, 9
Bookbinder, 2
Bookkeeper, 3
Border Patrol Agent, 11
Botanist, 6
Bricklayer, 4
Broadcast Technician, 2
Brokerage Clerk, 3
Building Custodian, 11
Building Inspector, 4
Business Family and Consumer
    Scientist, 5
Business Machine Operator, 3

Cable Television Engineer, 2
Cable Television Technician, 2
CAD Specialist, 6
Cafeteria Attendant, 8
CAM Operator, 9
Camera Operator, 2
Candy, Soft Drink, and Ice Cream
    Manufacturing Worker, 1
Car Rental Agent, 12
Car Wash Worker, 12
Cardiac-Monitor Technician/
    Perfusionist, 7

Cardiology Technologist, 7
Carpenter, 4
Cartographer, 1
Cartoonist, 2
Cashier, 10
Casino Worker, 8
Caterer, 8
Cement Mason, 4
Ceramic Engineer, 6
Ceramics Industry, 9
Chauffeur, 5
Cheese Industry Worker, 1
Chemical Engineer, 6
Chemical Technician, 6
Chemist, 6
Child Care Worker, Private, 5
Chiropractor, 7
Choreographer, 2
City Manager, 11
Civil Engineer, 4
Civil Engineering Technician, 4
Claim Adjuster, 3
Claim Examiner, 3
College Student Personnel Worker, 11
College/University Administrator, 3
Commercial Artist, 2
Companion, 5
Comparison Shopper, 10
Compensation Specialist, 3
Composer, 2
Composite Technician, 9
Computer Artist, 2
Computer Consultant, 3
Computer Database Manager, 3
Computer Network Technician, 3
Computer Operator, 3
Computer Programmer, 3
Computer Security Engineer, 3
Computer Servicer, 3
Computer Software Documentation
    Writer, 3
Construction Electrician, 4
Construction Equipment Dealer, 4
Construction Equipment Mechanic, 4
Construction Laborer, 4
Construction Millwright, 4
Construction Supervisor, 4
Consumer Advocate, 5
Consumer Credit Counselor, 5
Controller, 3
Convention Specialist, 8
Cook and Chef, 8
Cooperative Extension Service Worker, 1
Corrections Officer, 11
Correspondence Clerk, 3
Cosmetologist, 5
Court Clerk, 11
Craftsperson, 2

Looking Into Consumer, Homemaking, and Personal Services

Although consumer, homemaking, and personal services are as diverse as dog grooming, wedding consulting, window cleaning, and consumer advocacy, they all have one important thing in common: service. Service-producing industries can be divided into several areas including transportation, business, communications, finance, health, retail trade, utilities, and government.

The service-producing industries are the largest and fastest-growing segment of the American economy. A primary reason for this rapid growth is that women have been moving into the labor force in unprecedented numbers since the early 1960s. Before that time, most women worked within the home as homemakers. They took care of such jobs as housecleaning, cooking, laundry, shopping, errands, and child care. Times have changed, however, and the majority of women now work outside the home. Consequently, they have less time for traditional homemaking tasks. For this reason, many of these tasks have been transferred to the marketplace.

The growth of technology also has created a demand for services. As everyday lifestyles become more complicated, Americans have come to depend on the specialized knowledge of others. Many Americans now also have more disposable income to spend on the services of others.

Another reason for the growth of the service sector is the increase in the number of unmarried people who often live alone and hold jobs. Single people do not have spouses to share household tasks or run errands. On a typical day, for example, a single person may get up in the morning and put on clothes that were washed and pressed at a local laundry. Before leaving for work, she may leave a note for the house-cleaning service and telephone the dog-walking service with instructions. At lunchtime, she may make an appointment with her personal shopper to select clothes for an upcoming business function. On her way home from work, she may stop at the gym for a workout with her personal trainer and then meet a friend at a favorite restaurant. In just one day, this single person has used a wide range of consumer, homemaking, and personal services.

Unlike workers in many other industries, people employed in the service industries do not produce a tangible commodity, such as a television. Instead, they help people. Their work may involve caring for people, entertaining them, supplying them with information, motivating them, or making their lives easier in countless ways.

Variety is a key feature of the jobs in consumer, homemaking, and personal services. There are jobs to suit a wide range of interests, skills, and education. Some jobs have a long history, whereas others are new to the workplace. Despite their great variety, these jobs do have one major trait in common—they are all concerned with helping individuals and families in their daily lives.

Many people employ service workers to perform time-saving services, such as dog training.

CONSUMER SERVICES

The United States is a nation of shoppers. Americans buy most of their food, clothing, and household items. Some even hire people to help them care for the things they own. The workers they hire groom dogs, organize closets and drawers, tune pianos, and dry-clean clothes. Other consumer services workers repair products such as washing machines, cameras, and VCRs. Another area of consumer services provides purchasing assistance, from wedding consulting to home shopping via computer. Workers in this area also include credit counselors and consumer advocates.

Pet Care

Americans own a total of about 124 million cats and dogs, and they spend millions of dollars caring for their pets. Boarding kennels, obedience classes, and grooming salons have become well-established businesses in many communities. New services are being offered as well, such as self-service dog washes, pet-walking and pet-finding services, and home pet day care. Pet owners can even consult a pet psychologist if their pet shows signs of emotional problems.

Repair and Maintenance

Technological advances have affected jobs in repair and maintenance. On the one hand, technology has led to a decrease in the number of workers in certain jobs. For example, the need for watch repairers has declined dramatically. Modern technology, mass production techniques, and new materials have resulted in the availability of inexpensive watches. Now many consumers choose to buy a new watch rather than pay to have an inexpensive watch repaired.

At the same time, technology has increased the number of other jobs. For example, modern homes are equipped with a variety of complex and expensive electronic appliances. Few Americans have the specialized knowledge or tools to maintain and repair them. As a result, they turn to experts for the maintenance and repair of these items.

A weak economy is usually a bonanza for repair and maintenance. During an economic slowdown,

Industry Snapshots

CHILD CARE

With more mothers entering the workforce, the demand for well-trained child care workers will remain high. Increased corporate involvement in child care is one reason why the number of public child care workers is expected to grow by more than 36 percent through the beginning of the next century.

FUNERAL SERVICES

The funeral business is highly regulated. Nearly one-third of all funeral directors are self-employed, but the current trend is for national companies to take over family-run chains. Many funeral homes are now offering related services such as support groups for dealing with grief.

APPLIANCE REPAIR

Technological advances have led to a decrease in the number of workers needed in certain occupations in the appliance industry. Other jobs have been created, however, because of technological advancements that have led to the development of appliances requiring specialized knowledge to repair. The repair and maintenance industry usually fluctuates with the economy, as people's budget priorities change.

PERSONAL SERVICES

Personal service agencies primarily offer services that people could do themselves if they had the time. Personal service workers provide an array of time-saving services—from running errands to planning birthday parties. As the demand for such services has increased, some personal service agencies have begun franchising.

PET CARE

Every year Americans spend millions of dollars on pet care, and this trend is expected to continue. In particular, services that pamper pets will increase. Owners who are so inclined can treat their animals to a day at the pet salon. Pet psychologists may be consulted if cats and dogs show signs of emotional problems.

CONSUMER ADVOCACY

Since its inception in the 1960s, consumer advocacy has grown into a large industry employing thousands of workers. Most jobs for consumer advocates can be found in government. Nearly every state has an office of consumer protection. At the federal level the office is known as the U.S. Office of Consumer Affairs.

such as the recession of the early 1990s, people are less likely to buy expensive, new items. Instead they spend smaller sums of money to make their old, worn items last longer. This means jobs for repair and maintenance workers.

Fashion Services

Buying clothes can be not only expensive but also time-consuming. Fashions change, and professionals who want to "dress for success" must keep up with these changes. It also takes time to comparison shop and look for bargains. Because working Americans have less and less free time to devote to shopping, a new group of workers has emerged to assist consumers.

Personal Shoppers Many personal shoppers work for large department stores, where they assist customers in choosing clothing and building a wardrobe. Their service is usually free to customers. Most personal shoppers earn a salary plus commission, so while it is their job to assist customers, it is also their job to sell clothing. As personal shoppers get to know each customer's lifestyle and tastes, they are better able to meet the customer's needs and save the customer time.

A busy executive, for example, may call her personal shopper about an upcoming business trip. By the time the executive gets to the store, the personal shopper has already set aside several items that she thinks are suitable for both the customer and the occasion. The executive examines the personal shopper's selections, makes a few decisions, and pays for the clothes. Less than an hour later, her shopping trip is finished. Personal shoppers may cut down on shopping time even more by delivering clothes to the customer.

Image Consultants Image consultants take personal shopping a step further. They may visit clients' homes to look over clothes in their closet, help them decide what look is best for their line of work, and then advise them on how to achieve that look. Many professionals have found that having an image consultant is a boost to their confidence on the job.

Personal shoppers work in the field of consumer services. They provide purchasing assistance to consumers who hire them.

Wedding Consulting

An area similar to image consulting is wedding consulting. Wedding consultants assist the bride-to-be in purchasing her bridal gown, choosing dresses for her attendants, and selecting items such as jewelry, shoes, and flowers. Many wedding consultants know the rules of etiquette and can advise a nervous bride or groom on almost any wedding-related matter. Wedding consultants may also assist with the other purchases required of a large traditional wedding, from caterers and reception halls to limousine services and the gift registry.

Shopping for a wedding gift has become easier since the advent of computerized registries. Most stores that have these registries employ wedding consultants to help brides and grooms select everything from china to bath towels. The consultants enter the choices on a computer and then provide wedding guests with a printed list to refer to as they shop for a gift.

Home Shopping

Another area of consumer services that is growing rapidly is home shopping—any means of purchasing products from home, including catalogs, phone sales, cable TV shopping networks, and on-line computer shopping. After the purchase is made, the products are delivered directly to the consumer's home.

Summer Jobs in Consumer, Homemaking, and Personal Services

FAMILY AND CONSUMER SCIENCE

Summer internships are available in nutrition, research, family and consumer science, and social services. Clerical, laboratory assistant, and catering assistant jobs are also available. Contact:
- hospitals
- food, clothing, and home care products companies
- public and private research facilities
- Cooperative Extension Service

Sources of Information

The American Association of Family and Consumer Sciences
1555 King Street, Suite 400
Alexandria, VA 22314
(703) 706-4600
www.aafcs.org

National Association of Extension Home Economists
3900 East Camelback, Suite 200
Phoenix, AZ 85018
(602)412-5386

CHILD CARE

Many summer jobs are available for both daytime and live-in child care workers. Working parents may hire child care workers or babysitters to care for schoolchildren during the summer vacation. Sometimes it is possible to find a child care position that involves travel. Contact:
- families with young children
- employment agencies
- local school and community groups
- day care facilities

Sources of Information

National Association for Family Child Care
206 Sixth Avenue, Suite 900
Des Moines, IA 50309-4018

National Association of Child Care Resource and Referral Agencies
1319 F Street, NW, Suite 810
Washington, DC 20004
(202) 393-5501

HOUSEKEEPERS AND COMPANIONS

Companions are often needed to accompany people during summer travel and vacations. Housekeepers can help keep homes running smoothly during the summer or can look after homes while people are away. Contact:
- employment agencies
- social service agencies
- newspapers

Sources of Information

National Association for Home Care
228 Seventh Street, SE
Washington, DC 20003
www.nahc.org

National Council on the Aging
409 Third Street, SW, Second Floor
Washington, DC 20024
(202)479-1700
www.ncoa.org

Many experts predict that interactive TV technology and electronic catalogs will soon replace the catalog business that was popularized by such stores as J.C. Penney and Sears. Customers will shop from home computers and select products ranging from apparel to furniture to food.

Credit Counseling

The term *credit* means that payment is expected at some time in the future for goods given on trust. With the growth in the use of credit in the United States, a new career has emerged—that of consumer credit counselor. Some credit counselors offer advice to consumers and help them manage their financial affairs. Counselors help consumers devise a plan for paying back creditors, staying out of debt, and developing a budget.

Department stores, banks, and other credit organizations also employ consumer credit counselors. The counselors look into credit applications, assess the credit worthiness of applicants, and advise their employer on whether to extend credit to people who apply for it.

Consumer Advocacy

With so many products on the market, consumers need a means of protecting themselves from unscrupulous sellers. Consumer advocates investigate product claims and company practices, handle consumer complaints, inform consumers about product quality, and safeguard consumer rights.

The consumer advocacy movement began in the 1960s. Led by Ralph Nader, supporters of the movement battled giant corporations, identifying unsafe products and exposing unfair practices. Today many TV news shows and newspaper and magazine articles deal with these issues. Laws protecting consumer rights have been passed, and the public is much more aware of consumer issues.

HOMEMAKING SERVICES

Jobs in homemaking services include in-home services provided on a regular basis by homemakers and domestics. Homemaking services also include other services that are often provided outside the home and may be on a short-term basis. This category includes services provided by family and consumer scientists, dietitians, nutritionists, and interior designers.

In-Home Services

People who work within the home, such as housekeepers, cooks, nannies, and gardeners, are often referred to as *domestics*. These workers perform the daily chores that help a household run smoothly. The demand for private household workers far exceeds the supply. The situation is not likely to improve because women who formerly took jobs as private household workers now find jobs that offer better pay and benefits in industry. The decline in the number of teenagers and young adults—another

Top-Dollar Jobs in Consumer, Homemaking, and Personal Services

These are high-paying jobs described in this volume. The figures represent typical salaries or earnings for experienced workers.

$30,000–$50,000	Dietitian and Nutritionist
	Embalmer
	Funeral Director
	Business Family and Consumer Scientist
$20,000–$30,000	Cosmetologist
	Locksmith
	Pest Control Worker

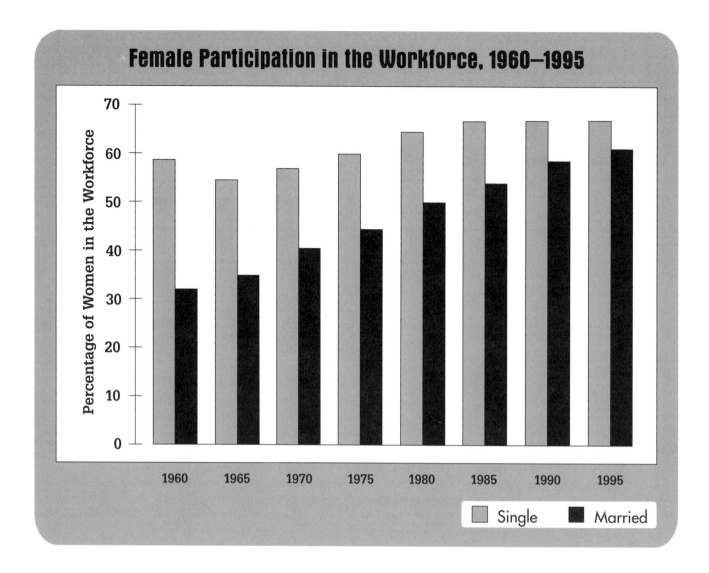

Female Participation in the Workforce, 1960–1995

Percentage of Women in the Workforce

	Single	Married

traditional source of household workers—has also contributed to the labor shortage. To fill the void, many families hire foreign workers, but immigration laws make this difficult. Consequently, employers are turning to domestic cleaning firms, day care centers, and temporary agencies for help.

Other Services

In the mid-1990s, the term *home economics* was replaced with the term *family and consumer science*. Family and consumer scientists provide homemaking services through research, education, and marketing. Their information provides help to homemakers as they decide how to best feed and clothe their families, how to manage their home efficiently and economically, and how to improve the quality of the home environment in many other ways.

Family and consumer scientists are employed in many occupations, including teaching, research, and writing, and in a variety of settings, such as schools, businesses, hospitals, and government. Some family

and consumer scientists provide information by writing brochures and newspaper articles and by conducting demonstrations and classes. Others help businesses develop products and services for homemakers and advise businesses on people's needs. Still others lobby for laws that will improve the well-being of families.

Family and consumer science curricula in schools and colleges emphasize overall household management. Included are courses in consumer education, interior design, nutritional analysis, child development, and family life. More men are entering the field of family and consumer science, as the increase in the variety of occupations is making family and consumer science more appealing.

PERSONAL SERVICES

The area of personal services has four main functions. One is to help people feel and look better. Cosmetologists, electrologists, and personal exercise trainers work toward this goal. A second function is to provide physical and emotional care to the young, the elderly, and others who need such help. Child care workers and companions meet this need. A third function is to help people in times of crisis or change. Divorce mediators and funeral directors perform these personal services. A fourth function is to provide time-saving services. Home caterers and professional organizers are two examples of the many personal service workers who provide this type of assistance.

Cosmetology

Cosmetology is the care of people's hair, skin, and nails. The field includes barbers, beauticians, hairstylists, beauty consultants, and makeup artists. Estheticians cleanse and beautify the skin. Electrology, the permanent removal of unwanted hair, is a related field.

Because American society values an attractive appearance, the demand for cosmetologists will continue to increase. As more women enter the business world, they want to look their best, and they have money to spend on beauty products and services. To be competitive in the business world, men, too, are discovering the need to present an attractive, vigorous appearance.

Trends and fads in cosmetology change often as new products and services are introduced into the market. One popular new product, introduced in the mid-1990s, is face cream that contains alpha-hydroxy acids. These acids are believed to make a person look younger because they remove dead skin cells to expose new cells underneath. Another current trend is toward the use of organic or natural products, including sea-derived cosmetics. In addition, many consumers are concerned with the issue of animal cruelty and look for cosmetics that have not been tested on animals. People who work in cosmetology must keep up-to-date on the latest consumer trends.

Fitness Services

Fitness services—professional guidance on exercise—are often provided by personal exercise trainers. Although personal exercise trainers were once thought of as a luxury only the wealthy could afford, they have recently become more popular as the cost for their services has decreased. Some personal exercise trainers work at a gym or other fitness facility, whereas others go to their clients' homes. In either case, the trainer sets up an individualized fitness program for each client. Some personal trainers have degrees in anatomy, exercise physiology, or related fields. Some are also certified by one or more fitness organizations.

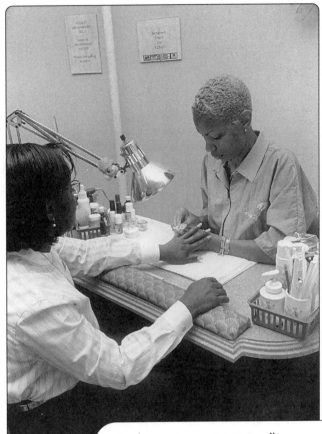

Employment opportunities will continue to be plentiful for cosmetologists as population growth leads to greater demand for their services.

Child Care

With more mothers entering the workforce, the demand for well-trained child care workers has risen significantly. Child care workers take care of other people's children on a full-time or part-time basis. Child care includes the full-time care of infants, toddlers, and preschoolers. It also includes before- and after-school care for school-age children.

The most common type of child care takes place in private homes. In family-operated day care, a worker opens his or her home to other people's children. These day care workers often care for their own children as well. Many such caregivers are licensed, and some have degrees in child development.

Many working parents use the services of child care centers. Some centers are affiliated with a church or synagogue, while others are owned by public companies. One such company is Kindercare—the largest public provider of child care in the United States. Because most centers do not take children who are ill, some centers specialize in the care of sick children. Besides providing child care workers,

Many parents in the labor force depend on child care workers to care for their children while they work.

the centers also provide a nurse and separate rooms for children with contagious diseases such as the flu. Another child care option is for parents to get together with other parents and form a cooperative in which they share the expenses and take part in hiring the workers.

Although relatively few businesses—usually only very large corporations—provide on-site child care, job-site care is in great demand by working parents. Taking children to work with them alleviates the need for dropping off and picking up children from day care. Parents are also nearby in case of emergency or illness. In lieu of on-site care, some businesses are offering child care referral services and flexible work schedules.

Elder Care

Whereas many working parents need help finding affordable, reliable child care, many other Americans need help finding care for an elderly relative. With the average life span of American men and women increasing, experts predict that almost every family will soon have an aged relative to care for. Often, however, family members are unable to provide the needed

level of care because they live too far away, work during the day, or lack the necessary skills.

As a result of the increasing need for elder care, adult day care centers are becoming more common. Adult day care centers provide transportation, meals, rehabilitation and social services, and assistance with physical needs.

Other workers provide in-home care for elderly people. These workers may prepare meals, do housekeeping, and assist with a variety of other tasks. Their goal is to help the elderly meet their needs and maintain their independence without having to move from their homes into a hospital or nursing care facility.

Divorce Mediation

Marriage meant "forever"—until the 1980s, when half of all marriages ended in divorce. This trend has continued into the 1990s and will most likely last well into the 21st century. To avoid costly litigation and attorney fees, many divorcing couples turn to mediators for help. A divorce mediator helps both parties work together to find mutual solutions, from dividing assets to determining child custody

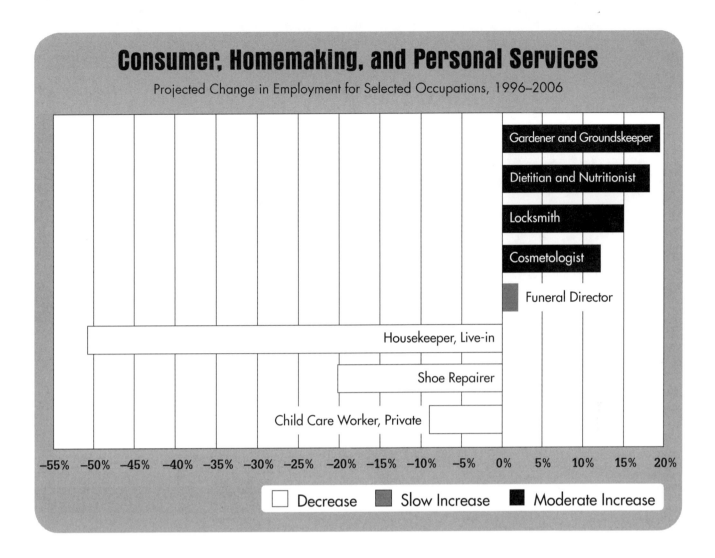

Consumer, Homemaking, and Personal Services

Projected Change in Employment for Selected Occupations, 1996–2006

Gardener and Groundskeeper

Dietitian and Nutritionist

Locksmith

Cosmetologist

Funeral Director

Housekeeper, Live-in

Shoe Repairer

Child Care Worker, Private

−55% −50% −45% −40% −35% −30% −25% −20% −15% −10% −5% 0% 5% 10% 15% 20%

☐ Decrease   ▨ Slow Increase   ■ Moderate Increase

and care. Although divorce mediators do not take the place of lawyers, they can help the two parties avoid court disputes and speed the process.

Funeral Services

When a family member dies, the family needs assistance in handling the logistics of a funeral. Funeral directors and embalmers provide these services. Many funeral homes are now recommending that people plan their own funerals and pay for them in advance to help reduce the number of difficult decisions that survivors must make. Funeral homes are also beginning to offer additional services such as video tributes to the deceased person and grief support groups.

Time-Saving Services

Many Americans complain that they do not have enough time to get everything done. For a fee, they can hire a personal service worker to save them time

by performing a wide range of tasks, such as running errands, standing in line for tickets to a concert, or waiting at a client's house while an appliance is repaired. Personal service workers might plan a child's birthday party, search for a rare book, or supervise the redecorating of a home. Professional organizers will even clean and organize a client's closets and drawers for maximum efficiency.

THE OUTLOOK FOR SERVICE JOBS

The United States is changing from a land of factories to a land of office buildings. Currently, the economy is gaining thousands of service jobs every year, while the number of manufacturing jobs is decreasing. In fact, service-producing industries will account for virtually all of the job growth over the 1996–2006 period. Many service workers enjoy their jobs, finding that their greatest reward is the feeling of satisfaction that comes from helping other people.

ood jobs rarely, if ever, just fall out of the sky. As anybody who has ever been in the job market knows, getting the right job takes planning, perseverance, and patience. There are, however, a number of ways to make the process easier and more rewarding. This is true whether you are looking for your first job, reentering the job market, trying to get a new job, or planning a mid-career change. This essay is designed to serve as your guide to the process of finding a job in the field of consumer, homemaking, and personal services. It starts off with the basics—helping you define your career objectives. Then it takes you through a number of steps you can use to work out a strategy to achieve these goals.

EVALUATING YOURSELF

Most people enjoy doing a job well. Apart from any praise from employers or fellow workers, there is an inner satisfaction in knowing that you've taken on a challenge and then succeeded in accomplishing something worthwhile. If you are unhappy or dissatisfied in your job and are just trying to do enough to get by, you may not be in the right job or the right field.

Making a Self-Inventory Chart

Before you make any career decisions, think about areas that interest you and things you do well. One way to go about this is to compile a self-inventory chart. Such a chart will be helpful when you decide what jobs you want to consider. It will also save time when you write cover letters and resumes, fill in applications, and prepare for job interviews.

Begin your self-inventory chart by listing all the jobs you have ever had, including summer employment, part-time jobs, volunteer work, and any freelance or short-term assignments you have done. Include the dates of employment, the names and addresses of supervisors, and the amount of money you earned. Then add a similar list of your hobbies and other activities, including any special experiences you have had, such as travel. Next, do the same for your education, listing your schools, major courses of study, grades, special honors or awards, courses you particularly enjoyed, and extracurricular activities.

In determining what you do well and what you enjoy doing, you may find a career pattern beginning to develop. If the picture still lacks detail or focus, try making a list of aptitudes, and then rate yourself *above average, average,* or *below average* for each one. Some of the qualities you might include in your list are administrative, analytic, athletic, clerical, language, leadership, managerial, manual, mathematical, mechanical, sales, and verbal abilities. You might also rate your willingness to accept responsibility and your ability to get along with people.

Compiling a Work Characteristics Checklist

Another way to choose a career path is to compile a checklist. Go through the questions in the "Work Characteristics Checklist" and then make a list of the work characteristics that are most important to you.

Do not expect a job to meet all your requirements. You have to consider which job characteristics are most important to you. If the characteristics of a job match most of your preferences, you might want to give the position serious consideration.

Work Characteristics Checklist

Do you want a job in which you can

- work outdoors?
- be physically active?
- work with your hands?
- be challenged mentally?
- work with machines?
- work independently?
- work on a team?
- follow clear instructions?
- earn a lot of money?
- have a chance for quick promotion?
- have good benefits?
- travel in your work?
- work close to home?
- work regular hours?
- have a flexible schedule?
- have a variety of tasks?
- have supervisory power?
- express your own ideas?
- be a decision maker?

Evaluating Your Career Options

It's important to evaluate yourself and your career options realistically. If you need help doing this, you can consult an experienced career counselor or take on-line aptitude tests.

Most guidance and counseling departments of high schools, vocational schools, and colleges provide vocational testing and counseling. Some local offices of the state employment services affiliated with the federal employment service offer free counseling. Career centers also offer these services.

Although vocational interest and aptitude testing can be done with paper and pencil, a variety of on-line programs can be used to test your interests and aptitudes. The results are measured against job skills and your personal profile is matched with potential jobs to show the training that is necessary. Some of these programs are self-administered on a personal computer whereas others must be administered and interpreted by a counselor.

Most major cities have professional career consultants and career counseling firms. You should, however, check their reputations before paying for their services. A list of counseling services in your area is available from the American Counseling Association, 5999 Stevenson Avenue, Alexandria, VA 22304 (www.counseling.org). (If you write, send a stamped, self-addressed envelope.)

You can also use the World Wide Web for services that career counselors would provide. Some sites have on-line counselors who can help you with a variety of tasks, such as obtaining information on jobs, careers, and training. They may be able to provide information on available services, including housing assistance, day care facilities, and transportation.

EVALUATING SPECIFIC JOBS

After you have taken a good look at what you do well and what you enjoy doing, you need to see how different jobs measure up to your abilities and interests. First, make a note of all the jobs in this volume that interest you. Then examine the education and training required for these jobs. Decide whether you qualify and, if not, whether you have the resources available to gain the qualifications. If possible, talk with someone who has such a job. Firsthand information can be invaluable. Also look through the appropriate trade and professional journals listed at the end of this essay and check the sections in this volume called "Resources" for books, audiovisual materials, and web sites that contain more detailed information about the job. In addition, counselors usually have helpful information on careers in consumer, homemaking, and personal services. For more detailed information, you can write to any of the trade and professional associations listed at the end of each occupational profile.

Once you have found out all you can about a particular job, compare the features of the job with your work characteristics checklist. See how many characteristics of the job match your work preferences. By completing these steps for all the jobs that appeal to you, you should be able to come up with a list of jobs that match your interests and abilities.

WAYS TO FIND JOB OPENINGS

Once you've decided what kind of job suits you, the next step is to look for available positions. Obviously, the more openings you can find, the better your chance of landing a job. People usually apply for a number of job openings before they are finally accepted.

There are many ways to find out about job openings. A number of job-hunting techniques are explained on the pages that follow and information is given on how you can follow up on job leads.

Applying in Person

For some jobs, especially entry-level positions, your best method may be to apply directly to the company or companies for which you would like to work. If you are looking for a position as a window cleaner or as a dry cleaning worker, for example, you might make an appointment to see the person responsible for hiring. This is a good method to use when jobs are plentiful or when a company is expanding. However, applicants for professional or supervisory positions generally need to send a cover letter and resume to the company first.

Applying in person will sharpen your interviewing techniques and give you a look at different places of employment. However, in most fields, it is not the method to use unless you are directed to do so.

Phone and Letter Campaigns

To conduct a phone campaign, use the Yellow Pages of your telephone directory to build a list of companies for which you might like to work. Call their personnel departments and find out whether they have any openings. This technique is not useful in all situations, however. If you're calling from out of town, a phone campaign can be very expensive. You may not be able to make a strong impression by phone. You also will not have a written record of your contacts.

Letter-writing campaigns can be very effective if the letters are well thought-out and carefully prepared. Your letters should always be typed. Handwritten letters and photocopied letters convey a lack of interest or motivation.

You may be able to get good lists of company addresses in your field of interest by reading the trade and professional publications listed at the end of this essay. Many of the periodicals publish directories or directory issues. Other sources you can use to compile lists of companies are the trade unions and professional organizations listed at the end of each job profile in this volume. The reference librarian at your local library can also help you find appropriate directories.

You can e-mail letters to human resource departments of companies with web sites, too. Be sure, however, that you follow all the same guidelines as you would for a letter you mail.

Your letters should be addressed to the personnel or human resources department of the organization. If possible, send it to a specific person. If you don't know who the correct person is, try to find the name of the personnel director through the directories in the library. You can also call on the phone and say, "I'm writing to ask about employment at your company. To whom should I address my letter?" If you can't find a name, use a standard salutation. It's a good idea to enclose a resume (described later in this essay) with the letter to give the employer a brief description of your education and work experience.

Keep a list of all the people you write to, along with the date each letter was mailed, or keep a photocopy of each letter. Then you can follow up by writing a brief note or calling people who do not reply within about 3 weeks.

Job Databases on the Web

The latest tool to use in looking for a job is the World Wide Web. The Internet currently has thousands of career-related sites to use to find job openings and to post your resume. Some sites, such as The Monster Board (www.monsterboard.com), help you build a resume and post it on-line as well as allow you to search through a massive database of help-wanted listings. Others, including E.span (www.espan.com), employ a search engine to find jobs that match your background, then post your resume on-line for employers. Another site called CareerBuilder (www.careerbuilder.com) has an interactive personal search agent that lets you key in job criteria such as location, title, and salary, and then it e-mails you when a matching position is posted in the database.

If you find a job that interests you in an ad on the web, you can respond by sending your resume and cover letter directly to the employer. Many companies even post job openings of their own in their company's human resource web pages. This allows you to target specific firms. Job hunters in many fields can also use professional associations to find jobs.

Some states, such as New Jersey, even have a home page (www.wnjpin.state.nj.us) designed to meet the needs of four groups: job seekers, students looking to make career choices, career counselors, and employers looking for workers. This one-stop career center has direct links to a variety of job listing sites on the web. You can post your resume, get information on training and education required for various jobs, read about occupations in demand, and even find out about job fairs.

Job Finder's Checklist

The following list of job-hunting tips may seem obvious, but getting all the bits and pieces in order beforehand helps when you're looking for a job.

Resume. Find out whether you will need a resume. If so, bring your resume up-to-date or prepare a new one. Assemble a supply of neatly typed copies or have a resume ready to e-mail to prospective employers.

References. Line up your references. Ask permission of the people whose names you would like to use. Write down their addresses, phone numbers, and job titles.

Contacts. Put the word out to everyone you know that you are looking for a job.

Job market. Find out where the jobs are. Make a list of possible employers in your field of interest.

Research. Do a little homework ahead of time—it can make a big difference in the long run. Find out as much as you can about a job—the field, the company—before you apply for it. A well-informed job applicant makes a good impression.

Organization. Keep a file on your job-hunting campaign with names and dates of employers contacted, ads answered, results, and follow-up.

Appearance. Make sure that the clothes you plan to wear to an interview are neat and clean. You may need to dress more formally than you would on the job, particularly if you are visiting a personnel office or meeting with a manager. Keep in mind that people may form an opinion of you based on their first impressions.

Help-Wanted Ads

Many people find out about job openings by reading the help-wanted sections of newspapers, trade journals, and professional magazines. Many employers and employment agencies use help-wanted classifieds to advertise available jobs.

Classified ads have their own telegraphic language. You will find some common abbreviations in the chart in this essay entitled "Reading the Classifieds." You can usually decode the abbreviations by using common sense, but if one puzzles you, call the newspaper and ask for a translation. Classified ads explain how to contact the employer, and they usually list the qualifications that are required.

As you find openings that interest you, follow up on each ad by using the method requested. You may be asked to call a specific person or send a resume. Record the date of your follow-up, and if you don't hear from the employer within 2 to 3 weeks, place another call or send a polite note asking whether the job is still open. Don't forget to include your phone number and address.

Some help-wanted ads are "blind ads." These ads give a box number but no name, phone number, or address. Employers and employment agencies may place these ads to avoid having to reply to all of the job applicants. In other words, you may not receive a response after answering a blind ad.

Situation-Wanted Ads

Another way to get the attention of potential employers is with a situation-wanted ad. You can place one of these in the classified section of your local newspaper or of a trade journal in your field of interest. Many personnel offices and employment agencies scan these columns when they're looking for new employees. The situation-wanted ad is usually most effective for people who have advanced education, training, or experience, or who are in fields that are in great demand.

A situation-wanted ad should be brief, clear, and to the point. Its main purpose is to interest the employer enough so you are contacted for an interview. It should tell exactly what kind of job you want, why you qualify, and whether you are available for full-time or part-time work. Use abbreviations that are appropriate.

If you are already employed and do not want it known that you are looking for a new position, you can run a blind ad. A blind ad protects your privacy by listing a box number at the publication to which all replies can be sent. They are then forwarded to you.

Reading the Classifieds

HELP WANTED

BEAUTICIAN— exp. stylist needed to grow w/new shop. Melissa's, 27 Park Street, 000-0000

DRY CLEANING COUNTER CLERK—p/t perm. Exp only. Some pressing. 5-day wk incl Saturdays. Mario's Spotless, 000-0000. Call bet 9 & 5.

FAMILY AND CONSUMER SCIENTEST
F/t & p/t temp positions avail immed for indiv w/1–2 yrs exp in home decorating, design. Publications exp pfd. 2–3 yrs teaching exp pfd. Excellent sal. Call Pat MacDonald for appt. 000-0000. Equal Opportunity Employer.

HOUSEKEEPER
Perm. sleep-in position. Working parents & 3-yr. old daughter. Plain cooking, thorough cleaning. Must be responsible, happy, energetic, and adore children. Own room, bath in dntn apt. Weekends off. No smokers. Excellent refs nec. Call Mrs. Jefferson, 000-0000

INTERIOR DESIGNER   **FEE NEG.**
Admin asst for partner in exciting prestige firm. Contact w/customers & mfrs. Degree and/or exp w/design & typ 50 wpm. WP exp. a plus. 000-0000. Art Associates (agency)

JEWELRY   **GROUP MGR**   **f/pd**
Exp w/fine jewelry. Exclusive dept stores throughout country. Must have impeccable bkgd and be accustomed to serving fine clientele. Top sal & gd. co. bnfts. Call Dennis Walker for this unique oppty.
FIFTY AVENUE AGENCY
000-0000

LOCKSMITH—3 yrs. exp., min. Industrial, commercial, residential work. Top quality shop. Top pay. Health insurance, other benefits. 000-0000.

REAL ESTATE APPRAISERS
Immediate openings for col grads w/2 yrs appraisal-type exp. No travel. Mr. Russo. 000-0000

CLASSIFIED ABBREVIATIONS

appt.	appointment
bet.	between
bkgd.	background
col.	college
dntn.	downtown
exp., expd.	experience, experienced
fee neg.	fee negotiable (fee can be worked out with employer)
f/p., f/pd.	fee paid (agency fee paid by employer)
f/t	full time
gd. bnfts.	good benefits
K	thousand
M	thousand
mfr.	manufacturer
mgr.	manager
nec.	necessary
neg.	negotiable
oppty.	opportunity
perm.	permanent
pfd.	preferred
p/t	part time
refs.	references
sal.	salary
sec., secy.	secretary
trnee.	trainee
typ.	typist, typing
w/	with
wk.	week
WP	word processing
wpm	words per minute
yrs.	years

SITUATION WANTED

BABYSITTER—mature and responsible student avail eves & weekends. Gd refs.
Call Matt 000-0000

CHILD CARE
Warm outgoing man, excellent Spanish & English, seeks live-out position caring for children 5 days a week. Firm but caring. Checkable references. Call 000-0000.

DAYWORKER—Thorough, dependable. Avail 3 to 5 days a week. Cleaning, laundry. Love children & pets. 000-0000

GARDENER/GROUNDSKEEPER
Industrial, residential. Handle all phases sowing to mowing. Reliable, refs. 000-0000.

HAIR STYLIST with devoted following seeks the right full-time position. Exp trendy blow cuts and roller styling. I offer excellent manner with customers and 5 yrs exp. Call 000-0000

FAMILY AND CONSUMER SCIENTIST
Highly competent woman w/4 yrs exp. teaching adults seeks extension position in community outreach program. Bilingual.
GRACE GEORGE
555 Livingston Street
000-0000

JEWELRY
MODELMAKER
Experienced with ability to sculpt in wax. Seeks position with costume jewelry manufacturer. Call 000-0000.

NO WALL TOO SMALL
Custom interior and exterior painting. Original supergraphics. Photomurals. Free estimates.
Call Steve 000-0000

SHOE REPAIRER—8 yrs. all-around shop exp avail p/t work. 000-0000.

You do not need to give your name, address, or phone number in the ad.

Networking

A very important source of information about job openings is networking. This means talking with friends and acquaintances about jobs in your area of interest. For example, if you would like to work in family and consumer science, get in touch with the people you know who work in family and consumer science, the food industry, consumer goods, or social services. Speak with all the people you know who have friends or relatives in the field.

There's nothing wrong with telling everyone who will listen that you are looking for a job—family, friends, counselors, and former employers. This will multiply your sources of information many times over.

You can use the web to make contacts, too. You can meet people with similar interests in news groups, which are organized by topic. Then you can write to them by e-mailing back and forth. Many fields have professional organizations that maintain web sites. You might use them to keep current on news affecting your field.

Sometimes a contact knows about a job vacancy before it is advertised. You can have an advantage, then, when you get in touch with the employer. Don't, however, use the contact's name without permission. Don't assume that a contact will go out on a limb by recommending you, either. Once you have received the inside information, rely on your own ability to get the job.

Placement Services

Most vocational schools, high schools, and colleges have a placement or career service that maintains a list of job openings and schedules visits from companies. If you are a student or recent graduate, you should check there for job leads. Many employers look first in technical or trade schools and colleges for qualified applicants for certain jobs. Recruiters often visit colleges to look for people to fill technical and scientific positions. These recruiters usually represent large companies. Visit your placement office regularly to check the job listings, and watch for scheduled visits by company recruiters.

State Employment Services

Another source of information about job openings is the local office of the state employment service. Many employers automatically list job openings at the local office. Whether you're looking for a job in private industry or with the state, these offices, which

Notes on Networking

Let people know you're looking. Tell friends, acquaintances, teachers, business associates, former employers—anyone who might know of job openings in your field.

Read newspapers and professional and trade journals. Look for news of developments in your field and for names of people and companies you might contact.

Use the World Wide Web. Make contacts through news groups, or find out information on web sites for professional organizations in your field.

Join professional or trade associations in your field. Contacts you make at meetings could provide valuable job leads. Association newsletters generally carry useful information about people and developments in the field.

Attend classes or seminars. You will meet other people in your field at job-training classes and professional development seminars.

Participate in local support groups. You can gain information about people and places to contact though support groups such as Women in Business, Job Seekers, Forty Plus, Homemakers Reentering the Job Market, as well as through alumni associations.

Be on the lookout. Always be prepared to make the most of any opportunity that comes along. Talk with anyone who can provide useful information about your field.

are affiliated with the federal employment service, are worth visiting.

State employment service offices are public agencies that do not charge for their services. They can direct you to special programs run by the government in conjunction with private industry. These programs, such as the Work Incentive Program for families on welfare, are designed to meet special needs. Some, but not all, of these offices offer vocational aptitude and interest tests and can refer interested people to vocational training centers. The state employment service can be a valuable first stop in your search for work, especially if there are special circumstances in your background. For example, if you did not finish high school, if you have had any difficulties with the law, or if you are living in a difficult home environment, your state employment service office is equipped to help you.

Private Employment Agencies

State employment services, though free, are usually very busy. If you are looking for more personal service and want a qualified employment counselor to help you find a job, you might want to approach a private employment agency.

Private employment agencies will help you get a job if they think they can place you. Most of them get paid only if they're successful in finding you a job, so you need to show them that you are a good prospect. These agencies will help you prepare a resume if you need one, and they will contact employers they think might be interested in you.

Private employment agencies are in the business of bringing together people who are looking for jobs and companies that are looking for workers. For some positions, usually middle- and higher-level jobs, the employment agency's fee is often paid by the employer. In such cases, the job seeker pays no fee. In other cases, you may be required to pay the fee, which is usually a percentage of your annual salary. Paying a fee is a worthwhile investment if it leads to a rewarding career. In addition, the fee may be tax deductible.

Some agencies may also ask for a small registration fee whether or not you get a job through them. Some agencies may demand that you pay even if you find one of the jobs they are trying to fill through your other contacts. Just be sure to read and understand the fine print of any contract you're about to sign, and ask for a copy to take home. Since the quality of these agencies varies, check to see if an agency is a certified member of a state or national association.

Some employment agencies, called staffing services, operate in a different way. They are usually paid by employers to screen and refer good candidates for job openings. They earn money when they refer a candidate who is hired by the employer. The employee pays no fee. Staffing firms, however, only spend time on candidates they think they may be able to place.

Private employment agencies are usually helping many people at one time. They may not have the time to contact you every time they find a job opening. Therefore, you may need to phone them at reasonable intervals after you have registered.

Computer Placement Services

Computer placement services are basically data banks (computerized information files) to which you send your resume or employment profile. When a company that subscribes to the service has a job to fill, it can call up on its computer a certain combination of qualifications and quickly receive information on qualified candidates.

Computer placement is very limited in scope and in the number of users. It seems to be most useful for people looking for technical or scientific jobs.

Civil Service

In your search for work, don't forget that the civil service—federal, state, and local—may have many consumer, homemaking, and personal services jobs. You may contact the state employment office or apply directly to the appropriate state or federal agency. The armed services also train and employ civilians in many fields, including consumer, homemaking, and personal services. Don't neglect these avenues for finding jobs. Civil service positions usually require you to take a civil service examination. Books are available to help you prepare for these exams, and your local civil service office can give you information, too.

Unions

In certain areas of consumer, homemaking, and personal services, such as dry cleaning, gardening, and window cleaning, unions can be useful sources of information. If you are a member of a union in your field of interest, you may be able to find out about jobs in the union periodical or through people at the union local. If you do not belong to a union, you may contact a union in the field you are interested in for information about available employment services. You will find addresses for some unions in the job profiles in this book.

Temporary Employment

A good way to get a feel for the job market—what's available and what certain jobs are like—is to work in a temporary job. There are many agencies that specialize in placing people in short-term jobs in consumer, homemaking, and personal services. Nannies and child care workers are in demand. Some jobs need extra workers on a temporary basis because they are seasonal, such as in gardening.

Temporary employment can increase your job skills, your knowledge of a particular field, and your chances of hearing of permanent positions. In today's tight labor market, many companies are using the services of temporary workers in increasing numbers. In fact, temporary agencies may sign multimillion-dollar contracts to provide businesses with a range of temporary workers. In some cases, temporary workers are in such demand that they may receive benefits, bonuses, and the same hourly wages as equivalent full-time workers. Some temporary agencies are even joining with companies to create long-term career paths for their temporary workers.

PRESENTING YOURSELF ON PAPER

An employer's first impression of you is likely to be based on the way you present yourself on paper. Whether it is in an application form or on a resume, you will want to make a good impression so that employers will be interested in giving you a personal interview. A potential employer is likely to equate a well-written presentation that is neat with good work habits and a sloppy, poorly written one with bad work habits.

Writing an Effective Resume

When you write to follow up a lead or to ask about job openings, you should also send information about yourself. The accepted way of doing this is to send a resume with a cover letter.

The work *resume* is derived from the French word *résumer*, meaning "to summarize." A resume does just that—it briefly outlines your education, work experience, and special abilities and skills. A resume may also be called a curriculum vitae, a personal profile, or a personal data sheet. This summary can act as your introduction by mail or e-mail, as your calling card if you apply in person, and as a convenient reference for you to use when filling out an application form or when being interviewed.

A resume is a useful tool in applying for almost any job in the field of consumer, homemaking, and personal services. It is valuable, even if you use it only to keep a record of where you have worked, for whom, and the dates of employment. A resume is usually required if you are being considered for professional or executive jobs. Prepare it carefully. It's well worth the effort.

The goal of a resume is to capture the interest of potential employers so they will call you for a personal interview. Since employers are busy people, the resume should be as brief and as neat as possible. You should, however, include as much relevant information about yourself as you can. This is usually presented under at least two headings: "Education" and "Experience." The latter is sometimes called "Employment History." Many people add a third section titled "Related Skills," "Professional Qualifications," or "Related Qualifications."

If you prepare a self-inventory such as the one described earlier, it will be a useful tool in preparing a resume. Go through your inventory, and select the items that show your ability to do the job or jobs in which you are interested. Plan to highlight these items on your resume. Select only those facts that point out your relevant skills and experience.

Once you have chosen the special points to include, prepare the resume. At the top, put your name, address, and phone number. After that, decide which items will be most relevant to the employer you plan to contact.

State Your Objective Some employment counselors advise that you state a job objective or describe briefly the type of position for which you are applying. The job objective usually follows your name and address. Don't be too specific if you plan to use the same resume a number of times. It's better to give a general career goal. Then, in a cover letter, you can be more specific about the position in which you are interested.

Describe What You've Done Every interested employer will check your educational background and employment history carefully. It is best to present these sections in order of importance. For instance, if you've held many relevant jobs, you should list your work experience first, followed by your educational background. On the other hand, if you are just out of school with little or no work experience, it's probably best to list your educational background first and then, under employment history, to mention any part-time and summer jobs or volunteer work you've done.

Under educational background, list the schools you have attended in reverse chronological order, starting with your most recent training and ending with the least recent. Employers want to know at a glance your highest qualifications. For each educational experience, include years attended, name and location of the school, and degree or certificate earned, if any. If you have advanced degrees (college and beyond), it isn't necessary to include high school and elementary school education. Don't forget to highlight any special courses you took or awards you won, if they are relevant to the kind of job you are seeking.

Chronological and Functional Resume Information about your employment history can be presented in two basic ways. The most common format is the chronological resume. In a chronological resume, you summarize your work experience year by year. Begin with your current or most recent employment and then work backward. For each job, list the name and location of the company for which you worked, the years you were employed, and the position or positions you held. The order in which you present these facts will depend on what you are trying to emphasize. If you want to call attention to the type or level of job you held, for example, you should put the job title first. Regardless of the order you choose, be consistent. Summer employment or part-time work should be identified as such. If you held a job for less than a year, specify months in the dates of employment.

It is important to include a brief description of the responsibilities you had in each job. This often reveals more about your abilities than the job title. Remember, too, that you do not have to mention the names of former supervisors or how much you earned. You can discuss these points during the interview or explain them on an application form.

The functional resume, on the other hand, emphasizes *what you can do* rather than *what you have done*. It is useful for people who have large gaps in their work history or who have relevant skills that would not be properly highlighted in a chronological listing of jobs. The functional resume concentrates on qualifications—such as familiarity with computers to organizational skills or managerial experience. Specific jobs may be mentioned, but they are not the primary focus of this particular type of resume.

Explain Special Skills You may wish to include a third section called "Related Skills," "Professional Qualifications," or "Related Qualifications." This is

DO YOU KNOW YOUR RIGHTS?

JOB DISCRIMINATION—WHAT IT IS

Federal and State Law

An employer cannot discriminate against you for any reason other than your ability to do the job. By federal law, an employer cannot discriminate against you because of your race, color, religion, sex, or national origin. The law applies to decisions about hiring, promotion, working conditions, and firing. The law specifically protects workers who are over the age of 40 from discrimination on the basis of age.

The law also protects workers with disabilities. Employers must make their workplaces accessible to individuals with disabilities—for example, by making them accessible to wheelchairs or by hiring readers or interpreters for blind or deaf employees.

Federal law offers additional protection to employees who work for the federal government or for employers who contract with the federal government. State law often provides protection also, for instance, by prohibiting discrimination on the basis of marital status, arrest record, political affiliations, or sexual orientation.

Affirmative Action

Affirmative action programs are set up by businesses that want to make a special effort to hire women and members of minority groups. Federal employers and many businesses that have contracts with the federal government are required by law to set up affirmative action programs. Employers with a history of discriminatory practices may also be required to establish affirmative action programs.

Discrimination Against Job Applicants

A job application form or interviewer may ask for information that can be used to discriminate against you illegally. The law prohibits such questions. If you are asked such questions and are turned down for the job, you may be a victim of discrimination. However, under federal law, employers must require you

to prove that you are an American citizen or that you have a valid work permit.

Discrimination on the Job

Discrimination on the job is illegal. Being denied a promotion for which you are qualified or being paid less than coworkers are paid for the same job may be forms of illegal discrimination.

Sexual, racial, and religious harassment are forms of discrimination and are prohibited in the workplace. On-the-job harassment includes sexual, racial, or religious jokes or comments. Sexual harassment includes not only requests or demands for sexual favors but also verbal or physical conduct of a sexual nature.

JOB DISCRIMINATION— WHAT YOU CAN DO

Contact Federal or State Commissions

If you believe that your employer practices unfair discrimination, you can complain to the state civil rights commission or the federal Equal Employment Opportunity Commission (EEOC). If, after investigating your complaint, the commission finds that there has been unfair discrimination, it will take action against the employer. You may be entitled to the job or promotion you were denied or to reinstatement if you were fired. You may also receive back pay or other financial compensation.

Contact a Private Organization

There are many private organizations that can help you fight job discrimination. For example, the American Civil Liberties Union (ACLU) works to protect all people from infringement on their civil rights. The National Association for the Advancement of Colored People (NAACP), National Organization for Women (NOW), and Native American Rights Fund may negotiate with your employer, sue on your behalf,

useful if there are points you want to highlight that do not apply directly to educational background or work experience. Be sure these points are relevant to the kind of work you are seeking. This section is most effective if you can mention any special recognition, awards, or other evidence of excellence. It is also useful to mention if you are willing to relocate or can work unusual hours.

Have References Available Employers may also want to know whom they can contact to find out more about you. At the start of your job search, you should ask three or four people if you may use them as references. If you haven't seen these people for a while, you may want to send them a copy of your resume and let them know what kind of position you're seeking. Your references should be the kind of people your potential employer will respect, and they should be able to comment favorably on your abilities, personality, and work habits. You should indicate whether these people are personal references or former work supervisors. Avoid using any

or start a class action suit—a lawsuit brought on behalf of all individuals in your situation.

WHAT TO DO IF YOU LOSE YOUR JOB

Being Fired and Being Laid Off

An employer usually has the right to fire an employee at any time. In many cases, however, an employer can fire you only if there is good cause, such as your inability to do the job, violation of safety rules, dishonesty, or chronic absenteeism.

Firing an employee because of that employee's race, color, religion, sex, national origin, or age (if the employee is over 40) is illegal. Firing an employee for joining a union or for reporting an employer's violation (called whistle-blowing) is also prohibited. If you believe you have been wrongfully discharged, you should contact the EEOC or the state civil rights commission.

At times, employers may need to let a number of employees go to reduce costs. This reduction in staff is called a layoff. Laying off an employee has nothing to do with the employee's job performance. Federal law requires employers who lay off large numbers of employees to give these employees at least two months' notice of the cutback.

Unemployment Compensation

Unemployment insurance is a state-run fund that provides payments to people who lose their jobs through no fault of their own. Not everyone is entitled to unemployment compensation. Those who quit their jobs or who worked only a few months before losing their jobs may not be eligible.

The amount of money you receive depends on the amount you earned at your last job. You may receive unemployment payments for only a limited period of time and only so long as you can prove that you are actively looking for a new position.

Each claim for unemployment compensation is investigated before the state makes any payments. If the state unemployment agency decides to deny you compensation, you may ask the agency for instructions on how to appeal that decision.

OTHER PROTECTIONS FOR EMPLOYEES

Honesty and Drug Testing

Many employers ask job applicants or employees to submit to lie-detector tests or drug tests. Lie-detector tests are permitted in the case of high-security positions, such as police officers. Some states prohibit or restrict the testing of applicants or employees for drug use. Aptitude and personality tests are generally permitted.

Other Federal Laws

The Fair Labor Standards Act prescribes certain minimum wages and rules about working hours and overtime payments. Workers' compensation laws provide payment for injuries that occur in the workplace and wages lost as a result of those injuries.

The Occupational Safety and Health Act sets minimum requirements for workplace safety. Any employee who discovers a workplace hazard should report it to the Occupational Safety and Health Administration (OSHA). The administration will investigate the claim and may require the employer to correct the problem or pay a fine.

Rights Guaranteed by Contract

Not every employee has a written contract. If you do, however, that contract may grant you additional rights, such as the right to severance pay in the event you are laid off. In addition, employees who are members of a union may have certain rights guaranteed through their union contract.

Before you sign any contract, make sure you understand every part of it. Read it thoroughly and ask the employer questions. Checking the details of a contract before signing it may prevent misunderstanding later on.

BRYAN COSTELLO

83 Langford Avenue

Santa Clara, CA 22105

(215) 382-3940

OBJECTIVE	Full-time position as hairstylist.
EDUCATION	
Certificate	ProStyle Barber Institute, Santa Clara, CA, 1999
Diploma	Parktown High School, San Jose, CA, 1998
HAIRSTYLING EXPERIENCE	
Hairstylist	ProStyle Barber Institute Student Barber Service, 1998–1999, part-time
	Performed variety of hairdressing services, including shampoo, hair cut and style, shave, beard and mustache trim, and scalp treatment. Duties occasionally included operating cash register and managing appointments calendar.
OTHER BUSINESS EXPERIENCE	
Dining Room Attendant	Cafe Antonio Restaurant, San Jos~~e, CA, 1997–1998~~
	Set tables; cleared tables; assisted ~~waitstaff in dining~~ room, bar, and entrance areas.
Attendant	A & B Service Station, Santa Clar~~a, CA, 1996–1997~~
	Operated gas pumps; performed ~~minor services~~ including tire and oil change.
REFERENCES	Available upon request.

State your name, address, and telephone number first.

State job objective or general career goal in a few words.

List education and work experience in reverse chronological order, with most recent item first.

ERIN O'MALLEY

16 Snowcrest Drive
Stamford, CT 05159
(213) 555-4567

OBJECTIVE	Position as writer or consultant in family and consumer science.
EXPERIENCE 1997 to present	**COLUMNIST** Community Health Care News, Darien, CT Write monthly column on new ideas in nutrition for journal of Community Health Care Workers Association. Propose story ideas; do research; prepare copy, photographs, and captions; and reply to reader correspondence. Part-time.
1995 to 1998	**FAMILY AND CONSUMER SCIENCE TEACHER** Northeastern Public High School, Bridgeport, CT Taught high school courses covering various subjects including:

child care	cooking	nutrition
clothing care	home finances	sewing
consumer awareness		

Served as head of department for one year. Supervised major annual fund-raising event that included baking and crafts preparations.

1993 to 1995	**DIETITIAN** Community General Hospital, Stamford, CT Planned menus, schedules, and budgets. Supervised food purchases and preparation, equipment, and storage facilities. Devised recipes and menus for restricted diets.
PROFESSIONAL CERTIFICATION	State teaching certificate, secondary education, home economics Member, Community Health Care Workers Association (treasurer, 1994–1998)
EDUCATION 1993	Bachelor of Science, major in Nutrition Lakeview College, Stamford, CT

References and writing samples available upon request.

List your work experience first if it is more important than your educational background.

Keep descriptions of your education and work experience brief.

List special skills and qualifications if they are relevant to the job.

relatives. You can list the names and addresses of your references at the end of your resume or in a cover letter. Or you can simply write, "References available upon request." Just be sure you have their names, addresses, and phone numbers ready if you are asked.

Present Yourself Concisely Tips for making your resume concise include using phrases instead of sentences and omitting unnecessary words. When appropriate, start a sentence with a verb, such as *maintained* or *coordinated*. There is no need to say "I"—that is obvious and repetitive.

Present Yourself Well Employment counselors often recommend that resumes be no longer than one page because employers won't take the time to read a second page. If you've held many positions related to your occupation, go on to the second page, but don't include beginning or irrelevant jobs. If you have a lot of work experience, limit the education section to just the essentials.

You should also concentrate on the appearance of your resume. It should be typed on a good grade of 8½" × 11" white bond paper. If you can't type, a professional typist can do it for you for a small charge. Be sure that it is neatly typed with adequate margins. The data should be spaced and indented so that each item stands out. This enables a busy executive or personnel director to see at a glance the facts of greatest interest.

You will probably need many copies of your resume during your job search. Each copy should be as neat and as clear as your original. If possible, input your resume on a computer and print copies on a good-quality printer. You may want to have your resume reproduced professionally. A photo-offset printer can make several hundred excellent copies for a moderate fee. A photocopying machine may be more economical for smaller quantities.

These suggestions for writing a resume are not hard-and-fast rules. Resumes may be adapted to special situations. For example, people with a variety of work experience often prepare several versions of their resume and use the experience that's most relevant when applying for a particular job.

If this is your first resume, show it to someone else, perhaps a guidance counselor, for constructive advice. No matter what, be truthful while emphasizing your assets. You can do that by showing the abilities, skills, and specific interests that qualify you for a particular job. Don't mention any weaknesses or deficiencies in your training. Do mention job-related aptitudes that showed up in previous employment or in school. Don't make up things about yourself; everything that's in your resume can, and sometimes will, be checked.

Writing Cover Letters

When you send your resume through the mail or the Internet, you should send a cover letter with it. This is the same whether you are writing to apply for a specific job or just to find out if there are any openings.

A good cover letter should be neat, brief, and well written with no more than three or four short paragraphs. Since you may use your resume for a variety of job openings, your cover letter should be very specific. Try to get the person who reads it to think that you are an ideal candidate for a particular job. If at all possible, send the letter to a specific person, either to the personnel director or to the person for whom you would be working. If necessary, call the company and ask to whom you should write.

Start your letter by explaining why you are writing. Say that you are inquiring about possible job openings at the company, that you are responding to an advertisement in a particular publication, or that someone recommended that you should write. (Use the person's name if you have received permission to do so.)

Let your letter lead into your resume. Use it to call attention to your qualifications. Add information that shows why you are well suited for that specific job. For example, the family and consumer scientist in the sample letter points out that she has experience as a magazine columnist. She also emphasizes the various fields of interest she could cover as a writer. In the second sample letter, the applicant for a hairstylist position shows that he practiced his trade while he was a student. He also expresses his willingness to relocate, since the job is in another city.

Completing the Application Form

Many employers ask job applicants to fill out an application form. This form usually duplicates much of the information on your resume, but it may ask some additional questions. Give complete answers to all questions except those that are discriminatory. If a question doesn't apply to you, put a dash next to it.

You may be given the application form when you arrive for an interview, or it may be sent to your home. When filling it out, print neatly in ink. Follow the instructions carefully. For instance, if the form asks you to put down your last name first, do so.

The most important sections of an application form are the education and work histories. As in your resume, many applications request that you write these in reverse chronological order, with the most recent experience first. Unlike your resume, however, the application form may request information about your earnings on previous jobs. It may also ask what rate of pay you are seeking on this job.

BRYAN COSTELLO

83 Langford Avenue

Santa Clara, CA 22105

(215) 382-3940

November 1, 1999

Mr. Martin Brown
Remington Beauty Salon
345 Groves End
San Francisco, CA 23109

Dear Mr. Brown:

I am writing in reply to the advertisement in the *Evening Post* for a beautician to work at the Remington Beauty Salon.

I have recently received my beautician's certificate from the ProStyle Barber Institute. While I attended the Institute I performed a variety of beauty salon services for clients of the Institute. I expect to take the state beauty operator's licensing exam in January.

I am very interested in beginning my career as a beautician with your salon. I would enjoy working to provide the many services offered by your salon. I am willing to relocate to San Francisco for this position.

I enclose my resume and hope that you will schedule an intervie

Very truly yours,

Bryan Costello

Bryan Costello

Enclosure

ERIN O'MALLEY

16 Snowcrest Drive
Stamford, CT 05159
(213) 555-4567

April 5, 1999

Mr. Gregory Polanski
Editor in Chief
Leisure & Living Magazine
200 Regents Avenue
Westport, CT 05345

Dear Mr. Polanski:

I am writing with regard to the advertisement in *The Reporter's Newsletter* for a family and consumer science writer for *Leisure & Living* magazine. I am an experienced writer and family and consumer scientist, and I would like to apply for the position.

I have been writing a column on nutrition for several years for the journal of the Community Health Care Workers Association. My areas of interest include nutrition and cuisine, fashion, child care, home management and finances, home improvement, and interior decorating. I have also worked as a family and consumer science instructor and hospital dietitian.

I am interested in working full-time as a writer and would like to be associated with a widely circulated publication such as *Leisure & Living*. I enclose my resume, and I can supply writing samples for your consideration. I would be pleased to meet with you to discuss the position. I look forward to hearing from you.

Very truly yours,

Erin O'Malley

Erin O'Malley

Enclosure

Be prepared to answer these and other topics not addressed on your resume. Look at the sample application form, and make note of the kinds of questions that you are likely to be asked—for example, your Social Security number, the names of previous supervisors, your salary, and your reason for leaving. If necessary, carry notes on such topics with you to an interview. You have a responsibility to tell prospective employers what they need to know to make an informed decision.

Neatness Counts Think before you write on an application form so you avoid crossing things out. An employer's opinion of you may be influenced just by the general appearance of your application form. A neat, clearly detailed form may indicate an orderly mind and the ability to think clearly, follow instructions, and organize information.

Know Your Rights Under federal and some state laws, an employer cannot demand that you answer any questions about race, color, creed, national origin, ancestry, sex, marital status, age (with certain exceptions), number of dependents, property, car ownership (unless needed for the job), or arrest record. Refer to the information on job discrimination in this essay for more information about your rights.

PRESENTING YOURSELF IN AN INTERVIEW

An interview is the climax of your job-hunting efforts. On the basis of this meeting, the prospective employer will decide whether or not to hire you, and you will decide whether or not you want the job.

Prepare in Advance

Before an interview, there are a number of things you can do to prepare. Begin by giving some more thought to why you want the job and what you have to offer. Then review your resume and any lists you made when you were evaluating yourself so that you can keep your qualifications firmly in mind.

Learn as much as you can about the organization. Check with friends who work there, read company brochures, search the Internet, or devise other information-gathering strategies. Showing that you know something about the company and what it does will indicate your interest.

Try to anticipate some of the questions the interviewer may ask and think of how you would answer. For example, you may be asked: Will you work overtime when necessary? Are you ready to go to night school to improve some of your skills? Preparing answers in advance will make the process easier for you. It is also wise to prepare any questions you may

have about the company or the position for which you are applying. The more information you have, the better you can evaluate both the company and the job.

Employers may want you to demonstrate specific skills for some jobs. An applicant for a job as a hairstylist, for example, may be asked to style a person's hair. Some employers may ask to see relevant licenses or certificates confirming an applicant's qualifications.

On the appointed day, dress neatly and in a style appropriate for the job you're seeking. When in doubt, it's safer to dress on the conservative side, wearing a tie rather than a turtleneck or wearing a dress or blouse and skirt rather than pants and a T-shirt. Be on time. Find out in advance exactly where the company is located and how to get there. Allow extra time in case you get lost, get caught in a traffic jam, can't find a parking spot, or encounter another type of delay.

Maintain a Balance

When your appointment begins, remember that a good interview is largely a matter of balance. Don't undersell yourself by sitting back silently, and don't oversell yourself by talking nonstop about how wonderful you are. Answer all questions directly and simply, and let the interviewer take the lead.

Instead of saying, "I'm reliable and hardworking," give the interviewer an example. Allow the interviewer to draw conclusions from your example.

It's natural to be nervous before and during a job interview. However, you need to try to relax and be yourself. You may even enjoy the conversation. Your chances of being hired and being happy if you get the job are better if the employer likes you as you are.

Avoid discussing money until the employer brings it up or until you are offered the job. Employers usually know in advance what they are willing to pay. If you are the one to begin a discussion about the salary you want, you may set an amount that's either too low or too high.

Be prepared to ask questions, but don't force them on your interviewer. Part of the purpose of the interview is for you to evaluate the company while you are being evaluated. For instance, you might want to ask about the company's training programs and its policy on promotions.

Don't stay too long. Most business people have busy schedules. It is likely that the interviewer will let you know when it's time for the interview to end.

Don't expect a definite answer at the first interview. Employers usually thank you for coming and say that you will be notified shortly. Most employers want to interview all the applicants before they

1 Always print neatly in blue or black ink. When completing an application at home, type it, if possible.

2 Read the application carefully *before* you start to fill it out. Follow instructions precisely. Use standard abbreviations.

3 If you aren't applying for a specific job, indicate the kind of work you're willing to do.

4 You don't have to commit to a specific rate of pay. Write "open" or "negotiable" if you are uncertain.

5 Traffic violations and so on do not belong here. Nor do offenses for which you were charged but not convicted.

6 If a question doesn't apply to you, write "NA" (for not applicable) or put a dash through the space.

7 Take notes along to remind you of school names, addresses, and dates.

8 If you're short on "real" employment, mention jobs such as babysitting, lawn mowing, or any occasional work.

9 Your references should be people who can be objective about you, such as former employers, teachers, and community leaders.

10 Under the heading "Reason for Leaving," a simple answer will do. Avoid saying "better pay"—even if it's so.

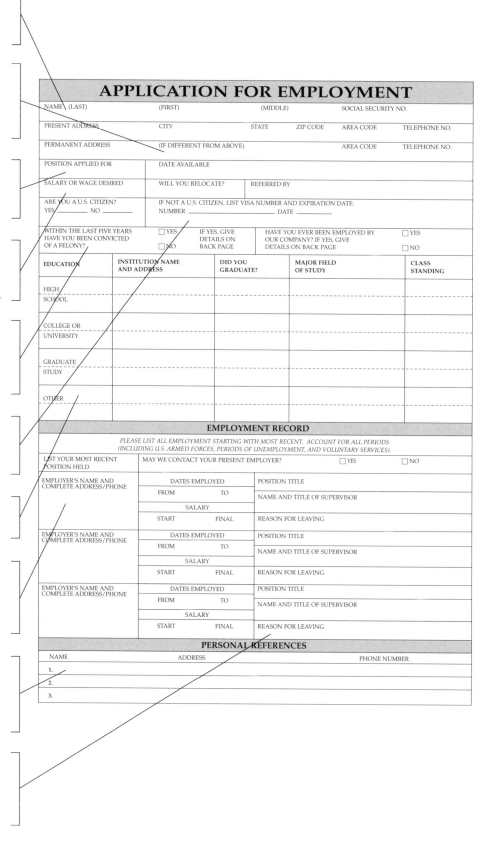

make a hiring decision. If the position is offered at the time of the interview, you can ask for a little time to think about it. If the interviewer tells you that you are not suitable for the job, try to be polite. Say, "I'm sorry, but thank you for taking the time to meet with me." After all, the company may have the right job for you next week.

Follow Up After the Interview

If the job sounds interesting and you would like to be considered for it, say so as you leave. Follow up after the interview by writing a brief thank-you note to the employer. Express your continued interest in the position and thank the interviewer for taking the time to meet with you.

It's a good idea to make some notes and evaluations of the interview while it is still fresh in your mind. Write down the important facts about the job—the duties, salary, promotion prospects, and so on. Also evaluate your own performance in the interview. List the things you wish you had said and things you wish you had not said. These notes will help you make a decision later. They will also help you prepare for future interviews.

Finally, don't hesitate to contact your interviewer if you haven't heard from the company after a week or two (unless you were told it would be longer). Write a brief note or make a phone call in which you ask when a decision might be reached. Making such an effort will show the employer that you are genuinely interested in the job. Your call will remind the interviewer about you and could work to your advantage.

TAKE CHARGE

The field of consumer, homemaking, and personal services offers many job opportunities. Job hunting is primarily a matter of organizing a well-thought-out campaign. Scan the classified ads, search through online job banks, watch for trends in local industry that might be reported in the news, and check with people you know in the field. Take the initiative. Send out well-crafted resumes and letters. Respond to ads. Finally, in an interview, state your qualifications and experience in a straightforward and confident manner.

TRADE AND PROFESSIONAL JOURNALS

The following is a list of some of the major journals in the field of consumer, homemaking, and personal services. These journals can keep you up-to-date with what's happening in your field of interest. These publications can also lead you to jobs through their own specialized classified advertising sections.

Consumer Services

Car and Driver, 1633 Broadway, New York, NY 10009.
Consumer Reports, Consumers Union of the United States, Inc., 101 Truman Avenue, Yonkers, NY 10703-1057.
www.consumerinternational.org/links
Footwear News, Fairchild Fashion and Merchandising Group, 7 West 34th Street, New York, NY 10001.
www.footwearnews.com.htm
Popular Mechanics, C.D.S., 959 Eighth Avenue, New York, NY 10019.
Workbench, KC Publishing Inc., 700 West 47th Street, Suite 310, Kansas City, MO 64112.

Homemaking Services

Better Homes and Gardens, 1716 Locust Street, Des Moines, IA 50309.
www.bhglive.com
Garden Design, Meigher Communications, 100 Sixth Avenue, Seventh Floor, New York, NY 10013-1605.
Interior Design, Reed Elsevier Business Information, 245 West 17th Street, New York, NY 10011.
Interiors: For the Contract Design Professional, 1515 Broadway, 39th Floor, New York, NY 10036.
Journal of Nutrition, 9650 Rockville Pike, Bethesda, MD 20814-3990.
www.faseb.org/ain/journal/tocs/jnjan.html
Ladies Home Journal, Myrna Blyth-Meredith Corporation, 100 Park Avenue, New York, NY 10017.
Scholastic Choices, 555 Broadway, New York, NY 10012.
www.scholastic.com

Chauffeur

Definition and Nature of the Work

Chauffeurs drive and maintain cars for private households, government agencies, business firms, and limousine companies. Chauffeurs who work for private households may drive family members to and from their daily activities, which may include school, work, and various business and social functions. They help their passengers to get in and out of the car, carry packages and luggage, and run errands. Since they are responsible for keeping their employers' cars in good condition, chauffeurs spend some of their working hours washing, waxing, and polishing the cars. They make arrangements to have the cars serviced and repaired. They often make minor repairs and adjustments themselves. Many chauffeurs who work for private households also have other duties, such as cleaning walks and driveways and exercising pets.

Chauffeurs who work for business firms and government agencies drive office staff and visitors, meet people at airports, and sometimes serve as messengers and run errands. Industrial firms, airports, private schools, health resorts, funeral homes, motion picture and television studios, and other businesses also employ chauffeurs. Chauffeurs who work for car rental and delivery companies may pick up and deliver rented cars and drive cars from one city to another.

Some chauffeurs are self-employed. They offer their services to those who need drivers only part-time or for special occasions. Many limousine chauffeurs own or lease their vehicles, and limousine companies inform them of their driving assignments by radiotelephone.

Education and Training Requirements

Many employers hire only high school graduates as chauffeurs. In most cases, you must be at least 21 years old. Because of insurance regulations, some employers do not hire drivers under the age of 25 or drivers who have been held liable for an accident in the last 5 years. You can prepare for a career as a chauffeur by taking a high school course in driver education. If you plan to work for a government agency, you may have to pass a civil service test. For some employers, you need to take a defensive driving course, and you must pass a special driving test to obtain a chauffeur's license. Most employers demand a good driving record.

Getting the Job

If you want to work for a private household, you can register with an employment agency that specializes in placing household service workers. To chauffeur for a business or government agency, apply directly to the agency or firm. Your state or local civil service office can give you information about getting a civil service job. You can also check newspaper classifieds and job banks on the Internet.

Advancement Possibilities and Employment Outlook

Chauffeurs advance by moving to jobs with employers who provide higher wages and better working conditions. Some chauffeurs start their own limousine

Education and Training
License

Salary Range
Average—$30,000 to $50,000

Employment Outlook
Fair

services. Some chauffeurs work part-time. The number of job openings for chauffeurs is expected to increase slower than the average through the year 2006.

Working Conditions

Working conditions for chauffeurs are usually pleasant. They are subject to little direct supervision and have considerable opportunity to travel and meet people. Self-employed chauffeurs may set their own hours. Private household chauffeurs may have their own living quarters.

The disadvantages of this work may include irregular hours and weekend and holiday work. Many chauffeurs are always on call. Also, chauffeurs frequently drive in heavy traffic and are required to meet deadlines.

Earnings and Benefits

Earnings of chauffeurs vary greatly. Chauffeurs who work full-time earn between $30,000 and $50,000 a year, including tips. Some limousine companies pay chauffeurs an hourly rate. Other companies pay chauffeurs commissions that are 20 to 25 percent of the fare. Chauffeurs can expect an additional 15 to 20 percent in tips. Chauffeurs employed by government agencies and business firms usually receive benefits that include uniforms, paid holidays and vacations, health insurance, and pension plans. Benefits for chauffeurs in private households vary widely. Many employers provide free room and board. Self-employed chauffeurs must provide their own benefits.

Where to Go for More Information

International Brotherhood of Teamsters, AFL-CIO
25 Louisiana Avenue, NW
Washington, DC 20001-2198
(202) 624-6800

Child Care Worker, Private

Education and Training
None

Salary Range
Varies—see profile

Employment Outlook
Very good

Definition and Nature of the Work

Child care workers look after young children. Those who care for children on a short-term or part-time basis are sometimes called *babysitters*. Child care workers who live in the family's home and work full-time are called *nannies*. In family day care, children from different families are cared for in the child care workers' homes or in day care centers.

The duties of child care workers are many and varied. They may prepare, serve, and feed meals to the children. They may bathe and dress the children or help them bathe and dress themselves. In some cases, they do the laundry or tidy the children's rooms. Child care workers may take the children for walks, play games with them, or entertain them in other ways. They keep a watchful eye while the children are playing to make sure they are safe.

Family day care workers must be aware of state regulations for the sanitation, safety, and health of the children. For example, these regulations call for smoke detectors on each floor and for electrical outlets to be covered.

Education and Training Requirements

Entry-level positions for child care workers usually require little or no experience. Although employers have no specific educational requirements, some prefer applicants with a high school diploma.

Private child care workers provide a fun, stimulating environment for children in addition to caring for their needs and ensuring their safety.

High school students who plan to work with small children should take courses in psychology, family and consumer science, nutrition, art, drama, and physical education. Local babysitting jobs and summer camp counseling provide valuable experience.

Formal training or certification is recommended for those who wish to advance. Many 2- and 4-year colleges offer certificate and associate degree programs in child care and guidance.

Getting the Job

You can get a job by registering with an employment agency that specializes in placing child care workers. You can go to local nursery schools and see if they need help, and you can check the classified ads in the newspaper and job banks on the Internet.

Many states and counties have their own family day care referral offices through which day care providers and parents can contact each other. For addresses of these offices, look up your local social services department in the phone book.

Advancement Possibilities and Employment Outlook

Some child care workers go into business for themselves by starting babysitting agencies. With some additional training, they may transfer to work in a nursery school or as teachers' aides in elementary schools.

Growth in the number of preschool-age children with working parents will lead to faster than average growth in job opportunities for child care workers through the year 2006. Many openings will arise from the need to replace the high proportion of child care workers who leave this occupation every year. There is a high job turnover rate because of the limited education and training requirements and the relatively low pay. Family day care is also expanding as social service agencies recognize and coordinate day care provision.

Working Conditions

There are a wide variety of working conditions when child care workers babysit in the homes of their employers. Hours are usually irregular and often include evenings and weekends. Many work part-time. On the other hand, family day care workers create their own work environment because they work at home. However, they may find the child care intrusive if the home is small.

Child care workers must be able to deal with the demands of children patiently and firmly. They may confront parents with attitudes that are different from their own. They should also be able to handle emergencies.

Earnings and Benefits

Wages of child care workers vary depending on their location and the situation in which they work. Wages are highest in the western United States and lowest in the Southeast. Self-employed babysitters earn between $190 and $310 a week. If they hold an unskilled job in a child care center, they may receive minimum wage.

Family day care workers who use their own homes must make initial expenditures for toys, outdoor equipment, first aid kits, extra toilets, and furniture. However, after this initial investment, some family day care workers earn up to $750 a week. Self-employed child care workers must provide their own health insurance.

Where to Go for More Information

National Association for the Education of
   Young Children
1509 Sixteenth Street, NW
Washington, DC 20036-1426
(202) 232-8777
www.naeyc.org

National Association for Family Child Care
206 Sixth Avenue, Suite 900
Des Moines, IA 50309-4018
(515) 282-8192

National Child Care Association
1016 Rosser Street
Conyers, GA 30012
(800) 543-7161
www.mccanet.com

Companion

Education and Training
None

Salary Range
Varies—see profile

Employment Outlook
Very good

Definition and Nature of the Work

Companions perform homemaking, personal care, social, and business services for people who are elderly, disabled, or recovering from illness. The duties of companions vary depending on the needs of their employers. They may read to their employers, talk to them, and play cards or other games with them. Companions may accompany and drive their employers, to social events, such as dinners and parties. They may also plan trips and outings for their employers as well as travel with them. Some companions handle their employers' business affairs, which include writing letters, paying bills, and going to the bank.

In attending to their employers' personal needs, companions may give medication and oversee exercise programs. They may plan, prepare, and serve meals and shop for food. They may do light housekeeping, such as dusting, sweeping, and making beds. Sometimes they also take care of washing and ironing clothes. Many companions live in their employers' homes. In some cases, companions speak with employers in their employers' native languages.

Education and Training Requirements

Age and educational requirements for companions vary. They are set by individual employers, who usually look for companions with social, cultural, and educational backgrounds similar to their own. In general, most employers prefer high school graduates. Some require companions to have a college education. Courses in family and consumer science, psychology, English, foreign languages, music, and art are good preparation for a career as a companion. Many companions also have a nursing background. However, some of the skills required of companions, such as cooking and cleaning, can be learned informally. Almost all employers require good references. Many prefer to hire those who have had experience in caring for people.

Getting the Job

You can get a job as a companion by contacting employment agencies that specialize in placing private household workers. You can also answer newspaper classifieds, check Internet job banks, or place your own ad in the "situation-wanted" section of a newspaper's classifieds. New employers often contact experienced workers who have a good reputation as a companion.

Advancement Possibilities and Employment Outlook

Companions advance by moving to a job with an employer who provides better working conditions and higher wages. Employment opportunities in the field are expected to grow faster than average through the year 2006. The number of people employed is not expected to change, as few people are willing to enter and remain in the field due to limited benefits and advancement. However, as the cost of nursing home care rises and the number of elderly people increases, there should be many job openings for companions.

Companions perform homemaking, personal care, social, and business services for people who are elderly, disabled, or recovering from illness.

Working Conditions

Most companions work in pleasant surroundings. Companions who live in their employers' homes generally have comfortable private rooms. Most companions work irregular hours, including nights and weekends. The amount of time they have off varies. Companions for the sick or elderly need patience, understanding, and a pleasant personality.

Earnings and Benefits

The earnings of companions vary according to their experience and the location and income of the employers. Earnings vary from $10 an hour in a big city to minimum wage— $5.15 an hour—in some rural areas. Some companions employed by wealthy families in urban areas can earn up to $800 to $1,200 a week. Live-in companions usually earn more than dayworkers and receive free room and board. Benefits may include paid vacations and bonuses.

Where to Go for More Information

National Association for Home Care
228 Seventh Avenue, SE
Washington, DC 20003
(202) 547-7424

National Council on the Aging
409 Third Street, SW, Second Floor
Washington, DC 20024
(202) 479-1200
www.ncoa.org

Dry Cleaning Worker

Education and Training
None

Salary Range
Varies—see profile

Employment Outlook
Very good

Definition and Nature of the Work

Dry cleaning workers clean, repair, and press clothes, linens, and other fabric items that cannot be cleaned in water. Dry cleaning involves the use of a variety of chemicals to clean fabrics. Most of the workers in this industry are employed by dry cleaning plants. Some workers have their own businesses.

There are many different kinds of jobs in the dry cleaning industry. *Route workers* pick up and deliver clothing at customers' homes and collect money from them. They often solicit new customers along their routes. *Counter clerks* receive soiled clothing from customers, give them receipts, and collect money when customers pick up the cleaned clothing. *Markers* tag or mark the soiled clothing so that it can be returned to the right customer. They are responsible for removing loose buttons and articles left in pockets. *Dry cleaners* sort the clothing according to its color and fabric type. They weigh the clothing and operate the cleaning machines. When the clothing is finished, they dry it in a tumbler or in a hot-air cabinet. *Spotters* remove stubborn stains by using chemicals, brushes, sponges, and other equipment. They may do this either before or after items are dry-cleaned.

Finishers place some of the clean clothing in steam tunnels to remove wrinkles. They press other clothing by using special steam irons and presses. Some finishers specialize in delicate clothing, and others may do only sturdy clothing, such as suits or coats. *Inspectors* check the finished clothing and decide whether it needs recleaning or refinishing. If necessary they send it to a *mender* for hand or machine sewing. *Assemblers* sort the clothing by matching it to the invoices. They put the clothing and invoices together so that the items can be returned to the right customer. Finally, *baggers* place bags over the clothing and attach the invoices. Sometimes one person does more than one of these jobs. Other

There are many different types of dry cleaning workers. This counter clerk receives soiled clothing from customers, gives them receipts, and charges customers when they pick up the cleaned clothing.

workers employed in this industry include office workers, plant managers, mechanics, and maintenance workers.

Education and Training Requirements

There are no educational requirements for many dry cleaning jobs. However, some employers prefer high school graduates for some positions. Although most dry cleaning workers learn on the job, some trade schools and vocational schools offer courses in dry cleaning, finishing, and spotting. Home study courses are also available. Some jobs take only a few days to learn whereas others require a full year of on-the-job experience.

Getting the Job

You can get a job in this field by applying directly to dry cleaning plants. You may find a job opening by reading the classifieds in newspapers or by checking Internet job banks. State and private employment agencies can also give you job information.

Advancement Possibilities and Employment Outlook

Some dry cleaning workers advance to more difficult jobs that pay higher wages. They can learn these jobs either on the job or by taking special courses organized by the International Fabricare Institute. These courses last from 2 to 4 weeks. They are designed to upgrade or expand a worker's skills or to provide a refresher course. Some dry cleaning workers become supervisors or managers.

Dry cleaners and spotters sometimes start their own businesses. An initial investment is needed to set up a small dry cleaning plant, and loans are available to qualified people. Some get started by renting equipment or buying used equipment.

The total number of jobs in the dry cleaning field is expected to increase faster than the average through the year 2006. However, new methods and machinery used for dry cleaning will eliminate some jobs. There will be openings to replace workers who leave the field.

Working Conditions

Dry cleaning workers usually work 40 hours a week. Hours may increase during busy seasons, which vary depending on the climate. There may also be slow seasons with reduced hours.

Modern dry cleaning plants are usually clean and well-lighted. Workers may be uncomfortable, however, because of the heat and odors created by the dry cleaning process. Many dry cleaning tasks are repetitive. Workers have to stand for long periods of time. There is some danger of injury from hot irons, presses, and chemicals. Some workers belong to unions.

Earnings and Benefits

Wages vary depending on the type of work. Entry-level workers earn around minimum wage. Spotters and dry cleaners may earn between $18,000 and $31,000 a year. Finishers who press items can earn between $13,000 and $20,000 a year. Employers often offer benefits that include paid holidays and vacations, health insurance, and pension plans.

Where to Go for More Information

International Drycleaners Congress
c/o North East Fabricare Association
343 Salem Street
Wakefield, MA 01880
(800) 442-6848

International Fabricare Institute
12251 Tech Road
Silver Spring, MD 20904-1976
(301) 622-1900
www.ifi.org

Textile Processors, Service Trades, Health
    Care, Professional and Technical
    Employees International Union
303 East Wacker Drive, Suite 1109
Chicago, IL 60601
(312) 946-0450

Gardener and Groundskeeper

Education and Training
None

Salary Range
Average—$220
to $410 a week

Employment Outlook
Good

Gardeners and groundskeepers take care of lawns and gardens. They often plant and maintain flowers, shrubs, and trees.

Definition and Nature of the Work

Gardeners and groundskeepers take care of lawns and gardens. They are sometimes called landscape gardeners or grounds custodians. Those who specialize in caring for lawns and have technical training are called turfgrass management technicians. Gardeners and groundskeepers work wherever lawns, trees, shrubs, and flowers need professional care. Many work at cemeteries, parks, golf courses, and other sports fields. Others work for arboretums, botanical gardens, and conservatories where different types of plants and trees are grown and displayed. Some schools, zoos, and museums have extensive grounds and employ gardeners and groundskeepers.

In addition, gardeners and groundskeepers maintain the grounds of factories, office buildings, shopping centers, housing developments, apartment complexes, highways, and resort hotels. Some workers take care of the lawns and gardens of individual families. Groundskeepers also work on farms that grow, harvest, and sell sod. The sod is grown as a lawn and is delivered to the buyer in pieces that are laid down as ground cover.

Some gardeners and groundskeepers work for landscaping services that are under contract to care for the grounds of several different firms, agencies, or homeowners. Many gardeners and groundskeepers have their own businesses.

The duties of gardeners and groundskeepers vary with the seasons and with their employers. They are usually responsible for keeping the soil in good condition. They often plant bulbs, flowers, shrubs, or trees. They may water, feed, transplant, and prune them. They often use chemicals to control insects, disease, and weeds. They may put down mulch, such as wood chips or peat moss, to control weeds and maintain soil moisture. Groundskeepers cut, fertilize, water, and renovate lawns.

Gardeners and groundskeepers often have other duties as well. For example, they may have to remove snow, leaves, and dead or diseased trees. They may paint or refinish outdoor furniture. They sometimes move benches and picnic tables, and they may be responsible for picking up litter and emptying trash cans.

Gardeners and groundskeepers use such tools as hoes, rakes, and spades. They also use power tools, such as gas-powered mowers and tillers and electric clippers and edgers. Sometimes they take care of underground watering systems. Gardeners and groundskeepers often maintain and repair their tools and equipment. They may sharpen lawn mower blades and oil hedge clippers.

Greenskeepers, sometimes called golf course superintendents, supervise the workers who care for golf courses. They decide what work needs to be done to keep the greens healthy and attractive. They make up schedules and assign duties. They sometimes help to take care of the greens themselves. In addition, greenskeepers often notify the public about the rules that must be followed on the golf course.

Education and Training Requirements

There are no specific educational requirements for gardeners and groundskeepers. However, many employers prefer to hire high school graduates. You can take high school, vocational school, or college courses in gardening and related subjects, such as biology, botany, and horticulture. Business subjects are useful if you want to start your own landscaping service.

Most gardeners and groundskeepers get their training on the job. Some colleges have 2-year programs in landscaping, horticulture, and lawn or turfgrass management. A few enter formal apprenticeship programs that combine classroom instruction with on-the-job training. Part-time and summer jobs caring for lawns and gardens or working in a greenhouse or on a farm are good ways to start your training.

Getting the Job

You can apply directly for a job at government agencies, business firms, landscape services, or private estates that employ gardeners and groundskeepers. Check newspaper classifieds and job banks on the Internet for openings listed in this field. If you attend a vocational school, you can ask the placement office to help you find a job. You may be able to get job information from professional associations and unions that include gardeners and groundskeepers in their membership.

Advancement Possibilities and Employment Outlook

Experienced gardeners and groundskeepers sometimes become head gardeners or supervisors. These workers can then get additional training or experience and become greenskeepers. Some go into business for themselves as landscape contractors. Other gardeners and groundskeepers advance by improving their skills in a special field through experience or further training. For example, gardeners can become tree surgeons and groundskeepers can become turfgrass specialists.

The employment outlook for gardeners and groundskeepers is expected to grow about as fast as the average for all occupations through the year 2006. There will be many job openings to replace workers who leave the field. Good gardeners and groundskeepers are always in demand. Growth in the construction of commercial and industrial buildings, shopping malls, homes, and highways should contribute to the demand for gardeners and groundskeepers.

Working Conditions

Gardeners and groundskeepers usually work alone or in small crews. They need to be able to work well with their hands and with tools and machinery. They must also be strong and healthy since their work requires much reaching, bending, lifting, and walking. The work is generally safe although tools and chemicals can be dangerous if not used properly. Gardeners and groundskeepers spend most of their working hours outdoors. Sometimes they also work in greenhouses, indoor gardens, or shops where equipment is kept. The hours are often irregular and depend on the climate, the season, and the type of job. There may be long workweeks of 44 to 48 hours in the spring and summer with shorter hours or even layoffs in the winter. Some gardeners and groundskeepers belong to unions.

Earnings and Benefits

Earnings vary widely depending on experience, location, and employer. Beginners usually earn about $5 to $8.75 an hour. The middle 50 percent of full-time gardeners and groundskeepers earn between $220 and $410 a week. Those who start their own businesses often earn higher incomes. With a degree in horticulture or plant science, experienced groundskeepers may make over $24,700 a year. Golf course superintendents earn about $38,600 a year.

Benefits also vary. Gardeners and groundskeepers who work for private estates may receive free housing in addition to their wages. Small landscape contracting services may provide few benefits. Self-employed workers must provide their own benefits. Workers employed by government agencies or business firms often receive benefits that include paid holidays and vacations, health insurance, and pension plans.

Where to Go for More Information

Professional Grounds Management Society
120 Cockeysville Road, Suite 104
Hunt Valley, MD 21030-2133
(410) 584-9754

Professional Lawn Care Association of
    America
1000 Johnson Ferry Road, NE, Suite C-135
Marietta, GA 30068-2112
(404) 977-5222
www.plcaa.org

Home Caterer

Education and Training
None

Salary Range
Varies—see profile

Employment Outlook
Good

Definition and Nature of the Work

Home cooks or caterers prepare food at home and serve it at parties and other functions. A good, well-organized cook can start a small catering business and serve gourmet food to large and small gatherings.

Catering offers people the opportunity to be their own bosses. It also can be a part-time occupation, which makes it attractive to homemakers and others who need supplementary incomes. Home caterers have flexible schedules because they can accept or pass up engagements. In addition, the evening and weekend hours required for most catered events make it possible for caterers to pursue other interests or jobs during the day or the week.

Unlike opening a restaurant, a catering business can be a low-investment, low-risk enterprise. Caterers who combine good food and practical organization with prime serving locations are often successful. In addition to the financial reward, there is the personal satisfaction of seeing people enjoy your food and having clients who continue to hire you for future engagements.

Education and Training Requirements

Many home caterers have no formal training. However, successful caterers are skillful in preparing traditional and new or unfamiliar dishes. They are also well-organized and can work under pressure.

Culinary degrees are offered by colleges and trade schools. It may prove useful to the home caterer to take courses that involve designing menus; estimating quantities and prices; and health, zoning, and insurance regulations related to the food industry.

Getting the Job

Although home catering businesses tend to expand by word of mouth, finding clients initially requires a good strategy. People who know fine food and can afford to pay for it often shop in gourmet and specialty stores. It may be possible to leave business cards and sample menus in these shops or even to set up a table with free samples. Florists, bakers, and rental company managers often provide services for special events such as weddings and reunions, which also need caterers. Contact these people for a good springboard to finding catering jobs. Also, museums, churches, and businesses frequently need caterers. You should contact the person in charge of food for social functions.

Home caterers must not only be skilled cooks, but they must also be able to get along with customers whose tastes may differ from their own. Promptness, good organizational skills, and good business sense are necessities.

Advancement Possibilities and Employment Outlook

There is a growing market for catering services, and caterers no longer limit their services to restaurant lunches and annual holiday dinners. People who work full-time are often too busy to cook and entertain. They may hire home caterers to prepare dinners for parties, or intimate, tasteful dinners.

Home catering services often start out small and then become large businesses. Some successful caterers decide to open retail stores with gourmet take-out and frozen dinners. Others decide to expand and become restaurant owners.

Home caterers cook and prepare food at home and serve it at parties and other functions.

Working Conditions

Cooking and catering services offer a variety of working conditions. Most small caterers work out of their own kitchens or out of the homes of friends or family members. Others prepare and serve meals at the locations of the parties or dinners including banquet rooms, outdoor patios, or private homes. Some caterers find that their own kitchen enables them to work more efficiently, whereas others are comfortable in any location with the proper equipment. Home caterers must also take into consideration state laws that govern food preparation when deciding on the location of their business.

Being a self-employed caterer offers the advantages of working either full- or part-time and being able to set your own hours. However, those hours are irregular and often include evenings and weekends.

Earnings and Benefits

Catering can be extremely profitable. Even inexperienced caterers earn over $250 a day after expenses. However, salaries vary because there are many factors which determine a caterer's earnings, such as food costs, labor, services, transportation, cancellation fees, insurance, and helpers' wages. Self-employed caterers must provide their own health insurance, vacation pay, and pension benefits.

Where to Go for More Information

National Association for the Specialty Food
    Trade, Inc.
120 Wall Street, 27th Floor
New York, NY 10005-4001
(212) 482-6440

Homemaker

Education and Training
None

Salary Range
Varies—see profile

Employment Outlook
Varies—see profile

Definition and Nature of the Work

People who take care of households for themselves and for the other people who live with them are called homemakers. They are responsible for managing the resources of their household. Homemakers may also perform general housekeeping chores and personal services, or they may assign them to other members of the household. Sometimes they employ people outside the household to do these tasks. Every household is unique, and the duties of each homemaker vary according to the ages, habits, needs, and incomes of the people in the household.

Homemakers are generally responsible for keeping their homes clean and running smoothly. They decide what cleaning jobs need to be done, and they arrange to have them completed. Cleaning tasks may include dusting, sweeping, making beds, washing and waxing floors, vacuuming, and a wide variety of other chores. Many homemakers also make sure that clothing and household items are laundered, dry-cleaned, or mended when needed. In many cases, they shop for food, clothing, and other household needs. Homemakers often plan, cook, and serve many of the meals for their households. Sometimes they make arrangements to have others cook meals in the home or to buy meals from outside sources.

Maintaining the household budget may be another responsibility of homemakers. They may take care of bills, banking, tax filing, and other financial matters. They often are responsible for day-to-day expenses, and they sometimes do long-range financial planning for their households. With other household members they make decisions about buying insurance, taking vacations, getting loans, and other important matters. Consumer skills are very important in making these decisions concerning the use of a household's resources.

In households with young children, homemakers have a great deal of responsibility for their care. If the children are very young, homemakers may feed, dress, and bathe them. As the children are growing, homemakers are responsible for creating a happy, healthy environment that will foster positive emotional and physical development. They may teach the children good health and personal habits, and make sure that they have proper medical and dental care. They may help them with their homework. As the children grow older, homemakers spend less time overseeing them. In some cases, homemakers care for adult members of the household who are ill or infirm.

Many homemakers drive household members to and from their daily activities. They may also have cars serviced. Some do minor repairs on cars and household appliances.

Improving the appearance of their homes may be another household responsibility. Homemakers often decorate their houses or apartments. They may paint or paper walls and ceilings, apply floor coverings, or refinish furniture. Sometimes they care for lawns and gardens. Often homemakers arrange to have these jobs done by outside contractors.

Since many homemakers have full- or part-time jobs outside the home, two or more household members may share the work of running a home. Homemakers spend varying periods of time in their occupations, and the needs of every household change. Homemakers' careers are flexible and diverse.

Education and Training Requirements

There are not any minimum age or educational requirements for homemakers. They learn such skills as cooking, cleaning, and child care informally at home.

You can prepare yourself for homemaking by taking high school and college courses in family and consumer science, psychology, sociology, mathematics, and first aid. Contact experienced homemakers for suggestions on ways to improve your homemaking skills. There are also many books, magazines, and television and radio programs that teach homemaking skills.

Getting the Job

Most people enter this field when they become responsible for the care of a home. In most cases, other household members work outside the home to provide the income that the homemaker uses to care for the home. Choosing to become a homemaker is a personal issue and a career decision. Because each situation is unique, there are no formal agencies that can help you to enter the field.

Advancement Possibilities and Employment Outlook

Since homemaking is not a formal job, there is no formal advancement in the field. However, homemakers usually improve their skills with experience. As they become more experienced as consumers, for example, they often learn to make better use of the resources available to them. Many homemakers believe the highest form of advancement is being satisfied with the management of their home and knowing that other members of the household are satisfied in their home. Other homemakers see a decrease in the number of chores or an increase in the household income as a form of advancement. Both the job of homemaking and its form of advancement are defined by the individual members of the household.

Many households are expected to need homemakers through the year 2006. Since needs change, the household that needs a full-time homemaker in one decade may need only a part-time homemaker in the next.

Working Conditions

Homemakers work in a great variety of physical surroundings, determined in part by family income and by their own skills as a homemaker. There are no set hours for homemakers.

Discipline and motivation are two qualities homemakers need to have. Patience, understanding, and a good sense of humor can help them to deal with the many demands of running a household. Successful homemakers are successful managers who can balance the many changing needs of household members and achieve a smoothly running household.

Earnings and Benefits

Homemakers are not paid salaries. They share the household income with other members of the household. One benefit is a flexible work schedule. They are able to pursue leisure or work activities inside and outside the household. Homemakers sometimes use some of the household income to provide themselves with such benefits as health or life insurance. In some cases, homemakers receive benefits from jobs they hold outside the home. They may share in benefits extended to other members of the household who have jobs outside the home. Some lawmakers are trying to pass laws that would change the financial status of homemakers.

Where to Go for More Information

American Association of Family and
   Consumer Sciences
1555 King Street, Fourth Floor
Alexandria, VA 22314
(703) 706-4600

Housekeeper, Domestic

Education and Training
None

Salary Range
Average—$5.15
to $10 an hour

Employment Outlook
Very good

Definition and Nature of the Work

Housekeepers clean private homes, buy food, cook and serve meals, and do laundry for family members. Some housekeepers work for several households, spending one or two days a week with each one. These housekeepers are called *dayworkers*. Other housekeepers work full-time for one family. Some full-time workers are *live-in housekeepers*, who live with the family for whom they work. In some cases, housekeepers work through social service agencies to housekeep for families with absent or ill parents.

The duties of individual domestic housekeepers vary widely. Some housekeepers have complete responsibility and authority to plan and carry out many household duties. Others are given very specific duties and are closely supervised. Housekeepers may plan, cook, and serve meals and clean up after food is eaten. They may buy food and household supplies. Sometimes they care for children, helping them to eat, dress, and bathe. They may also be responsible for disciplining children and entertaining them by reading to them or playing games with them.

Domestic housekeepers may clean floors, windows, furniture, and other areas. They sometimes make beds and change linens. They may wash, iron, and mend clothes and linens. Sometimes housekeepers perform such services as answering the telephone, receiving visitors, and exercising pets.

Education and Training Requirements

There are no specific educational requirements for housekeepers. Some employers prefer people who have a high school education. Experience and skill in caring for a home are generally more important than formal education. Housekeepers should know how to use such appliances as clothes washers, should be familiar with household cleaning products, and should know the basics of good nutrition.

Live-in housekeepers often clean the home, wash clothes, and cook and serve meals. Sometimes their responsibilities also include caring for children.

You can improve your skills in cooking, child care, and house cleaning by working as a helper to an experienced housekeeper. High school courses in family and consumer science may be helpful. Some community service organizations, social service agencies, vocational schools, and community colleges offer courses in food service, child development, and consumer studies.

Getting the Job

You can get a job as a housekeeper by registering with an employment agency that specializes in finding jobs for household workers. Formal training programs often have placement services that can help you. You can also apply directly to social service agencies or to firms that provide housekeeping services to families. Job openings are often listed in newspaper classifieds and you can place your own ad in the "situations-wanted" section of a newspaper. Once you have gained some job experience and a good reputation, you may be contacted by people who want to hire you.

Advancement Possibilities and Employment Outlook

Housekeepers usually advance by getting a raise in salary. They can also take jobs in households that offer better working conditions. Or they can move into a job requiring greater skill, such as a cook or a companion. In a few large households that employ several workers, housekeepers can become head housekeepers, who supervise other workers. Some housekeepers advance by working in day care centers, hotels, or restaurants. Others start their own firms that provide housekeeping services.

The employment outlook for housekeepers is expected to be very good through the year 2006. There has been a shortage of qualified household workers for some years, and they often work past retirement age. As more homemakers work outside the home, there should be more openings for part-time and full-time housekeepers.

Working Conditions

Because housekeepers work in private homes, working conditions vary greatly. Those who live in their employers' homes generally have pleasant surroundings and comfortable private rooms, although they may feel cut off from family and friends. Most home housekeepers, however, live in their own homes. They may have a key to the house or apartment and work on their own during the day. Housekeepers who work for social service agencies often work in difficult and unpleasant situations.

Housekeepers who work without direct supervision often have a great deal of responsibility. Some housekeepers must be able to deal with children. They must accept employers' attitudes and values that may differ from their own. Some of the work housekeepers do is physically demanding. They may have to lift and carry heavy objects during cleaning and shopping tasks.

Working hours vary. Dayworkers may work half-days or only a few days a week. Live-in housekeepers work longer hours. They often begin working before breakfast and do not finish until the children are in bed in the evening. Live-in housekeepers usually have some time off during the week.

Earnings and Benefits

Earnings for housekeepers vary with experience, location, and hours. Minimum wage laws now apply to most private household workers. Housekeepers earn from

Where to Go for More Information

Cleaning Management Institute
13 Century Hill Drive
Latham, NY 12110-2197
(518) 783-1281

the minimum wage—$5.15 an hour—in some rural areas, to $10 or more an hour in large cities such as New York. They also may receive meals and transportation costs. Live-in housekeepers receive free room and board. A few employers offer benefits, such as paid holidays and vacations and health insurance. Employers, by law, must make payments for the worker to the Social Security Administration. Housekeepers who work for social service agencies and housekeeping firms receive standard benefits.

Laundry Worker

Education and Training
None

Salary Range
Average—$5.15 to $8 an hour

Employment Outlook
Very good

Definition and Nature of the Work

Laundry workers take part in the washing, drying, and ironing of clothes and other fabric items. Most laundry workers are employed by commercial laundries, which may be independent plants or parts of large institutions, such as hospitals or hotels. Some laundry workers are employed by firms that specialize in renting and cleaning uniforms, diapers, towels, or other linens. A few laundry workers have their own businesses.

There are several different kinds of jobs in the laundry business. *Route workers* pick up soiled clothing and linens at customers' homes. Sometimes they try to solicit new customers along their routes. They also deliver clean laundry, bill customers, and collect money. *Counter clerks* receive soiled linens and clothing from customers, give back clean laundry, and collect payments from customers. *Markers* or *sorters* tag and mark the soiled clothing and linens so that they can be returned to the right customer. They usually remove loose buttons and mark items that need to be mended.

Machine washers weigh laundry and place it in huge washing machines. Machine washers control the machine settings for each kind of material. This includes setting the proper temperature, washing speed, and water and suds level and adding the right amount of bleaches and rinses. After the laundry is washed and rinsed, *extractor operators* place it in extractors, which spin most of the water out of it. The laundry then goes to *tumbler operators* who put it in drying machines that tumble it dry. Some items, such as blankets and rugs, may be hung in heated rooms to dry.

Finishers fold and press the clean, dry laundry. Some finishers specialize in flatwork, such as sheets and tablecloths. When requested, they press the flatwork using special ironing machines. They also may just fold and stack sheets, towels, diapers, or other flatwork. Other finishers work on shirts, ruffled curtains, blankets, or other items that require special pressing and finishing. To get professional results, they use forms designed for certain parts of clothing, such as shirt sleeves, shirt collars, or the bodies of skirts. They also use hand irons to finish certain items that cannot be done on the forms. The finished items are then folded or placed on hangers.

Inspectors check the finished laundry. If it needs rewashing or repressing, they send it back to the proper department. They send some pieces to *menders,* who do repairs by hand or machine. *Assemblers* collect all the items belonging to each customer. Finally, *baggers* or *bundle wrappers* place the laundry in bags or bundles and attach invoices, which indicate how much money the customer owes. Sometimes one person does more than one of these jobs. Other workers employed in the laundry industry include office workers, plant managers, mechanics, sales workers, and maintenance people.

Education and Training Requirements

In most cases, there are no educational requirements for laundry workers. Most workers learn on the job. Some jobs, such as flatwork folding, take only a few days to learn. It may take several weeks to learn to be a marker, inspector, or assembler. Some employers prefer high school graduates for jobs as managers and supervisors.

Getting the Job

You can get a job by applying directly to a laundry. You can also check the classifieds in newspapers and Internet job banks. State and private employment agencies can also give you job information.

Advancement Possibilities and Employment Outlook

Some laundry workers advance to better paying jobs that require more skill. They can learn new skills either on the job or by taking special courses organized by the International Fabricare Institute. These courses are designed to upgrade or expand a laundry worker's skills and last from a few days to a few weeks. Some laundry workers become supervisors or managers. A few start their own businesses. Some capital is needed to set up a small laundry, but loans are available to qualified people.

The total number of jobs in the laundry business is expected to grow faster than average through the year 2006. New methods and machinery will eliminate some jobs. However, there will be numerous openings to replace laundry workers who leave the field.

Route workers pick up soiled clothing and linens at customers' homes and bring them to the laundry for cleaning. Then they return the clean clothing and linens to customers' homes.

Working Conditions

Laundry workers generally work 40 hours a week. Modern laundries are usually clean and well-lighted, but they are generally noisy, hot, and humid. Laundry jobs tend to be repetitious and require workers to stand for long periods of time. There is some danger of injury from hot water, irons, presses, and from lifting heavy loads of laundry. Some workers belong to unions.

Earnings and Benefits

Wages in this field vary depending on the type of work. Laundry workers who are not supervisors earn an average of $5.15 to $8 an hour. Those with more experience may earn up to $10 an hour. Employers often offer benefits that include paid holidays and vacations.

Where to Go for More Information

International Fabricare Institute
12251 Tech Road
Silver Spring, MD 20904-1976
(301) 622-1900
www.ifi.org

Textile Processors, Service Trades, Health
    Care, Professional and Technical
    Employees International Union
303 East Wacker Drive, Suite 1109
Chicago, IL 60601
(312) 946-0450

Personal Service Worker

Education and Training
Varies—see profile

Salary Range
Average—$5.15
to $25 an hour

Employment Outlook
Good

Definition and Nature of the Work

Personal service workers help people who are unable to perform certain tasks because of various reasons such as being too busy or too ill. They may stand in line for license renewals, organize retirement parties, index videotape collections, or take elderly people to their doctors' appointments. There are no limits to the sizes or types of jobs personal service workers do. Personal service workers may be self-employed, or they may work for agencies that provide such services.

Some workers specialize in certain services. For instance, a worker who provides stand-in services will wait in line to renew a passport or stay in a house while a new furnace is installed. Other workers who offer organizational services will alphabetize files, set up offices, or arrange garage sales. Some offer personal shopping services. These workers bring ranges of goods to choose from to the clients' homes, or they buy those items requested by the clients. Some agencies offer all of these services.

Education and Training Requirements

Education and training requirements for personal service workers vary according to the tasks to be done. For example, establishing a filing system may call for past office experience, whereas assembling a bookshelf kit may require some carpentry skills. Many personal services simply call for common sense, patience, and a willingness to help. Taking dogs for walks, opening a summer house, waiting for a telephone installer, and buying a funeral wreath fall into this category.

Getting the Job

You can get a job as a personal service worker by applying directly to agencies, which are usually located in large cities. You can also check newspaper classifieds and job banks on the Internet, both of which may list positions under "dispatcher," "messenger," "gal/guy Friday," or "handyman."

Advancement Possibilities and Employment Outlook

Many young people take part-time personal service jobs while they are studying at college. These jobs are also ideal for retired persons, people who like to set their own work schedules, or workers with minimum skills or experience. Because the work is so varied, the personal service worker benefits from a range of tasks and environments. Some tasks can lead to further interests or changes in occupations. For example, a worker who enjoys assembling a bookshelf kit might decide on a carpentry career; someone who cares for a disabled person might think about the possibility of nursing. Some personal service workers open their own agencies.

The employment outlook is good. However, the number of openings is dependent on the needs and income of the people who want these services. There are a large number of two-career couples who do not have the time for shopping, waiting in lines, keeping house, or other tasks. Their needs will continue to create openings for these workers.

Working Conditions

Personal service workers work in many different conditions. They work indoors or outdoors, during the daytime or evening, and at a frantic or a leisurely pace. Beginning service workers should seek the agency with the most suitable working conditions. Stand-in and dispatch services are often physically demanding.

Earnings and Benefits

Most personal service workers are paid by the task or by the hour—from $5.15 to $25 and up an hour—rather than receiving a weekly salary. Earnings depend on the skills required for the job. For example, a worker would be better paid for organizing a home than for collecting laundry from the dry cleaner. Personal service workers must arrange for their own benefits.

Where to Go for More Information

National Association of Professional
 Organizers
1033 La Posada Drive, Suite 220
Austin, TX 78752-3880
(512) 454-8626
www.ccsi.com

Personal Shopper

Definition and Nature of the Work

Personal shoppers help people to select and purchase clothing and other merchandise. The scope of the job ranges from gift buying for their clients to providing advice for a complete change of image. In this emerging field, several other job titles are used, including fashion consultant and personal image consultant.

Personal shoppers vary considerably in the services they offer and in their methods of working with clients. Those who work for a department or specialty store provide advice about purchases of clothes and other items from their store. These personal shoppers may coordinate items from several departments within the store to save the client time. Fashion consultants who work for consulting firms or who are self-employed usually meet with clients to learn their needs, budget requirements and professional status, and to analyze their current wardrobe. Then the consultant researches which stores have the clothing and accessories that will suit the client best. The consultant may then take the client shopping to make final selections. Many personal shoppers offer advice on makeup, hairstyling, and colors, in addition to shopping assistance. Some even provide an entire "makeover" service, including posture and public speaking skills, for clients who wish to change their image.

Education and Training
Varies—see profile

Salary Range
Varies—see profile

Employment Outlook
Good

Personal shoppers help people to select and purchase clothing and other merchandise. To be successful, they need to be able to analyze a client's needs and fulfill them.

Education and Training Requirements

Personal shoppers have emerged from a number of fields, including marketing, fashion design, and communications. There are no particular education or training requirements, but a potential personal shopper must have strong interpersonal skills and a good sense of style. Experience in retailing and buying is also helpful.

Getting the Job

Since many personal shoppers work on a consulting basis, breaking into the field may involve little more than finding a few initial clients, working with them successfully, and getting permission to use them as references to attract new customers. Working as a salesperson in a clothing store might give you a good start, enabling you either to work your way up to personal shopper for the store or to find your first clients from among the store's customers.

Advancement Possibilities and Employment Outlook

For personal shoppers who are self-employed, advancement usually comes in the form of gaining a good reputation, expanding their clientele, and charging higher rates for their services. Some become consultants for design companies, and some offer training to aspiring consultants. Personal shoppers for major stores may eventually manage the personal shopping department or start an independent service.

The outlook for personal shoppers is good through 2006. More and more men are seeking shopping assistance, and this trend will continue to create more opportunities.

Working Conditions

Personal shoppers are likely to have irregular hours, including some evenings and weekends, since most clients have jobs that make weekday consultations inconvenient. Personal shoppers spend most of their time in stores, and unless they work for one store, they may have to visit many shops in a short period of time. Tact and discretion are essential qualities for a fashion consultant.

Earnings and Benefits

Earnings in this field depend on the type and level of service provided as well as the reputation of the shopper. Independent personal shopping consultants may charge from $25 to $300 an hour for consultations. They may also charge from $20 to $80 an hour for shopping time. Some charge a commission based on the price of the items purchased. Benefits for personal shoppers who work for stores or large consulting firms include paid holidays and vacations, health insurance, and pension plans. Self-employed personal shoppers must provide their own benefits.

Where to Go for More Information

Association of Image Consultants
  International
1000 Connecticut Avenue, NW, Suite 9
Washington, DC 20036
(800) 383-8831
e-mail: aici@worldnet.att.net

Pest Control Worker

Education and Training
None

Salary Range
Starting—$5.15
  to $7.50 an hour
Average—$26,000
  to $29,000

Employment Outlook
Very good

Definition and Nature of the Work

Pest control workers help to eliminate and control undesirable insects and animals. These pests include rats, mice, and other rodents as well as termites, cockroaches, and wasps. Sometimes workers are also asked to rid buildings of birds or snakes. They control or remove pests in private homes, businesses, and institutions. Pest control workers are sometimes called exterminators.

Most pest control workers are employed by firms that specialize in pest control. These may be small independent firms or branches of nationwide chains. Some workers have their own businesses. A few work for local, state, or federal government agencies. Some large institutions and firms, such as food processing companies, have their own staffs of pest control workers. Pest control work is very important in preventing disease and property damage.

Many pest control workers travel regular routes. Route workers make scheduled visits to private homes and businesses, such as restaurants and food stores. They go back to these places regularly to make sure that pests do not return. Some pests, such as cockroaches and mice, are difficult to eliminate. Workers put poison or traps in places where pests are most likely to be found. They often spray large areas to force pests out of their hiding places. They may also advise customers about ways of sealing up holes and destroying nesting and breeding areas. Termite exterminators may need to drill holes in basement floors to pump chemicals into the ground under the house. To insure that termites do not return, foundations may be raised or wood replaced. Builders may be called in for major reconstruction.

Pest control workers are often contacted to solve a particular pest problem. The first thing the workers do is look at the damaged or infested area. They try to locate nests. They may track the pests' movements to uncover their hiding places. Workers must identify what kind of pest has invaded the area. If it is a rare species, they may ask another expert to identify it.

Pest control workers must decide on the best way to eliminate each type of pest. Sprays or liquids work best against some insects. A solid or powder might be most effective against rodents. The method used will also depend on the area that is infested. For example, workers would not use a spray where food is exposed. In some cases, such as in termite control, special drills, spraying equipment, and other machines are needed. Traps and poisoned baits are sometimes used. Pest control workers also inspect buildings for termites and give estimates of how much an extermination job will cost.

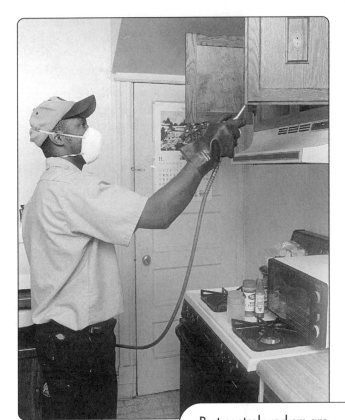

Pest control workers are trained and often state-certified in the use of sprays, liquids, and powders to eliminate undesirable insects and rodents.

Education and Training Requirements

Employers often prefer to hire high school graduates. Courses in chemistry, biology, and business mathematics are helpful. Termite exterminators will also find a knowledge of carpentry valuable. Pest control workers usually need a driver's license and a good driving record. Most employers give their workers on-the-job training. Beginners may be assigned to help an experienced worker, or they may be given some formal training either in a classroom or through a home-study course. It usually takes 2 or 3 months to learn the basics in pest control work. It takes a few years of experience to handle the more difficult pest control problems.

Technicians who apply or supervise the application of restricted-use pesticides must be certified by the state. A valid driver's license is also required.

Getting the Job

To get a job, apply directly to pest control companies. Check newspaper classifieds and Internet job banks, and contact state or private employment agencies. You can also apply to government agencies or to large institutions or businesses that have their own staffs of pest control workers. Some firms conduct training classes that last 2 to 3 weeks. New employees also accompany experienced workers on service calls.

Advancement Possibilities and Employment Outlook

Some pest control workers become supervisors, salespeople, or managers in large companies. Others save or borrow money to start their own pest control businesses. Workers can also advance to higher-paying, more responsible positions by getting additional training through college courses in science or business administration. Some workers become experts in one area of pest control, such as termite control.

The employment outlook for pest control is expected to increase faster than the average through the year 2006. There are currently 60,000 employed pest control workers.

Working Conditions

Working conditions depend on the job. A worker may spend one day working in the kitchen of a restaurant and the next day crawling through a dirty basement looking for rats' nests. Usually workers do their job alone, without supervision. They work both indoors and outdoors. Pest control workers often have to carry and lift equipment and materials weighing as much as 50 pounds. They must be very careful when using poisons, because some pesticides are harmful to humans if inhaled or touched. They should have manual dexterity as well as some mechanical skill.

Most pest control workers have workweeks of 40 to 44 hours. They may work longer hours during warm weather, when pests are more active. Some weekend, night, and emergency work may be required. Some clients, such as restaurants, ask that pest control workers visit them before or after normal business hours.

Earnings and Benefits

Today some beginning pest control workers earn between $5.15 and $7.50 an hour. Experienced workers earn anywhere from $26,000 to $29,000 a year, depending on the amount of education and experience they have. Some route workers are paid a commission or percentage of the customer's bill. Benefits vary, but they may include paid holidays and vacations, health insurance, and pension plans.

Where to Go for More Information

National Pest Control Association
8100 Oak Street
Dunn Loring, VA 22027
(703) 573-8330

Pet Care Worker

Education and Training
None

Salary Range
Varies—see profile

Employment Outlook
Very good

Definition and Nature of the Work

Pet care workers provide a wide variety of services for the owners of small animals, such as dogs, cats, and birds. Pet care workers are employed in animal hospitals, boarding kennels, animal shelters, pet grooming establishments, pet training schools, and pet shops. Some pet care workers have their own businesses.

There are many kinds of pet care workers. *Kennel attendants* care for animals and keep their quarters clean. They feed and give water to the animals in their care. They watch the animals closely to make sure that they are in good health. They often exercise animals and keep records on the animals' health, feeding, and breeding patterns. At times they may have to euthanize (put to death) some diseased or unwanted animals.

Animal groomers bathe pets and use special solutions to keep them free of fleas, ticks, and other pests. They often brush and trim their hair and cut their nails. *Dog trainers* teach dogs to hunt or track, to obey signals or commands, to guard lives or property, to run races, or to lead the blind. *Dog guide instructors* train dogs to assist blind people in finding their way to such routine places as their offices and grocery stores. They may also train dogs to assist other disabled people in the completion of daily activities. *Handlers* hold and command trained animals during a show, sporting match, or hunt. *Animal breeders* arrange for the mating of animals and care for the mother and the young. They usually train or sell the young animals when they reach a certain age. They often specialize in one breed, such as German shepherd dogs or Siamese cats.

Pet shop owners care for the birds, fish, cats, dogs, and other animals that they offer for sale. They also interact with customers. In addition, they must take care of the business details involved in running a store.

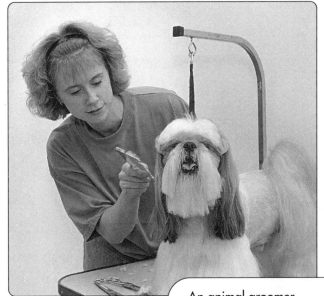

An animal groomer combs and trims a dog's hair. Groomers use special solutions to keep pets free of fleas, ticks, and other pests.

Education and Training Requirements

There are no special education requirements for most jobs in pet care. Many employers prefer to hire high school graduates. You need to know about the needs and habits of animals to work in this field. You can learn about animals by having pets of your own or by working part-time or during summers in a kennel or pet shop. Some people get started by taking care of pets when the animals' owners are away.

To prepare for a job in this field, you may want to take courses in biology and animal husbandry. In some cases, you will need special training. For example, schools that train guide dogs for the blind have programs to train the instructors. You learn to teach the guide dogs and their blind owners to work together. In other cases, you learn on the job. If you want to start your own kennel or pet shop, take courses in business management, such as bookkeeping.

Getting the Job

Apply directly to animal hospitals, boarding kennels, animal shelters, pet shops, and other places that employ pet care workers. You can check newspaper classifieds and Internet job banks. Private and state employment agencies may also be able to help you find a job.

Advancement Possibilities and Employment Outlook

Pet care workers can advance to become supervisors in large animal hospitals, kennels, or pet shops. Some experienced workers start their own kennels or pet shops. A few pet care workers go on to college and become veterinarians. Pet care workers can also increase their earnings by developing skills in special fields, such as grooming, training, or breeding animals.

There are many qualified people looking for beginning jobs in pet care. The best jobs will go to those who have the most experience in caring for animals. There will be openings to replace workers who leave the field. Since more people are keeping pets, the number of jobs should increase, and job opportunities should be very good through the year 2006.

Working Conditions

Pet care workers must enjoy being around animals. They may work indoors or outdoors. They must get used to the odor of animals and should not mind cleaning up after them. Their work may involve lifting heavy animals and equipment. Sometimes they must drive station wagons or trucks to pick up or deliver pets. The work involves interacting with people, so workers should be friendly and courteous.

Many pet care workers work 40 hours a week. Some workers must also work or be on call evenings or weekends. There are some jobs for part-time workers to care for animals at night or on weekends. Some workers care for animals on an around-the-clock basis with some time off during each day. In these situations, the employers often provide attendants with living quarters near the kennel. Pet shop workers and owners often work more than 40 hours a week.

Earnings and Benefits

Earnings vary widely depending on the location, the type of job, and the worker's experience. Many pet care workers begin at the minimum wage. Experienced kennel attendants earn about $200 to $300 a week. Experienced groomers who work in a pet shop may get a percentage of the price charged to groom the animal. Pet shop owners average $30,000 a year, but many make much less.

Benefits vary, but employers may provide paid vacations and holidays, health insurance, and pension plans. Self-employed workers must provide their own benefits.

Where to Go for More Information

American Veterinary Medical Association
1931 North Meacham Road, Suite 100
Schaumburg, IL 60173-4360
(708) 925-8070

National Dog Groomers Association of America
P.O. Box 101
Clark, PA 16113
(412) 962-2711

Pet Industry Joint Advisory Council
1220 Nineteenth Street, NW, Suite 400
Washington, DC 20036
(202) 452-1525

Professional Organizer

Education and Training
None

Salary Range
Average—$25 to $125 an hour

Employment Outlook
Very good

Definition and Nature of the Work

Professional organizers bring order to everything from office filing systems and medical records to family budgets and bedroom closets. They help businesses and individuals gain more control over time and space, reduce stress, and increase productivity by providing information and ideas, structure, and comprehensive organizational systems.

While some professional organizers will organize just about anything for a client, others specialize in a particular area. Those who specialize usually choose an area related to the field in which they worked before becoming organizers. For example, an organizer who previously worked in banking may specialize in organizing financial matters such as bill paying and retirement accounts. Other specialties include residential or office organizing, closet/storage design and organizing, relocation management, records or filing systems management, memorabilia organizing, and time and space management.

Education and Training

There are no specific educational or training requirements needed to become a professional organizer. However, organizers should be well-versed in their area of expertise and be able to provide references for potential clients. Most professional organizers enter the field after working for several years in other professions. All organizers must have good communication and management skills and must be detail oriented.

Professional organizers may be hired to organize anything from a family's budget to the bedroom closets. This organizer is bringing order to a home kitchen.

Getting the Job

You can consult the member directory of the National Association of Professional Organizers for names of organization/management consulting firms in your area. Many people who enter the field begin work as freelancers and set up their own small businesses. They advertise in newspapers, magazines, and professional journals to attract clients.

Advancement Possibilities and Employment Outlook

Advancement in this field depends on gaining a reputation for performing quality service. Some professional organizers advance by moving from smaller rural markets to more lucrative metropolitan areas. Others start their own businesses after holding positions in large management firms.

The field of professional organizing is growing rapidly, primarily due to the increasing demands placed on people by the complex technology of the Information Age. More and more people are turning to organizers to help them put aspects of their personal and professional lives in order. Therefore, the job outlook for professional organizers is very good through the year 2006.

Working Conditions

Professional organizers generally work out of offices or their own homes. They spend a great deal of time meeting with clients and working at clients' homes and business offices. Many work flexible hours. Professional organizers also spend time designing organizational plans and negotiating with suppliers.

Where to Go for More Information

National Association of Professional
   Organizers
1033 La Posada Drive, Suite 220
Austin, TX 78752-3880
(512) 454-8626
www.ccsi.com/~asmi/GROUPS/NAPO
   /napo.html

Earnings and Benefits

Earnings for professional organizers vary widely according to qualifications, experience, type of service offered, and geographic area. Hourly fees range from $25 to $125. Some organizers charge by the day, collecting as much as $1,500 for an 8- to 10-hour day.

Large management consulting firms usually provide health insurance, paid vacations, and retirement plans to their employees. Professional organizers who work on a freelance basis must provide their own benefits.

Rug and Carpet Cleaner

Education and Training
None

Salary Range
Average—$240
to $500 a week

Employment Outlook
Good

Definition and Nature of the Work

Rug and carpet cleaners use chemical solutions, soap and water, and a variety of hand brushes and mechanical equipment to clean rugs and carpets. Carpets are usually sewed together and tacked to the floor. They are cleaned in a customer's home. Rugs usually do not cover an entire floor. They are often cleaned in a rug cleaning plant. Most rug and carpet cleaners work for firms that specialize in cleaning rugs and carpets for homeowners, business firms, and other customers. Some rug and carpet cleaners work for building maintenance firms. Others are employed by large establishments, such as hotels and apartment complexes.

When workers clean carpets in a customer's home or business, they first decide on the proper chemical solution and cleaning method to use, depending on the general condition and fiber content of the carpet. Then they apply the chemical solutions to the carpet to break down dirt and stains. Most cleaners use steam vacuums or mechanical circular scrubbers to extract the dirt. The carpet then dries naturally. Some methods require only an hour, others need 6 to 8 hours.

Rug and carpet cleaners also examine floor coverings for stubborn stains that were not removed by the vacuum machines. They select the right type of stain remover for each kind of fiber and for each kind of stain. They work the stain remover into the rug or carpet until the stain is removed.

Rugs cleaned at a plant are usually fed into rug cleaning machines that scrub, rinse, and partly dry them. To finish drying, rugs are often hung in a heated room. Once the rugs are dry, rug cleaners may use a special machine to raise the pile. Sometimes they apply sizing to the back of the rug to help it keep its shape and resist soiling.

Rug cleaners sometimes clean delicate rugs by hand. They may repair and rebind edges using scissors, a knife, and needle and thread. Some rug and carpet cleaners also clean upholstered furniture. Workers are required to measure rugs and carpets and give customers estimates for the cleaning.

Education and Training Requirements

Many employers prefer to hire high school graduates. You can learn rug and carpet cleaning on the job. An informal training period under the supervision of an experienced worker lasts about 6 months. Trainees learn about the different cleaning solutions and rug fibers, how to identify and treat stains, and how to use and maintain equipment.

Getting the Job

Job openings for rug and carpet cleaners are often listed in newspaper classifieds and job banks on the Internet. You can also apply directly to rug and carpet cleaning firms, to building maintenance firms, and to businesses that employ their own rug and carpet cleaners, such as hotels. State and private employment agencies may also be able to help you find a job.

Advancement Possibilities and Employment Outlook

In large rug cleaning firms, experienced workers can become supervisors. Some workers open their own businesses. This requires an initial investment, but it is often possible to get a loan or rent the necessary equipment.

The employment outlook is good through the year 2006. As the demand for construction increases, so will the demand for carpet cleaners. There will also be jobs to replace workers who leave the field. However, some of the demand will be offset by people using home cleaning products or renting the necessary equipment to do the job themselves.

Rug and carpet cleaners must determine which chemical solution and cleaning method to use, depending on the general condition and fiber content of a rug or carpet.

Working Conditions

Rug and carpet cleaners generally work 40 hours a week. They may have to work some evening and Saturday hours. Since much of the work is done in customers' homes and businesses, working conditions vary. Workers usually drive to job sites in trucks provided by their employers. Rug and carpet cleaners who work in rug cleaning plants may find the heat and noise unpleasant. Certain chemicals used in cleaning rugs and carpets have unpleasant odors and may irritate the skin. Workers must use these chemicals with care. Rug and carpet cleaners often lift heavy machines and rugs. Workers who meet and talk with customers should be friendly and courteous.

Earnings and Benefits

Salaries are higher in the spring and summer than in the slower winter months. Experienced rug and carpet cleaners earn between $240 and $500 a week depending on the season. Trainees usually begin at the minimum wage and receive regular increases. Employers generally provide benefits that include paid holidays and vacations and health insurance. Self-employed workers must provide their own benefits.

Where to Go for More Information

Association of Specialists in Cleaning and Restoration
10830 Annapolis Junction Road, Suite 312
Annapolis Junction, MD 20701-1120
(800) 272-7012
www.ascr.org

The Carpet and Rug Institute
310 South Holiday Avenue
P.O. Box 2048
Dalton, GA 30722-2048
(706) 278-3176

International Fabricare Institute
12251 Tech Road
Silver Spring, MD 20904-1976
(301) 622-1900
www.ifi.org

Shoe Repairer

Education and Training
None

Salary Range
Average—$350
to $500 a week

Employment Outlook
Poor

Definition and Nature of the Work

Shoe repairers rebuild, remodel, and repair boots and shoes. They also mend luggage, handbags, and sports equipment, such as tents, saddles, and golf bags. Some shoe repairers specialize in making and repairing orthopedic shoes following a doctor's prescription. Most shoe repairers work in shoe repair shops. Some work in shops in variety stores, department stores, shoe stores, or dry cleaning shops. About half of all workers have their own shoe repair businesses.

Shoe repair workers generally spend much of their time replacing worn heels and soles. They remove the old sole and sand the bottom of the shoe to make it rough so that the new sole will stay in place. Then they choose a ready-made sole or cut one from a piece of leather. They attach the sole to the shoe with nails, cement, or stitching, and then trim it to size. To replace heels, they first pry off the old heel. Then they select a factory-made replacement or cut one to the proper size and shape. They fasten the heel to the shoe with cement and nails. They stain and buff the new sole and heel to match the color of the shoe. To complete a repair job, workers may restitch worn or ripped seams, replace inner soles, and polish the shoes.

Shoe repairers use a variety of hand and power tools including hammers, awls, automatic sole stitchers, heel-nailing machines, and sewing machines. In large shops some shoe repairers specialize in only one task, such as the restitching of torn seams. Other shoe repairers do a wide variety of jobs that may include stretching shoes that are too tight. Shoe repairers restyle shoes by changing their color or by reshaping the toes and heels. They add or remove ornaments. They sometimes repair or replace zippers in articles made of canvas, leather, or rubber. Many workers are also responsible for waiting on customers and taking care of the business details involved in running a shoe repair shop. In some shops they sell leather goods and accessories such as shoelaces, polishes, and foot comfort aids.

Education and Training Requirements

Most employers prefer to hire high school graduates. Shoe repairers usually get their training on the job. It takes from 6 months to 2 years to become fully qualified. You can also learn the shoe repair trade in a vocational or trade school. Most school programs take from 6 months to 2 years to complete. Students receive practical training in the use of the tools, machines, and materials used in the repairing and rebuilding of shoes. After completing such a program, workers usually need an additional year or so of experience before they are fully qualified as shoe repairers. Graduates of vocational schools may be hired more quickly than those who have no training or experience.

Getting the Job

You can get a job as a shoe repairer by applying directly to shoe repair shops. Large shoe repair shops employ the greatest number of workers, but you can also apply to the shoe repair departments of variety or department stores or to dry cleaning firms. Shoe stores that specialize in orthopedic shoes and shoes for people with uncommon sizes sometimes employ shoe repairers. You can also apply to firms that make and repair leather goods. Some jobs are listed in newspaper classifieds and job banks on the Internet. State or private employment agencies may also be able to help you find a job. If you attend a trade or vocational school, the placement office can give you job information.

Shoe repair workers generally work in shoe repair shops where they repair boots and shoes, restyle shoes, and mend other leather items.

Advancement Possibilities and Employment Outlook

Shoe repairers can advance by becoming supervisors or managers in large shops or by opening their own shops. Loans are available to qualified people.

Jobs for shoe repairers are expected to decrease steadily through the year 2006. People are buying more inexpensive shoes made of materials that cannot be repaired. Some jobs may be available in "while-you-wait" repair shops that have opened to offer customers more convenient service.

Working Conditions

Working conditions for shoe repairers vary. Most large shops are clean and well-lighted. Small shops may be noisy, crowded, or poorly ventilated. The strong odor of leather and dyes may bother some workers. Shoe repair employees generally work 40 hours a week. Self-employed repairers often work as many as 60 hours a week. Shops tend to be busiest in the spring and fall, but there are not usually any seasonal layoffs.

Shoe repairers spend most of the working day on their feet. Some mechanical ability and manual dexterity is required. Those who deal with customers should be patient and courteous.

Earnings and Benefits

Currently shoe repairers earn approximately $350 to $500 a week. Shop managers and owners of shoe repair shops earn substantially more. Salaries vary according to the worker's skill and experience and geographic location. Employers generally provide paid holidays and vacations. Large companies often give more benefits than small shops. Self-employed shoe repairers must provide their own benefits.

Where to Go for More Information

Shoe Service Institute of America
5024-R Campbell Boulevard
Baltimore, MD 21236-5974
(410) 931-8100
e-mail: lebovic@aol.com

Union of Needletrades, Industrial and
    Textile Employees
1710 Broadway
New York, NY 10019
(212) 265-7000

Swimming Pool Servicer

Education and Training
High school

Salary Range
Starting—$210
to $250 a week

Employment Outlook
Good

Definition and Nature of the Work

Swimming pool servicers clean and check the water in swimming pools. They maintain certain standards of water quality by adding chemicals such as chlorine, iodine, and hydrochloric acid to the water. Swimming pool servicers must follow strict rules for pool treatment and must handle and measure chemicals very carefully. Too little of a chemical may allow algae to grow; too much may cause eye or skin irritation and sickness.

When cleaning a pool, the servicer removes debris with a net, brushes the walls with a bristle brush, and vacuums the pool floor. Pool servicers must be alert for pool equipment problems, such as clogged pipes and rusted equipment. Their tools include pressure gauges, steel snakes, and rubber plungers.

Winter pool closings and summer openings are an important part of servicers' work. At the end of the summer season, the servicers must drain and clean filters and tanks. They also must remove and store diving boards and ladders. They may need to cover the pool with a heavy tarpaulin. At the beginning of the new swimming season, servicers clean the deck, paint the pool interior if necessary, and inspect and repair equipment as needed.

Education and Training Requirements

Swimming pool service contractors look for employees with a high school diploma or a background in the building trades. Beginning pool servicers receive 2 to 8 weeks of on-the-job training. Because the job requires a lot of driving, a driver's license is necessary.

Swimming pool servicers test the water quality of pools. They add chemicals such as chlorine, iodine, and hydrochloric acid to the water to maintain certain standards.

High school courses in chemistry, biology, metalwork, and pipe fitting will be useful. Bookkeeping will be helpful to servicers who want to start their own businesses. Swimming pool servicers must keep accurate records of their water tests and handle chemicals carefully. This calls for a high level of self-discipline and responsibility.

Getting the Job

Job seekers should visit or write to companies that build, install, and service pools. The job seeker should be willing to work on pool construction until servicing positions become available.

Advancement Possibilities and Employment Outlook

Swimming pools are often the focal points of health and sports clubs. As more and more of these clubs open, there will be a corresponding rise in the demand for pool servicers. Health departments, concerned about bacterial pollution in home pools, are calling for more pool inspections and controls. Workers who can increase the number of pools they service a day or who are expert troubleshooters will receive higher wages.

The employment outlook for swimming pool servicers is expected to increase about as fast as the average for all jobs through the year 2006. Nevertheless, there are still seasonal upswings and downturns, and some servicers may need to find other work during the winter.

Working Conditions

Most swimming pool servicers work for small- to medium-size contractors, and they usually work alone. Servicers wear long rubber gloves and special uniforms to protect themselves against chlorine and other harmful chemicals. The work is not overly strenuous but may require some lifting, and workers remain standing for long periods of time. In large servicing companies, workers may specialize in tasks such as repairing or painting.

A swimming pool servicer's schedule may vary from day to day, according to geographic location and seasonal changes. The average worker is sent out to service two or three private pools a day. At the height of the season, however, he or she may service twice that number. Large public pools must be cleaned every day. They often take six hours or more to clean. Sometimes they must be cleaned in the evening hours, when the pool is closed. For this type of job, servicers often work in teams of two or more.

Earnings and Benefits

Newly employed workers may receive about $160 a week during training and then $210 to $250 a week base pay. Wages may go up to $320 or more a week for workers who can service more than the average number of pools or who are expert troubleshooters and repairers. Swimming pool servicers receive uniforms and group health insurance. Vacation and sick time vary among pool servicing companies.

Where to Go for More Information

National Spa and Pool Institute
2111 Eisenhower Avenue
Alexandria, VA 22314
(703) 838-0083

Window Cleaner

Definition and Nature of the Work

Window cleaners wash and dry glass surfaces on the insides and outsides of buildings. They usually work for window cleaning companies or for building maintenance firms that do many different kinds of cleaning. Large business and industrial firms often hire window cleaners as permanent employees. Some window cleaners have their own businesses.

Windows cleaners wash glass surfaces in private homes, offices, and many other kinds of buildings. In addition to windows, they often wash glass partitions, mirrors, and other glass surfaces. Window cleaners use brushes, sponges, or wet cloths to apply soapy water or other cleaning solutions to the surfaces. They dry the wet glass with a cloth, chamois skin, or squeegee. When they work on windows above the ground floor, window cleaners use scaffolding, ladders, or special swinging seats. They sometimes crawl through windows from the inside and support themselves with safety belts hooked to brackets.

Education and Training
None

Salary Range
Average—$5.75 to $8 an hour

Employment Outlook
Good

Education and Training Requirements

There are no specific educational requirements for window cleaners. You must be at least 18 years old. You can learn window cleaning on the job. Some

Window cleaners must have a good sense of balance since they must often use scaffolding, ladders, or special swinging seats to wash windows and other glass surfaces on buildings.

employers give new workers a short demonstration of how to clean windows. Others offer supervised training for several weeks. Unions usually require an apprenticeship lasting 6 months or more. Training programs teach you about the different cleaning solutions, how to set up scaffolding, how to use belts and ladders safely, and how to use cleaning equipment properly.

Getting the Job

You can get a job as a window cleaner by applying directly to window cleaning companies, building maintenance companies, or large business or industrial firms that hire window cleaners as permanent employees. Some job openings can be found in newspaper classifieds. State and private employment agencies may also be able to help you find a job.

Advancement Possibilities and Employment Outlook

Experienced workers can become supervisors in large window cleaning companies. Some window cleaners go into business for themselves. Starting a window cleaning business requires a small investment in tools and equipment. There will continue to be a demand for building construction, so the employment outlook is expected to be good through the year 2006. There will also be job openings to replace workers who leave the field.

Working Conditions

Window cleaners work indoors and outdoors, sometimes in bad weather. Their work requires them to stoop, kneel, climb, and reach. Window cleaners do repetitive work. They must have good balance and not be afraid of heights. There is some risk of injury from slipping on wet surfaces and falling from ladders, scaffolding, and window ledges. However, such accidents are not common. Window cleaners must also lift heavy equipment. They may work alone or in teams. They usually work 35 to 40 hours a week. Many window cleaners belong to unions.

Earnings and Benefits

Beginning window cleaners in some cities earn the minimum wage. Experienced window cleaners earn an average wage of $5.75 to $8 an hour. Window cleaners who work at great heights and those who use scaffolding, ladders, and safety belts usually receive higher wages because of the greater risk of injury. Benefits that are provided by employers usually include paid vacations and holidays, health insurance, and pension plans.

Where to Go for More Information

Building Service Contractors Association
   International
10201 Lee Highway, Suite 225
Fairfax, VA 22030
(703) 359-7090

Cleaning Management Institute
c/o National Trade Publications
13 Century Hill Drive
Latham, NY 12110-2197
(518) 783-1281

Service Employees International Union
1313 L Street, NW
Washington, DC 20005
(202) 898-3200

Appliance Service Worker

Definition and Nature of the Work

Appliance service workers fix and sometimes install the wide variety of gas and electric appliances used in the home. They work on large appliances like refrigerators and freezers, as well as on small appliances such as toasters, blenders, and irons. Some service workers specialize in either gas or electric appliances. Others work on one particular group of appliances, such as clothes washers and dryers.

Field workers usually travel to a customer's home to repair large appliances. *Bench workers* repair appliances that are brought into an appliance repair shop. These shops may be independent repair shops or they may be part of an appliance or department store. Appliance manufacturers, wholesalers, and gas and electric companies sometimes have repair services and shops as well.

When they are called on to fix an appliance, service workers ask the customer about the problem. The customer may want an estimate on how much the repair will cost. Service workers try to find the problem by operating the appliance. They use special equipment, such as voltmeters, to check the power source and the electrical connections. They take the appliance apart and replace worn or broken parts or make adjustments. They use basic hand tools, such as pliers and wrenches. At times they use special tools designed for particular appliances. When appliance service workers install a new appliance, they often teach the customer how to use and care for it.

Education and Training Requirements

Employers usually prefer to hire high school graduates. Courses in mathematics, electronics, physics, mechanics, and shop are helpful. Some vocational high schools offer training in the repair of appliances. You can also take a formal course in a technical school or 2-year college. Another option is to take correspondence courses in such subjects as electronics, machinery, and motors. Most service workers, however, receive on-the-job training. This training can take up to 3 years. Appliance distributors, repair shops, or department stores can train you in this field. Trainees usually start as helpers and learn from experienced workers. Trainees may also receive some formal classroom instruction.

Getting the Job

You can apply directly to repair shops, to appliance dealers and manufacturers, and to gas and electric companies for a job. You can also answer newspaper classifieds and search job banks on the Internet. Your vocational or trade school may be able to help you find a job. You may also want to register with a state or private employment agency.

Advancement Possibilities and Employment Outlook

Appliance service workers can become supervisors or managers in repair shops. With some extra training they can become parts managers or dispatchers in

Education and Training
Varies—see profile

Salary Range
Average—$350 to $760 a week

Employment Outlook
Fair

large firms. Some experienced workers become teachers in vocational schools or teach other workers how to fix new models of appliances. A few become salespeople or technical writers of service manuals. Appliance service workers can also go into business for themselves if they have enough capital.

The demand for appliance service workers is expected to increase slower than the average through the year 2006. Many job openings will still be created to replace workers who leave the field. The increase in the purchase of household appliances will result in additional jobs becoming available. However, more of the new and improved appliances that appear on the market contain electronic parts, which reduce the frequency of repairs.

Working Conditions

Bench workers generally work in shops that are quiet and well-lighted. Field workers work in customers' homes, so their working conditions vary. Field workers often have to work in uncomfortable positions when they repair large appliances that are hard to move. They may have to lift heavy appliances. They must also be able to handle the questions and complaints of customers. Field workers often spend a large part of their workday driving. Both field workers and bench workers usually work without direct supervision.

Appliance service workers handle small tools and parts. They must have mechanical ability and work well with their hands. There is some danger of injury when they work with appliances. Appliance service workers often work more than 40 hours a week, but they receive extra pay for overtime.

Earnings and Benefits

Earnings vary depending on skill, location, the type of employer, and the kind of appliances serviced. Full-time workers earn between $350 and $760 a week. Experienced workers can make more. Employers generally provide benefits that include paid holidays and vacations, health insurance, and pension plans. Self-employed appliance service workers provide their own benefits.

Where to Go for More Information

Association of Home Appliance
    Manufacturers
20 North Wacker Drive, Suite 1231
Chicago, IL 60606
(312) 984-5800
www.aham.org

National Appliance Service Association
9247 North Meridian Street, Suite 216
Indianapolis, IN 46260
(317) 844-1602

Barber and Hairstylist

Education and Training
Voc/tech school; license

Salary Range
Starting—$15,660

Employment Outlook
Good

Definition and Nature of the Work

Barbers and hairstylists shampoo, cut, style, and color hair. They shave and cut beards and mustaches. They also give facial massages and hair and scalp treatments. At many salons they use, recommend, and sell a variety of grooming products such as shampoo, styling gels, and hairbrushes. Barbers usually work on men's hair, although many have both male and female customers.

Barbers and hairstylists usually work in barbershops. Some work in unisex salons. A few work in hotels, department stores, or government agencies. More than half of all barbers have their own businesses.

Some barbers, often called hairstylists, specialize in styling or coloring hair. They use equipment such as rollers, curling and straightening irons, and color treatments. They know how to perform various processes such as highlighting, frosting, or streaking hair. In addition, some hairstylists fit, shampoo, and style wigs and hairpieces. Sometimes they also sell wigs and hairpieces. Most states require a special license in cosmetology before a barber can do some of these jobs.

Barbers and hairstylists use such tools as scissors, clippers, razors, and combs. They also use lotions, gels, and powders to help groom their customers. Barbers and hairstylists must keep their work area clean. They must also keep their tools sterile and in good working order. Many barbers and hairstylists take care of the day-to-day concerns involved in running a small business. For example, they may order supplies, make appointments, and pay bills.

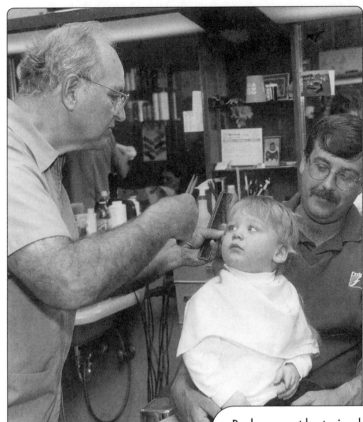

Barbers must be trained and licensed to groom customers' hair.

Education and Training Requirements

You can be trained as a barber in a vocational school or a barber college. A full-time course usually takes from 6 to 12 months to complete. All states require barbers to be licensed. The qualifications necessary to get a license vary from state to state, but generally you must be at least 16 years old, in good health, and a graduate of an approved barber school. In most cases you need to take a test to get an apprentice license after you graduate from barber school. Then you must serve 1 or 2 years as an apprentice. To qualify for a barber's license, you must take several tests including a written section and a practical demonstration of your skills. To do some procedures, such as giving a permanent wave, you will also need a cosmetology license.

Getting the Job

Most barber schools have placement services to help you get a job. Local unions or professional associations can also give you information about job openings. You can also apply directly to barbershops. Sometimes openings for barbers or hairstylists appear in newspaper classifieds. You can also check state and private employment agencies or search job banks on the Internet.

Advancement Possibilities and Employment Outlook

Experienced barbers can become managers or owners of barbershops. Loans are available to barbers, and used equipment can be bought at reduced prices. Some barbers get additional training and specialize in hairstyling or coloring. A few become teachers at barber schools.

Changing consumer preferences has led to a drop in demand for regular haircuts and shaves in barbershops. At the same time, more people are having their hair styled, which is a more costly alternative to the standard "cut and dry." Because of this trend, there will be fewer jobs for barbers who only offer conventional services but more jobs for those who specialize in hairstyling. There will also be numerous openings to replace barbers who leave the field. Overall, employment for barbers and hairstylists is expected to grow as fast as the average for all occupations through the year 2006.

Working Conditions

Barbershops are usually clean, attractive, well-lighted places. Most are small, although there are some very large shops in some cities and suburbs. Most barbers and hairstylists work more than 40 hours a week, including Saturdays. Some work part-time. There are often slow periods followed by rush periods. Some barbershops ask their customers to make appointments to even out the work load. Barbers and hairstylists must stand for long periods of time. They must work well with their hands. Since some customers are hard to please, barbers and hairstylists need patience and good humor. Barbers who set a cheerful mood sometimes find that their shops become local social centers. Some barbers and hairstylists are union members.

Earnings and Benefits

Barbers and hairstylists either receive wages or work on a commission basis, getting a percentage of the fee charged. Many also receive tips. Their earnings depend on the location of the shop, the tipping habits of the customers, and their own skill. Beginning barbers and hairstylists average a yearly salary of $15,660 plus tips. Workers with more skills and experience earn more, especially those who own their own businesses. Hairstylists usually make more than barbers because the services that hairstylists provide are usually more costly. Benefits vary from shop to shop. Under some union contracts, benefits include paid holidays and vacations and health insurance. Barbers and hairstylists with their own businesses provide their own benefits.

Where to Go for More Information

Association of Cosmetologists and
  Hairdressers
2547 Monroe Street
Dearborn, MI 48124-3013
(313) 563-0360

Hair International
P.O. Box 273
Palmyra, PA 17078-0273
(717) 838-0795
www.hairinternational.com

National Cosmetology Association
3510 Olive Street
St. Louis, MO 63103
(314) 534-7980

Consumer Credit Counselor

Education and Training
High school plus training

Salary Range
Starting—$13,000
to $20,000

Employment Outlook
Very good

Definition and Nature of the Work

Consumer credit counselors help customers to use credit wisely. Some of them work for businesses that give credit. These businesses include loan agencies, banks, credit unions, and large stores. Counselors in these businesses usually work under the supervision of a credit manager. Other counselors work for consumer credit counseling agencies, which do not give credit. The main purpose of these agencies is to give advice on the handling of money.

People often want to borrow money to make a major purchase such as a house or a car. Sometimes they ask for a loan to pay for a vacation or for college tuition expenses. They may want to open a charge account so that they can buy clothing or household needs. Sometimes people want to borrow money to pay back a large number of bills all at once.

Consumer credit counselors help decide whether customers are likely to pay back the money that they want to borrow. Counselors ask customers questions such as how much money they earn, where they live, how long they have lived there, and how many children they have. Counselors may also get additional financial information about their customers from banks or credit bureaus. They advise the customers and extend credit to those customers whom they consider able and willing to pay the money back on time.

Even people with good intentions sometimes have trouble paying all their bills on time. Consumer credit counselors can help these people manage their money better. Some credit counselors help people to make budgets and plan ahead. Sometimes people cannot pay their bills because of an unexpected crisis, such as an accident or illness. In such cases, counselors can sometimes arrange to stretch their clients' payments out over a longer period of time. Counselors can also help customers to avoid future trouble by teaching them how to handle their money wisely.

Consumer credit counselors spend much of their time talking to customers. They must also fill out forms and use formulas to help them make decisions. They often work with computerized information.

Education and Training Requirements

Consumer credit counselors need at least a high school education. An aptitude for math and numbers is important, and some business courses would be useful. A college education is also desirable for those who want to advance. Training or experience in social work is useful for counselors working in nonprofit agencies. Those who want to work for profit-making businesses will find that college courses in business administration are helpful.

Counselors learn most of their skills on the job. There are also several formal training courses that can help them to advance. After they have worked for a full year and have taken a series of courses, they can receive professional certification. Although certification is not always required by employers, it can speed advancement.

Getting the Job

You can apply directly to consumer credit counseling agencies or to loan agencies, banks, credit unions, or large stores. Your school placement office can also help you to find a job. State and private employment agencies often list job openings. Newspaper classifieds may provide other job leads. You might also try searching job banks on the Internet.

Advancement Possibilities and Employment Outlook

Advancement depends on location and experience. Some counselors become credit managers and supervise other workers. Others become directors of consumer credit counseling agencies.

The employment outlook for consumer credit counselors is very good through the year 2006. More people are using credit to buy the goods and services that they want or need. They often need help and advice with credit problems. Businesses are making greater use of electronic data processing machines to help them make credit decisions. However, the machines cannot take over the personal contact of counseling. Many jobs will be opening to replace counselors who leave the field.

Working Conditions

Consumer credit counselors generally work in pleasant offices. They usually work between 35 and 40 hours a week. Sometimes they must work in the evenings

Where to Go for More Information

American Financial Services Association
919 Eighteenth Street, NW, Third Floor
Washington, DC 20006
(202) 296-5544

International Credit Association
P.O. Box 419057
243 North Lindbergh Boulevard
St. Louis, MO 63141-1757
(314) 991-3030

or on Saturdays. Counselors need to be able to deal with all kinds of people. Credit problems make many people tense. Counselors must be able to make them feel at ease. Counselors often find great reward in helping people solve their money problems.

Earnings and Benefits

Salaries vary depending on education, experience, and location. Currently people entering the credit field earn about $13,000 to $20,000 a year. Benefits include paid holidays and vacations, health insurance, and pension plans.

Cosmetologist

Education and Training
Voc/tech school; license

Salary Range
Starting—$200
to $250 a week
Average—$20,000
to $30,000

Employment Outlook
Very good

Definition and Nature of the Work

Cosmetologists care for people's hair, skin, and nails. They are also called beauty operators, hairdressers, or beauticians. Most cosmetologists work in beauty salons. More than one-third have their own businesses. Some work in unisex shops, barbershops, department stores, hospitals, and hotels. Cosmetologists work with many types of beauty products and often sell them at their salons as well.

Most cosmetologists work chiefly with hair. They cut, shampoo, condition, style, color, permanent wave, or straighten it. They use a variety of chemical solutions, such as bleaches and dyes. They use equipment such as scissors, clippers, curlers, and dryers to give their customers fashionable hairstyles. Some cosmetologists care for wigs and hairpieces and in some cases sell them. Often cosmetologists specialize in one procedure, such as hair cutting or coloring.

Cosmetologists also care for the skin and nails. They give scalp treatments, massages, and facials. They use a variety of special creams and lotions. They also shape eyebrows and remove unwanted hair from the face. They give demonstrations and advice on the use of makeup. Cosmetologists who care for the nails, often called manicurists, soften and trim the cuticles. They shape the nails with files or emery boards and apply nail polish.

Cosmetologists must keep their work area and equipment clean. They may have other duties, such as answering the telephone or making appointments. They often recommend and sell a variety of grooming products, such as cosmetics or hairbrushes. Sometimes they take care of the day-to-day concerns involved in running a small business. For example, they may supervise other workers, order supplies, and keep records.

Education and Training Requirements

You can get training as a cosmetologist in a public or private vocational school. A full-time course usually takes from 6 to 12 months to complete. Courses cover hygiene, bacteriology, cosmetic chemistry, psychology, and sales techniques. Evening courses are available, but the program takes longer to complete. Some vocational schools offer the subjects needed for a high school diploma in addition to training in cosmetology. These programs take 2 or 3 years to complete. Cosmetologists may also get their training in 1- or 2-year apprenticeship programs.

Cosmetologists care for people's hair, skin, and nails. When caring for nails, cosmetologists soften and trim the cuticles. Then they shape the nails with files or emery boards and apply nail polish.

All states require cosmetologists to be licensed. However, requirements for a license vary from state to state. In most states you must be at least 16 years old, in good health, and a graduate of an approved cosmetology school. You must also pass a state licensing examination. This test usually includes both a written part and a practical demonstration of your skills. There may even be an oral exam in which you are asked to explain particular cosmetology procedures. The license must be renewed every year or every 2 years.

Getting the Job

Most schools of cosmetology help their students find jobs. Some of these schools offer a lifetime placement service so that graduates can return and receive assistance finding work or continuing their studies. The reputation of a school can greatly enhance a graduate's job opportunities. Professional associations, newspaper classifieds, and job banks on the Internet are also good sources of employment information.

Advancement Possibilities and Employment Outlook

Cosmetologists can advance by improving their skills and building up their clientele, or following of customers. They can specialize in one procedure, such as hair cutting or manicures, or they can become a manager or owner of a beauty salon. They need a small investment to start their own business. Loans are available and equipment can be rented. A few cosmetologists teach at schools of cosmetology or work as inspectors for state cosmetology boards. Others work for cosmetics manufacturers, demonstrating or selling their products.

The employment outlook is very good through the year 2006, with manicurists taking the lead in projected growth (nearly 70 percent). The need for personal cosmetologists is increasing, and there is a widening demand for cosmetologists to work with media and advertising productions. There will also be openings to replace workers who leave the field.

Working Conditions

Beauty salons are usually well-lighted, cheerful places. In small salons a cosmetologist may do everything from shampooing and manicuring to answering the telephone and sweeping up. In large shops workers may specialize in one area, such as hair cutting or coloring.

Many cosmetologists work more than 40 hours a week, including Saturdays and one or two evenings. Others work part-time, usually during the end of the week when beauty salons are busiest. Cosmetologists have to stand for many hours. They must sometimes use harsh chemicals. Some protect themselves by wearing rubber gloves. Cosmetologists must be able to work well with their hands and should have a good sense of style. They also need to keep up with the latest fashions in hairstyling and cosmetics. They must be able to deal with all kinds of customers. Some cosmetologists are union members.

Earnings and Benefits

Cosmetologists may receive wages or be paid a commission, which is a percentage of the fee charged for services rendered. They usually receive tips as well. Their earnings depend on where they work, their skill, and the tipping habits of their customers. Beginning cosmetologists average $200 to $250 a week plus tips. The earnings of experienced cosmetologists range from about $20,000 to $30,000 a year, including tips. Top cosmetologists can earn $650 to $775 a week plus tips. Self-employed cosmetologists and those who work for small beauty salons must provide their own benefits. Group insurance can be obtained through membership in a cosmetology association. Benefits for cosmetologists employed by large salons and department stores sometimes include paid holidays and vacations, health insurance, and pension plans.

Where to Go for More Information

American Association of Cosmetology
  Schools
901 North Washington Street, Suite 206
Alexandria, VA 22314-1535
(703) 683-1700

Association of Cosmetologists and
  Hairdressers
2547 Monroe Street
Dearborn, MI 48124-3013
(313) 563-0360

National Cosmetology Association
3510 Olive Street
St. Louis, MO 63103
(314) 534-7980

Custom Tailor and Dressmaker

Education and Training
High school plus training

Salary Range
Average—$8
to $12 an hour

Employment Outlook
Fair

Definition and Nature of the Work

Custom tailors and dressmakers make clothing according to the needs and requests of their customers. Custom tailors work on tailored or shaped garments, such as coats and suits for men or women. Custom dressmakers usually work on women's garments, such as dresses and blouses. Most custom tailors and dressmakers work in small shops. Many have their own businesses. A few work from their homes.

Custom tailors and dressmakers first help their customers choose the kind and color of fabric they want and the style of the garment to be made. Custom tailors and dressmakers need to know all about the different kinds of fabrics and the latest styles. Sometimes they stock fabric in their shops. Otherwise they get it from another store or use fabric that the customer supplies.

Custom tailors and dressmakers take a customer's measurements and note any special figure problems. They may work with a ready-made pattern or make one of their own. They place the pattern pieces on the fabric. Then they cut the fabric with shears along the pattern outlines. Custom tailors and dressmakers pin

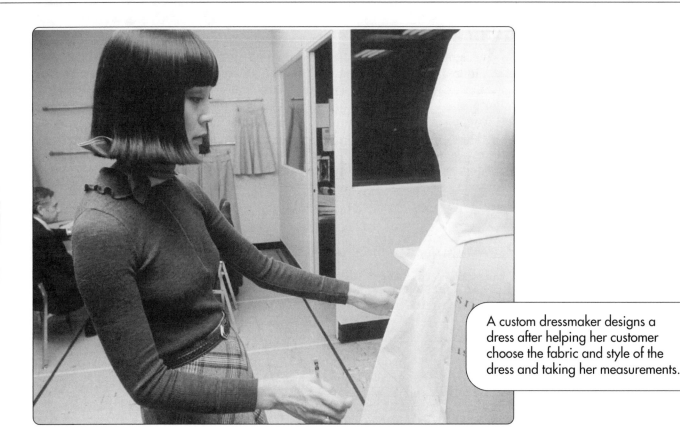

A custom dressmaker designs a dress after helping her customer choose the fabric and style of the dress and taking her measurements.

or baste the garment pieces together before doing the final sewing by hand or machine. They often use padding and stiff fabrics to add body and shape to the garment. They press the garment several times to shape it properly. The customer may try the garment on one or two times while it is being made to make sure that it fits properly. The custom tailor or dressmaker finishes the garment by hemming it, sewing on buttons and trim, and giving it a final pressing.

Some custom tailors and dressmakers specialize in one kind of garment, such as coats or wedding gowns. Others may perform one function, such as fitting clothing. They may also supervise other workers. Custom tailors and dressmakers sometimes repair or alter garments for their customers.

There are other people who do tailoring and sewing but who are not custom tailors or dressmakers. These people are known by a variety of names, such as shop tailor, alteration tailor, alterer, busheler, sewer, or mender. They work in clothing factories, in clothing or department stores, or in dry cleaning plants. They often do repairs or make alterations to factory-made clothing, or they may sew one specific part of a garment. For example, they may pad lapels or set in collars.

Education and Training Requirements

Custom tailors and dressmakers should have a high school education. However, retailers often place more emphasis on a person's previous experience in apparel manufacture, design, or alterations when making hiring decisions. In high school you should take courses in tailoring and sewing, art, design, and business. Sewing clothing for yourself or for your family and friends will help you to improve your skills. You can continue your training at a trade school or 2-year college. You can also get on-the-job training in a custom tailoring or dressmaking shop, in a garment factory, or in a clothing or department store. There are some formal apprenticeship programs for tailors.

Getting the Job

Some custom dressmakers start their own businesses right away by making their own clothes and then taking orders from those who like their work. You may have to work at related jobs for a few years, however, before becoming a custom tailor or dressmaker. For example, you may start as a sewer or alterer in a custom tailoring or dressmaking shop, in a garment factory, or in a clothing or department store. You can apply directly to these firms for a job. You can also register with the placement office of your trade school or college. Custom tailoring and dressmaking jobs are sometimes found through the newspaper classifieds or by searching job banks on the Internet. State and private employment agencies may also help you to find a job.

Advancement Possibilities and Employment Outlook

After custom tailors and dressmakers have gained enough experience and skill, they can apply to better shops. They can also become supervisors of other workers or open their own businesses.

Employment for custom tailors and dressmakers is expected to decline through the year 2006. More people are buying imports and factory-made clothing, which lessens the need for tailoring. Consumers also prefer to buy new clothes, rather than alter or repair old ones. There will be some jobs, however, to replace custom tailors and dressmakers who leave the field.

Working Conditions

Custom tailors and dressmakers usually work in shops that are pleasant and well-lighted. In many shops employees work 40 to 48 hours a week. This sometimes includes Saturdays. Those who are union members often work 35 to 40 hours a week. Custom tailors and dressmakers who have their own businesses often work longer hours. Sometimes they must rush to get orders ready on time. Spring and fall are usually the busiest times. Some custom tailors and dressmakers work part-time.

Custom tailors and dressmakers do much of their work sitting down. They must have good eyesight and work well with their hands. Successful custom tailors and dressmakers have a good sense of fit, color, and style. They should like detailed work. They must also be able to deal with customers who may be hard to please.

Where to Go for More Information

Custom Tailors and Designers Association
   of America
P.O. Box 53052
Washington, DC 20009-9052
(202) 387-7220

National Apparel, Garment, and Textile
   Workers Council
4207 Lebanon Road
Hermitage, TN 37076
(615) 889-9221

Union of Needletrades, Industrial and
   Textile Employees
1710 Broadway
New York, NY 10019
(212) 265-7000

Earnings and Benefits

Earnings for custom tailors and dressmakers vary widely, depending on experience, skill, and location. Experienced custom tailors may earn from about $8 to $12 an hour. Self-employed custom tailors earn weekly salaries of $450 to $650, and earnings are even higher for custom tailors who make high-quality, high-fashion garments in large metropolitan areas. The earnings of custom tailors and dressmakers who work part-time vary, too, ranging from about $5 to over $7.50 an hour. Workers may receive benefits that include paid holidays and vacations, health insurance, and pension plans. Self-employed custom tailors and dressmakers and those who work for small shops must usually provide their own benefits.

Custom Upholsterer

Definition and Nature of the Work

Custom upholsterers repair, rebuild, and re-cover upholstered furniture, such as sofas and chairs. Most custom upholsterers work in small upholstery shops. Some work for furniture or department stores. A few are employed by hospitals, hotels, and theaters. About one-third of custom upholsterers have their own businesses.

Custom upholsterers often help customers select an upholstery fabric and give them an estimate on how much a job will cost. A total upholstery job involves stripping a piece of furniture down to the bare wooden frame. Upholsterers usually put the furniture on padded wooden horses so that they can work comfortably. They pull out the anchoring tacks and take off the covering. They remove the padding and burlap that cover the springs. Upholsterers cut the cords or wires that hold the springs in the webbing. They remove worn or broken springs, as well as the webbing. To repair the frame, they may have to glue loose or broken pieces or refinish exposed wooden areas. Sometimes upholsterers use a saw and hammer to change the shape of the frame.

To rebuild the piece of furniture, upholsterers reweb the bottom and tie new springs in place. Then, they cover the springs with burlap. They pad the furniture using such materials as cotton batting and foam rubber. Then they cover the padding materials with a rough fabric, such as muslin. They attach the final covering, which they have cut and sewn using patterns and heavy-duty sewing machines. Once the covering is in place, upholsterers tack it tightly and sew the final seams by hand. They may finish the edges of the furniture with braid or other trim. Custom upholsterers also make fitted cushions and slipcovers.

Education and Training
Varies—see profile

Salary Range
Average—$370 a week

Employment Outlook
Fair

Custom upholsterers often strip a piece of furniture down to the bare wooden frame. After they remove and replace worn or broken springs and repair the frame, they apply the new padding and coverings.

Custom upholsterers use a variety of hand and power tools in their work. Some of these are special upholstery tools, such as upholstery needles and webbing stretchers. Many upholsterers also manage the day-to-day activities of running a small business.

In addition to custom upholsterers, there are other kinds of upholstery workers. Most work for furniture manufacturers, but some work for manufacturers of automobiles or airplanes. These workers are usually concerned with just one part of the upholstering process. For example, they may make only the arms or backs of seats in these vehicles. Depending on the type of work they do, these upholstery workers may be known as springers, cushion fitters, cutters, or sewers. Sometimes they are called industrial upholsterers.

Education and Training Requirements

Employers usually prefer to hire high school graduates, especially those with vocational training in woodworking, drafting, textiles, and upholstery repair. The most common way to enter the field of custom upholstery is through on-the-job training, which you can complete in about 3 years. You can get this training in a furniture factory or in a custom upholstery shop. You can also enter a formal apprenticeship program that lasts 3 or 4 years and includes both classroom and on-the-job training.

Getting the Job

The placement office of your high school or vocational school can help you to find a job. You can enter the upholstery field by applying directly to custom upholstery shops, to furniture or department stores, or to factories that make furniture. You can also answer newspaper classifieds, check with state or private employment agencies, or search job banks on the Internet.

Advancement Possibilities and Employment Outlook

Experienced custom upholsterers can become supervisors or managers in a large shop or firm. Many workers open their own custom upholstery shops. They need only a small amount of money to get started in this business. Competition is keen, however, and many small shops fail each year.

Little or no employment growth is expected through the year 2006. Most job openings will be created to replace workers who leave the field. Although manufacturers are expected to make more furniture, they are likely to use less upholstery on each piece of furniture. In addition, as the economy remains strong, people are preferring to buy new furniture rather than have their old pieces reupholstered. However, there will still be a demand for upholsterers to restore more valuable furniture.

Working Conditions

Although most upholstery workshops are well-lighted and well-ventilated, the air may contain dust and lint from the materials used in the trade. Workshops may also be noisy from the use of hand and power tools. Upholsterers may receive minor cuts and scratches when working with sharp tools and rough wood. Sometimes workers must lift heavy furniture. They often pick up and deliver the furniture that they upholster. They need to be strong and work well with their hands. Some artistic ability is helpful, too. Custom upholsterers who start their own shops need good business sense as well as the ability to deal with customers.

Most upholsterers work 40 hours a week. They may work overtime during the busy periods before holidays. There may also be slow periods with little work.

Self-employed workers generally work longer hours than those who are employed by others. Some upholsterers are union members.

Earnings and Benefits

Most upholstery trainees start at $5 to $7 an hour. Experienced custom upholsterers earn an average of $370 a week. The earnings of self-employed workers depend on the size and location of their shops, plus the amount of hours they work in each one. Benefits for upholsterers vary. Many small custom upholstery shops offer few benefits. Larger firms often give benefits that include paid holidays and vacations, health insurance, and pension plans.

Where to Go for More Information

Institute of Inspection Cleaning and
    Restoration
2715 East Mill Plain Boulevard
Vancouver, WA 98661
(360) 693-5675

National Association of Decorative Fabric
    Distributors
3008 Millwood Avenue
Columbia, SC 29205
(803) 252-5646

Dietetic Technician

Definition and Nature of the Work

Dietetic technicians help dietitians in the daily operation of food services. Technicians help to plan and prepare meals that are nutritious and satisfying. They work in hospitals, day care centers, nursing homes, and other institutions.

Many dietetic technicians work for schools, colleges, or factories that operate food service facilities. Some work for public health departments, visiting nurse associations, and other health agencies. They may also work in one of the growing number of neighborhood health centers that help families plan better meals. Some dietetic technicians work as supervisors. Others are involved in research.

Dietetic technicians who work in health care facilities often work directly with dietitians to plan patients' diets. They observe and record patients' eating habits and report changes to the dietitian. They also work with the food service staff in the kitchen to make sure that each menu is prepared according to nutrition guidelines.

Dietetic technicians who are supervisors often serve as the liaison between a professional dietitian and the food service employees who work in the kitchens of hospitals, factory cafeterias, schools, and other institutions. Technicians prepare work schedules and time cards. They also supervise the ordering, storing, preparing, and serving of food.

Education and Training Requirements

You must have an associate degree in order to be a dietetic technician. While in high school you should take courses in the sciences, including family and consumer science. Two-year courses in dietetics are offered by vocational schools and community and junior colleges. Most courses include some practical experience in a food service facility.

Getting the Job

In many cases, you can get a job with the hospital, health agency, school, or plant where you received your practical training. Your school placement office can also

Education and Training
Varies—see profile

Salary Range
Average—$300
to $400 a week

Employment Outlook
Very good

Dietetic technicians assist in planning and preparing nutritious menus.

help you to find a job. You might also try searching newspaper classifieds and job banks on the Internet. The job listings in health care magazines are another good source of information. You can also apply directly to the personnel office of the companies, institutions, or agencies for which you want to work.

Advancement Possibilities and Employment Outlook

Dietetic technicians begin as assistants to dietitians or food directors. They may then go on to become supervisors in kitchen management or administration. With a bachelor's degree and a year of internship, technicians can become professional dietitians.

Employment opportunities are very good. The number of patients requiring long-term care in nursing homes and other institutions will increase, so there will be a greater need for qualified dietetic technicians.

Working Conditions

The job is a very active one. There are times when technicians are under pressure to work fast and accurately. They usually work in 8-hour shifts. They work 40 hours a week. Holiday and weekend work is often required. During food preparation, technicians may have to stand for long periods. Wherever technicians work, the environment is clean and well-lighted. They generally work with up-to-date equipment.

Earnings and Benefits

Salaries vary depending on experience, geographic location, and the individual employer. Most dietetic technicians currently earn between $300 and $400 a week. Some dietetic technicians earn up to $500 a week. Benefits include paid vacations and holidays, health insurance, and meals during working hours.

Where to Go for More Information

American Dietetic Association
216 West Jackson Boulevard, Suite 800
Chicago, IL 60606
(312) 899-0040
www.eatright.org

American Society for Nutritional Sciences
9650 Rockville Pike
Bethesda, MD 20814-3990
(301) 530-7050
www.faseb.org/asns

Electrologist

Definition and Nature of the Work

Electrologists permanently remove unwanted hair from the face and body by a process called electrolysis. This process uses an electric current to destroy the tissue called the papilla that produces each hair. Electrologists work in private offices or salons. Many have their own businesses.

Most patrons of electrologists are women with excess facial hair. Male patrons often ask to have eyebrows and beards thinned or to have unwanted hair removed from their bodies. Electrologists also shape eyebrows and change hairlines permanently. In addition, they may remove hairs from moles but only with the written permission of a physician.

Patrons usually come to electrologists by appointment. Electrologists first make their patrons comfortable and sterilize their skin with an antiseptic solution. Then they slide a small, fine needle down the opening through which the hair grows to reach the papilla below the hair root. It is important that electrologists adjust the timing and flow of electricity before pressing the foot switch that sends the electric current into the papilla. They remove the needle and then lift the hair out with tweezers. Some hairs may require several treatments if earlier attempts have been made to remove them by temporary methods. Removing hair from large areas of the body may require several visits to an electrologist. Despite the use of electricity, electrolysis is a painless process. Patrons usually feel only a slight tingling sensation.

Education and Training Requirements

High school courses in chemistry, biology, psychology, business, and speech can help prepare you for training as an electrologist. There are special schools where you can study electrolysis. Full-time courses generally last about 4 weeks. You can also study part-time at these schools. Manufacturers of electrolysis machines and large electrolysis firms also offer training programs. In some cases you can earn a salary as you learn.

About one-third of the states require electrologists to be licensed. Requirements for licensing vary widely. Some states have minimum age, education, and training requirements. You may also be required to pass a test before you can be a licensed electrologist.

Getting the Job

If you attend a trade or professional school, you can get a job through the school placement service. You can also answer newspaper classifieds or apply to employment agencies. Try searching job banks on the Internet as well. If you have not attended electrolysis school, apply directly to firms that have their own training programs.

Advancement Possibilities and Employment Outlook

Electrologists who work for large electrolysis firms or salons can become supervisors or managers. They can also become teachers of electrolysis. Many electrologists open their own salons after getting some job experience. This requires a large sum of money, but loans are available to qualified electrologists. It usually takes self-employed electrologists 2 to 5 years to build up a steady practice.

Education and Training
Voc/tech school

Salary Range
Average—$35 to $75 an hour

Employment Outlook
Good

The employment outlook for electrologists is good. Many people are increasingly concerned about their personal appearance and have the money for electrolysis treatments. Therefore, the demand for electrologists' services should continue through the year 2006.

Working Conditions

Electrolysis salons are clean and attractive. Electrologists usually wear white uniforms that they buy themselves. They work regularly scheduled hours, including some evenings and Saturdays. There may be some slow periods. Electrologists are seated when they treat patrons. Removing unwanted hair is a slow and precise process, so electrologists should be patient and have steady hands. They are expected to respect the privacy of their patrons and should be able to make them feel at ease.

Earnings and Benefits

Employed electrologists often receive a salary plus a commission, which is a percentage of the fee charged. Others receive only a commission. Electrologists also accept tips from their patrons. Self-employed electrologists charge their patrons by the hour. The average hourly rate is about $35 to $75. Earnings vary greatly depending on the geographic location, the number of patrons, and the salon's business expenses. Self-employed electrologists must provide their own benefits. Benefits for salaried electrologists may include paid vacations and health insurance.

Where to Go for More Information

American Association of Cosmetology
  Schools
901 North Washington Street, Suite 206
Alexandria, VA 22314-1535
(703) 683-1700

Society of Clinical and Medical
  Electrologists
132 Great Road, Suite 200
Stow, MA 01775-1189
(978) 461-0313

Floral Designer

Education and Training
High school plus training

Salary Range
Starting—$5.75 an hour
Average—$7
to $10 an hour

Employment Outlook
Very good

Definition and Nature of the Work

Floral designers artistically arrange real and artificial flowers, leaves, and other decorations. They make corsages, bouquets, wreaths, wedding decorations, and other kinds of floral designs. They follow standard designs or fill special orders. Sometimes they create original designs. Floral designers generally work in retail flower shops. Some designers manage their own shops.

Floral designers need to be knowledgeable about a wide range of flowers, foliage, and potted plants. They must know their names, seasonal availability, and how long they will stay fresh. Designers must also keep up-to-date on the current fashions and styles in floral design, while at the same time understand the traditions of using certain flowers for weddings, funerals, and other occasions.

Designers usually work from the written orders of their customers. These orders may be very specific or may leave many details to the imagination of the designer. Floral designers select the appropriate flowers and cut the stems to the proper length. They may strengthen them with wire or wooden sticks. They arrange the flowers in a base of styrofoam or other material. Sometimes customers provide special containers for floral arrangements. Other times the designers may choose containers. Leafy branches and decorations such as bows, tiny bells, or artificial butterflies are often used to accentuate or complete the floral design.

Floral designers create visually appealing flower arrangements. They make traditional corsages, bouquets, wreaths, and wedding decorations, as well as other kinds of original designs.

Besides creating arrangements, floral designers also help out in other ways in a flower shop. Some wait on customers or give advice about floral purchases. Others arrange potted plants and terrariums or work on seasonal decorations. For example, they may wire together small pinecones for use in floral designs for winter. Designers also unpack flowers and prepare them for storage. They water potted plants and cut flowers. Sometimes they help prepare attractive window displays.

Education and Training Requirements

A high school diploma is necessary to enter this field. High school courses in art and business subjects are helpful. Most floral designers get their training on the job. It takes about 2 years of work experience to become a fully qualified designer. Students can get started by taking a part-time job as a designer's helper in a flower shop. Some high schools, junior colleges, and colleges also offer courses in floral design.

Getting the Job

The best way to get started in floral design is to apply directly to flower shops. Your school placement office may be able to help you with job information. You can also apply to state or private employment agencies. Newspaper classifieds sometimes list job openings in flower shops. You might also search job banks on the Internet.

Advancement Possibilities and Employment Outlook

Flower designers can become managers in large flower shops. If they have the capital, they can open their own shops. Loans are available to qualified people.

The employment of floral designers is expected to increase faster than the average through the year 2006, due in part to the continued demand for floral arrangements. However, it should also be taken into consideration that jobs are easy to find mainly due to the low pay and limited opportunities for advancement in this field.

Working Conditions

Floral designers work in attractive shops. Their work areas are usually cool and humid so that the flowers will keep well. Designers often get small cuts and scratches from the tools and materials that they handle. They may also need to stand for long hours. Floral designers generally work 40 to 48 hours a week, including Saturdays.

Floral designers need to have some artistic talent and the ability to work well with their hands. They should be able to get along with customers. Designers who want to start their own shops should also have good business sense.

Earnings and Benefits

Currently beginning floral designers earn starting salaries of about $5.75 an hour. Workers with 1 to 3 years of experience earn about $7 an hour. Workers with over 3 years of experience earn about $8 an hour, and managers make about $10 an hour. Small shops may offer few benefits to their workers. Benefits in larger shops may include paid holidays and vacations and health insurance.

Where to Go for More Information

American Institute of Floral Designers
720 Light Street
Baltimore, MD 21230
(410) 752-3318

Society of American Florists
1601 Duke Street
Alexandria, VA 22314
(703) 836-8700

Home Security Consultant

Education and Training
High school plus training

Salary Range
Varies—see profile

Employment Outlook
Good

Definition and Nature of the Work

Home security consultants provide hardware and customer support services to help homeowners prevent crime and fires in their homes and on their property. The home security consultant assesses a customer's risk of property and personal loss due to fire or crime and recommends a security system to reduce that risk in accordance with the customer's budget. The hardware used in home security most often includes electronic burglar and fire alarm systems and exterior lighting. More complex systems may include closed-circuit television. Customer support services include monitoring the alarm systems, notifying local police or firefighters when the alarm systems indicate problems, and maintaining the alarm systems.

Most home security consultants work for companies that maintain home security systems over an extended area. In general, there are four basic types of positions in the home security industry: salespeople, technicians, support personnel, and managers and administrators.

Salespeople meet with potential customers, go over the customers' needs, and recommend home security systems that are within the customers' budgets. *Technicians* install and maintain the home security systems in the buildings to be monitored. These complex systems usually include electronic sensors on windows and doors, motion detectors, and one or more keypad control centers for

A home security consultant meets with a client to discuss options for a home security plan before the client's house is built.

activating and deactivating the system. The systems are usually patched directly into a phone line and linked to the company monitoring the home security system.

Support personnel work in a central office, monitoring the home security system. When an alarm goes off in one of the homes on the system, the support personnel alert the homeowner, as well as the appropriate law enforcement or firefighting department. *Managers* and *administrators* oversee the entire operation and are responsible for billing, payroll, insurance, and other basic office functions.

Education and Training Requirements

In general, people working for a home security firm need a high school diploma, along with specialized training in their area of expertise. Technicians need to understand fundamental electronics and must be able to read electronics schematics. They must also be skilled electricians and should know the basics of telephone wiring. Salespeople should understand cost/risk analysis and must know the basic capabilities of the various electronic alarm systems they offer. Managers and administrators should know the principles of accounting and basic business administration.

Getting the Job

Individuals interested in working in this industry should apply to local home security businesses. Call local firms to learn what entry-level jobs are available and what sort of experience is necessary to get them. Chances are, if you have basic clerical skills and proven work habits, you could apply for an entry-level support position. If you have training in electronics, you might apply for an entry-level job as a technician-trainee.

Advancement Possibilities and Employment Outlook

Advances in electronics and telecommunications have made sophisticated home security systems readily available and more affordable, so the industry is expected to grow. Employees who do well as technicians or support personnel for a home security business may move up in the organization to more responsible and lucrative positions as managers or salespeople.

Employment depends to some extent on the state of the economy. Since the economy is expected to remain stable, there will be a steady demand for home construction. As a result, the employment outlook is good for home security consultants.

Where to Go for More Information

International Association of Home Safety
    and Security Professionals
P.O. Box 2044
Erie, PA 16512-2044
(814) 452-0592
www.members.aol.com/iahssp/private/
    homepage.htm

International Association of Professional
    Security Consultants
1444 I Street, NW, Suite 700
Washington, DC 20005
(202) 216-9623

National Burglar and Fire Alarm
    Association
Security Industry Association
7101 Wisconsin Avenue, Suite 901
Bethesda, MD 20814-4805
(301) 907-3202
www.alarm.org

Working Conditions

Support personnel and administrators work in modern, comfortable offices. Technicians and salespeople spend most of their time in the field, visiting customers' houses. Technicians spend a lot of time going up and down ladders, in basements, and generally moving all over a building to set up sensors at every possible point of entry. They might spend time outdoors, possibly in bad weather, installing or maintaining a system. Since around-the-clock coverage is essential to a home security business, both technicians and support personnel may have to work "graveyard shifts" through the night—and on holidays—to monitor or repair systems under their watch.

Earnings and Benefits

The earnings of home security consultants vary depending on the location of employment. Managers and administrators earn the highest salaries in this field—between $32,000 and $90,500 a year. Technicians earn between $13 and $18 an hour. Employers generally provide benefits that include paid holidays and vacations, health insurance, and pension plans.

Jeweler

Education and Training
Varies—see profile

Salary Range
Varies—see profile

Employment Outlook
Fair

Definition and Nature of the Work

Jewelers design, make, sell, and repair jewelry. Their field is a broad one, including many kinds of workers. Jewelers work in design and crafts studios, factories, retail stores, and repair shops. They work with gold, silver, diamonds, and other metals and gems. Jewelers deal with rings, necklaces, earrings, and other ornaments. They may work with fine jewelry, which is made of precious metals and gems. Or they may work with costume jewelry, which is made of less expensive metals and materials such as shells, wood, plastic, or imitation gems.

Some jewelers are artists who design jewelry. They draw pictures to show how a piece of jewelry will look. They either make the jewelry themselves or pass their designs on to another craftsworker. Jewelry craftspeople often make jewelry based on the design specifications of another jeweler. Sometimes they make expensive custom-made pieces that require a lot of handwork. At other times they

Jewelers must have several years of on-the-job training or technical school training to design and repair jewelry.

make jewelry using assembly-line methods. Even factory-made jewelry often needs some hand-finishing. Workers who make jewelry use a wide variety of hand and machine tools. They use special magnifying glasses to help them see details when they are working on intricate pieces.

Many jewelers work in retail shops. Over one-third of all jewelers are self-employed owners of jewelry stores and repair shops. They may design and make jewelry, but they spend most of their time running their businesses and selling and repairing jewelry. Jewelry stores often carry other items in addition to jewelry. They may carry watches, silverware, china, glassware, and a wide variety of gifts. Some employees in jewelry shops just sell merchandise. Others just repair jewelry and watches.

Within the larger profession, jewelers often narrow their field of work. *Gemologists,* for example, are experts in precious gems. They examine stones, such as diamonds and rubies, and estimate their value. They often buy and sell gems wholesale. *Gem cutters* are skilled workers who cut diamonds and other precious and synthetic gems. Other jewelers may specialize in engraving, setting stones, or repairing and restyling old jewelry.

Education and Training Requirements

Most jewelers are high school graduates. Training requirements vary with the type of work you want to do. Some people receive informal on-the-job training in a factory or retail jewelry shop. The training period may be 3 to 4 years, depending on what skills are being learned. Most people learn their skills in technical school programs, which last from 6 months to 2 years. Technical school courses include the use and care of jewelers' tools and stone setting. Employers usually want technical school graduates to have 3 years of additional training on the job. There are also college art programs that run for 4 years and lead to a bachelor's degree in fine arts. Some colleges also offer home-study courses. If you want to be a jeweler, you will probably find that high school or college courses in physics, chemistry, art, mechanical drawing, and business management are helpful.

Jewelers work with valuable materials, so many employers require that you be bonded before they will hire you. Bond companies provide a kind of insurance which guarantees that bonded employees will not steal. They check your background to make sure that you are honest before they will bond you.

Getting the Job

You can apply directly to design and crafts studios, to jewelry factories, or to retail shops for a job. Usually you will be able to continue working at the place where you trained. Trade organizations and the jewelers' union may be able to provide job information. You can also check with employment agencies, read the newspaper classifieds, or search job banks on the Internet.

If you want to open your own jewelry store, you should first get some experience selling, making, or repairing jewelry. Initially, you will need a lot of money to open your own store. Loans are available, but you will have to convince the lender that you are honest and know enough about the jewelry business to succeed.

Advancement Possibilities and Employment Outlook

Experienced jewelry workers can become supervisors in a studio or factory or managers in a retail store. Many become owners of their own shops or studios.

Employment for jewelers is expected to decline slightly through the year 2006. However, there will be openings to replace workers who leave the field. While there is a growing demand for jewelry, more of it is being made by machinery. People who have completed technical school courses in the design, making, and repair of jewelry have the best chances of getting jobs in jewelry making. Jobs in the retail jewelry business are available in all parts of the country, whereas opportunities for jobs in jewelry factories are more limited. As the economy fluctuates, so do opportunities. Jewelry retailers benefit during a strong economy, when people are willing to buy more. However, during an economic slowdown, opportunities are usually better for repairers as people decide to repair or restore existing pieces of jewelry rather than make purchases.

Working Conditions

Working conditions vary with the type of employment. Retail stores are usually quiet, clean, and attractive. Jewelers involved in selling must have good business sense and must be able to get along well with other people. Factories, repair shops, and studios are usually well-lighted and pleasant, but they may be noisy because of the machinery.

All jewelers should have some artistic ability. They must have good hand-eye coordination, as well as skill at working with their hands. Patience and attention to detail are essential.

Jewelers in factories often work 35 to 40 hours a week. Those working in retail stores and repair shops generally work 40 to 48 hours a week, including some evenings and weekends. Extra hours are required during holiday seasons when stores stay open longer. Both manufacturing and retail workers sometimes experience slow seasons when there may be layoffs. Some jewelers belong to labor unions.

Earnings and Benefits

Experienced, full-time unionized jewelry workers in manufacturing earn an average of $12.60 an hour. Jewelry repair workers in retail stores earn an average of $32,100 a year. Depending on the store, jewelers may receive commissions on what they sell. Earnings vary, depending on skill, union contracts, and place of employment. Benefits for employed jewelers sometimes include paid holidays and vacations, health insurance, and pension plans. Self-employed jewelers must provide their own benefits.

Where to Go for More Information

American Gem Society
8881 West Sahara Avenue
Las Vegas, NV 89117-5865
(702) 255-6500
www.AGS.org

Jewelers of America
1185 Avenue of the Americas, 30th Floor
New York, NY 10036
(212) 768-8777

Locksmith

Definition and Nature of the Work

Locksmiths install, adjust, repair, and open locks. They also change lock combinations and make keys. Most locksmiths work in locksmith shops. Many have their own businesses. Hardware and department stores sometimes employ locksmiths. Some locksmiths work for manufacturers of safes and locks, government agencies, and large industrial plants.

Locksmiths advise people about the best security measures for their homes or businesses. They sell and install the devices that they recommend. Locksmiths often drive to a worksite in a mobile shop. They may teach their customers how to use locks and keys properly.

Locksmiths often spend part of their working day opening locks for people who have lost or misplaced their keys. They may do this by picking the lock or by making a duplicate key. Sometimes locksmiths use the scratches that the lock leaves on a blank key as a guide for filing the blank key into the proper shape. At other times they get the key code number and make a duplicate key on a key cutting machine. Locksmiths open combination locks by turning the dial on the lock until the tumblers click into place. Or they may drill through the lock with an electric drill.

Locksmiths use screwdrivers, pliers, tweezers, lockpicks, and a variety of other hand and power tools in their trade. They repair locks by taking the mechanism apart and replacing worn and broken parts, such as springs and tumblers. They sometimes make new parts by hand. To protect homes and businesses, locksmiths often adjust and change locks. They also create new master key systems for businesses. Locksmiths with a knowledge of electricity and electronics install and repair alarm systems. In addition to their other duties, some locksmiths take care of the business details involved in running a shop.

Education and Training Requirements

You can learn to be a locksmith through on-the-job training, which usually takes 1 to 12 months. Employers prefer to hire high school graduates. Courses in

Education and Training
High school plus training

Salary Range
Average—$20,000 to $30,000

Employment Outlook
Good

Locksmiths repair locks by taking the mechanism apart and replacing worn and broken parts, such as springs and tumblers.

mathematics, mechanical drawing, and machine shop are useful. You can prepare for your on-the-job training by taking a correspondence course in locksmithing or attending courses at a vocational/technical school. In some areas locksmiths must be licensed.

Getting the Job

Locksmith shops are often family businesses. Locksmiths do hire people who are not part of their family, however. You can apply directly to locksmith shops or to industrial firms, schools, hospitals, and government agencies. Employers often place classified ads in trade magazines and newspapers. You can also try searching job banks on the Internet. State and private employment agencies may be able to help you find a job as well.

Advancement Possibilities and Employment Outlook

Experienced locksmiths can become supervisors or managers in large shops. Many locksmiths go into business for themselves. They often run their businesses right from their homes. A small investment is necessary to get started. Locksmiths can expand and upgrade their skills by reading technical journals and taking training classes given by the Associated Locksmiths of America.

The outlook for locksmiths is good. The field is expected to grow about as fast as the average for all occupations through the year 2006. People want and need better security devices for both their homes and their businesses. The employment outlook is especially good for locksmiths who can install and repair electronic alarm systems.

Working Conditions

Most locksmiths work out of small shops that are usually well-kept. Since much of their work is done on job sites, conditions vary. Locksmiths may have to work outdoors in bad weather. They sometimes work in uncomfortable positions for long periods of time. Their work often requires them to spend much time driving from job to job. Manual dexterity and good hand-eye coordination are important for locksmiths. They should also have some mechanical ability. Those who deal with customers must be able to get along with people.

Locksmiths generally work 40 to 48 hours a week. They are sometimes on call 24 hours a day for emergencies. Self-employed locksmiths often work more than 48 hours a week.

Earnings and Benefits

Experienced locksmiths can earn from about $10 to $14 an hour. Most locksmiths earn about $20,000 to $30,000 a year. Those with many years of experience earn $43,000 or more. Benefits vary depending on the employer. Some employers provide paid vacations and holidays, health insurance, and pension plans. Those who work for small shops and those who are self-employed must often provide their own benefits.

Where to Go for More Information

Associated Locksmiths of America
3003 Live Oak Street
Dallas, TX 75204
(214) 827-1701

Massage Therapist

Definition and Nature of the Work

Massage therapists massage their customers for therapeutic and remedial reasons. They also administer other kinds of body conditioning. Massage therapists are employed by community service associations, health clubs, resorts, and country clubs. They are sometimes called masseurs or masseuses.

Before giving a massage, therapists apply alcohol, lubricants, and other substances to the customer's body. They then massage the body by kneading, rubbing, and stroking the flesh. Massages stimulate blood circulation, relax tight muscles, and have other beneficial effects. Massage therapists use their hands and mechanical vibrating equipment to give massages.

Massage therapists also give steam and dry heat treatments, ultraviolet and infrared light treatments, and different types of water therapy. These treatments may be given at the customer's request or according to a physician's instructions. Therapists may instruct their customers in weight reduction, exercise, and body conditioning programs.

Education and Training
Voc/tech school

Salary Range
Average—$20 to $50 an hour

Employment Outlook
Good

Education and Training Requirements

You can become a massage therapist through formal training at a reputable school. Some schools will accept only those with a high school diploma or its equivalent. Training usually lasts from 6 to 12 months. Students are taught the theory and practice of massage, along with courses in anatomy, physiology, pathology, hygiene, public health, and professional ethics. More than one-fourth of the states require massage therapists to pass a written and practical licensing examination in order to enter this field.

Getting the Job

You can get a job as a massage therapist by registering with the placement service of the school you attend. You can also apply directly to health clubs, community

A massage therapist massages a customer to stimulate blood circulation, relax tight muscles, and for other beneficial effects.

service organizations, resorts, and country clubs. Some jobs are listed in newspaper classifieds or job banks on the Internet. State and private employment agencies may help you to find a job. You can also go into private practice.

Advancement Possibilities and Employment Outlook

Massage therapists who work in large health clubs, resorts, and country clubs can become supervisors. Those who are employed by community service organizations can become health service directors. Massage therapists in private practice advance by building a reputation and a loyal clientele and by commanding higher fees for their services.

The employment outlook for massage therapists is good through the year 2006. The rising popularity of health clubs should result in an increase in the number of jobs in the field. Also, more massage therapists are bringing their services into the workplace, since a brief midday massage is now believed to increase employee productivity.

Working Conditions

Most massage therapists work 35 to 40 hours a week, although self-employed workers may work longer hours. The workweek usually includes evenings and weekends, which are generally the busiest times for massage therapists. Most of the working day is spent standing. Massage therapists work in clean, pleasant rooms. In some states sanitary conditions are set by law.

Massage therapists must be able to work well with their hands. They should have a pleasant, courteous manner. The nature of their work demands that they be able to respect the privacy of their customers.

Earnings and Benefits

The wages of massage therapists range from minimum wage for beginning workers to $20 to $50 or more an hour for those with experience. In addition, therapists often receive tips from their customers. Many massage therapists add to their income by giving massages in their customers' homes or in their own homes. Employers generally provide benefits that include paid vacations and holidays and health insurance. Self-employed massage therapists must provide their own benefits.

Where to Go for More Information

American Massage Therapy Association
820 Davis Street, Suite 100
Evanston, IL 60201-4444
(847) 864-0123

Nanny

Definition and Nature of the Work

Nannies are child care specialists who provide full-time care for children in the employer's home. People sometimes confuse nannies with babysitters, teachers, or housekeepers. Although nannies need some of the same skills, their job is different from the jobs of these other workers. Unlike other child care workers, a nanny usually provides long-term care for the children in one family. These children may be infants, preschoolers, or older. Nannies work directly for a family, not for a school or an organization.

Duties may vary from household to household, but nannies generally tend to the basic needs of the children they care for, including shopping, cooking, preparing bottles, changing diapers, ironing and mending, supervising baths, and educating and amusing the children by reading and taking them on outings. They also discipline the children according to parents' wishes.

Education and Training
Varies—see profile

Salary Range
Starting—$300 to $375 a week

Employment Outlook
Excellent

Education and Training Requirements

A nanny must be a sensitive and stable person who understands and likes children. A typical nanny is a high school graduate who has received further training in child care and development. If you have been trained as a teacher, you may wish to pursue a governess position, which combines the roles of nanny and teacher. Governess jobs are available in some wealthy families.

High school students interested in becoming nannies should take courses in communication, psychology, health, family and consumer science, and biology. Babysitting and camp counseling will also provide valuable experience.

A number of nanny schools have opened in different parts of the country. Some private schools provide a 10- or 16-week training course for nannies that includes an internship. Applicants to nanny schools must be in good health, provide letters of reference, and show that they have a driver's license. Many 2-year colleges offer an associate degree program in child development, and some 4-year colleges offer a bachelor's degree in child development. Courses include child psychology, first aid, cardiopulmonary resuscitation (CPR), creative play,

Unlike other child care workers, a nanny usually provides long-term care for the children in one family.

and family dynamics. A few states offer certification for people who have successfully completed such courses.

Getting the Job

The three main paths to employment as a nanny are school placement services, employment agencies, and classified ads. Agencies may request a minimum commitment of a year, so job seekers should screen them carefully, perhaps by contacting some of the nannies the agencies have already placed. State employment offices and college newspapers may also advertise positions.

Advancement Possibilities and Employment Outlook

Advancement opportunities in the nanny profession are limited. Nannies are not promoted. However, they may leave one job for another that offers better wages and living conditions. Some nannies return to college and receive teaching credentials. Others may open nanny schools or agencies.

The employment outlook for nannies is excellent through the year 2006. As the number of families in which both parents work outside the home increases, so will the demand for nannies. Already the demand far exceeds the supply. Those with formal training and excellent references from past employers will be the most sought after.

Working Conditions

Most families who hire nannies live in apartments in large cities or in houses in suburban areas. In most cases, nannies work in agreeable surroundings. They may live in pleasant rooms in the homes of their employers, or they may have homes of their own and commute back and forth to work. Prior to accepting a position, a nanny should feel comfortable in the new surroundings.

Nannies do much of their work in the employer's home. However, they may also spend a good deal of their work time outside the home, driving the children to school, to the doctor's office, and to special events. They may take the children for walks, go shopping with them, or participate in some of their hobbies or athletic activities, such as ice skating. Nannies might also travel with the family on their vacations. Sometimes this may involve travel out of the country.

Nannies often work more than 40 hours a week. Occasionally they may be asked to work during the evening or on weekends. Working with children for long hours can be stressful. Some children are very demanding and resent being disciplined by a nanny. Parents, too, can make the nanny's job difficult, by interfering too much or by indulging the children and thus undermining the nanny's authority. The long hours and the demanding nature of the job may inhibit a nanny's social life. Nannies must be sure to set aside time to pursue personal interests. It is important for nannies to sit down with their future employers and discuss expectations on both sides and what their job entails. This will prevent disagreements and tension later. Nannies who live and work far away from their own families may experience homesickness and loneliness. But most nannies experience great professional and personal satisfaction in their jobs.

Earnings and Benefits

Nannies' salaries start at about $300 to $375 a week. Experienced nannies, especially ones working for wealthy families in major metropolitan areas, can earn $800 or more a week. In addition, they often receive room and board. Some have the use of a car. Nannies usually receive an annual raise, although some employers give them a raise every 6 months.

Employers must make payments for the worker to the Social Security Administration, and some states require that employers provide workers' compensation insurance. Other benefits vary according to the contract between employer and employee; benefits may include paid vacations and sick days, health insurance, and even such fringe benefits as a health club membership or the use of a car.

Where to Go for More Information

American Council of Nanny Schools
Delta College
University Center, MI 48710
(517) 686-9417

Piano and Organ Tuner and Technician

Definition and Nature of the Work

Piano and organ tuners and technicians tune, repair, and rebuild pianos and organs. Most work for independent repair shops, and many have their own shops. Some tuners and technicians work for piano and organ dealers. Others work for manufacturers of pianos and organs.

There are four different kinds of workers in this field. *Piano tuners* adjust the tuning pins that control the tension of the piano strings so they produce the correct pitches. Tuners are trained to hear the correct pitches, but they also use a tuning fork, which is a two-pronged device that gives a fixed tone when it is struck. Although piano tuners may replace worn parts or strings, further repairs require the skills of a piano technician. *Piano technicians* understand the overall mechanical operation of the instrument, and they find and correct problems such as loose pins or worn felt on hammers. Piano technicians use common hand tools as well as special repinning and restringing tools.

Education and Training
High school plus training

Salary Range
Average—$20,000 to $40,000

Employment Outlook
Varies—see profile

A piano tuner adjusts the tuning pins that control the tension of the piano strings so that they produce the correct pitches.

There are two kinds of organ technicians. *Pipe organ technicians* tune, install, and repair pipe organs. Most pipe organs are large and complex. They are usually installed in churches or auditoriums. Installing a pipe organ can take several weeks or months, depending on the size of the organ. Pipe organ technicians install air chests, blowers, pipes, and other parts of the organs. They also tune and repair the organs regularly. As with piano tuners, technicians have trained ears, and they use tuning forks. They move or adjust metal slides or reeds until each pipe of the organ sounds the correct pitch. Since the organ console and its blowers are in different sections of a building, organ technicians work in teams of at least two workers.

Electronic organ technicians tune and repair electronic organs by using special electronic test equipment. Electronic organ technicians use soldering irons, wire cutters, and other tools to fix the electrical wiring in electronic organs. Many technicians work on only one brand of electronic organ.

Education and Training Requirements

Employers prefer to hire high school graduates as piano and organ tuners and technicians. Courses in music, metallurgy, physics, and woodworking are useful. If you want to work on electronic organs, you should take courses in electronics. These courses are given in some high schools and in technical schools and 2-year colleges.

High school graduates interested in tuning pianos may go to work in a piano shop or with a qualified tuner-technician. Some colleges offer a program for piano technicians as well as courses in rebuilding pianos. Home-study courses should always be supplemented with on-the-job experience. A few schools teach piano tuning to visually handicapped persons whose acute hearing helps make them outstanding tuners. The Piano Technicians Guild publishes a list of schools offering these courses.

Both piano technicians and organ builders may employ apprentices. Larger organ builders have their own programs for advancement. Study in a technical school can shorten a piano-tuning apprenticeship. Apprentices become registered piano tuners or technicians by passing written and practical tests given by the Piano Technicians Guild.

Getting the Job

The best way to get a job as a piano or organ tuner or technician is to apply directly to repair shops, piano and organ dealers, or companies that make pianos and organs. You can also check with your school placement service. Employment agencies, newspaper classifieds, and Internet job banks can give you information about jobs. You can also open your own repair business, but you should get some job experience first.

Advancement Possibilities and Employment Outlook

Piano and organ tuners and technicians can advance to positions as supervisors in large stores or repair shops. Those who are very skilled can get jobs caring for fine pianos and organs in concert halls. Some tuners and technicians advance by going into business for themselves. Tools for tuning and repairing pianos and pipe organs are not costly, so large sums of money are not needed to open a business. On the other hand, tools and testing equipment needed to work on electronic organs are very expensive. Loans are available for those who qualify.

Job openings for piano tuners and piano technicians are expected to increase as fast as the average for all occupations through the year 2006. Employment of tuners and technicians is affected by the condition of the economy. Many will hold off on having their pianos or organs tuned and repaired during economic downturns. As long as the economy remains stable, there will be a steady demand for tuners and technicians. There will also be some job openings each year to replace workers who leave the field.

Employment opportunities for pipe organ technicians are not expected to increase. Most pipe organs are owned by churches and musical organizations, so employment is not as sensitive to the economy's fluctuations. Opportunities will continue to be few as it is a very small occupation area. However, some opportunities will be available to replace retired technicians.

Electronic organs are very popular, and the number in use is expected to increase. Many churches are beginning to use electronic organs. There should be an increase in the number of jobs available for electronic organ technicians.

Working Conditions

Piano and organ tuners and technicians spend many of their working hours in people's homes and in buildings such as churches and schools, so working conditions vary. They often use cars or trucks for service calls. Working hours may depend on the season. During fall and winter, people spend more time indoors playing the piano or organ. Many tuners and technicians work more than 40 hours a week during these times of the year. They may work evenings or weekends. Some tuners and technicians work part-time. They may also be music teachers, musicians, or television and radio repairers. Piano tuning and repairing is well suited to people who like to work independently.

Earnings and Benefits

Piano and organ tuners and repairers working for retail stores earn about $20,000 a year. Self-employed piano tuners average about $40,000 a year. Travel and tool expenses reduce the net income for tuners and technicians.

Benefits for employed tuners and technicians vary according to the size of the business. Benefits may include paid holidays and vacations, health insurance, and pension plans. Those who have their own businesses must provide their own benefits.

Where to Go for More Information

Piano Technicians Guild
3930 Washington Street
Kansas City, MO 64111
(816) 753-7747
www.ptg.org

Watch Repairer

Education and Training
Varies—see profile

Salary Range
Starting—$450
to $500 a week
Average—$30,000
to $35,000

Employment Outlook
Poor

Definition and Nature of the Work

Watch repairers clean, repair, and adjust watches and clocks. They work in watch and jewelry repair shops, in jewelry stores, or in factories that make clocks and watches. About two-fifths of all watch repairers are self-employed. Watch repairers are sometimes called watchmakers.

Watch repairers use small tools to take a watch out of its case. They examine the watch with a special magnifying glass called a loupe. They may give the owner an estimate of how much it will cost to fix the watch. Watch repairers then replace or repair the broken part or parts. Sometimes they have to make a new part or alter a factory-made part to fit a watch.

Watch repairers use delicate hand tools, as well as special machines. When they work on electronic watches, they use electric meters. Watch repairers clean and oil the watch movement and test it before putting it back into its case.

Some watch repairers also wait on customers. Many sell watches, jewelry, silverware, and related items. They may also repair jewelry and do engraving. A few teach in vocational schools.

Education and Training Requirements

Most employers prefer to hire high school graduates as watch repairers. A few vocational high schools give courses in watch repairing. Some watch repairers get informal on-the-job training from experienced workers. Most watch repairers, however, learn their trade in special watch repair schools. Courses in these schools usually last 1 to 3 years. Students learn to use the tools and machines of the trade, and they learn how to recognize and solve repair problems.

Some states require watch repairers to be licensed. To get a license, watch repairers must pass an exam that tests their skills and knowledge. Watch repairers in all states can obtain certification from the American Watchmakers Institute. Those who pass special tests given by the institute receive the title of Certified Watchmaker, Certified Master Watchmaker, Certified Electronic Watch Specialist, Certified Clockmaker, or Certified Master Clockmaker.

Getting the Job

If you attend a watch repair school, your school's placement service will help you find a job. Trade associations and unions for watch repairers also provide job information. You can apply directly to jewelry and department stores or to watch repair shops. You can check newspaper classifieds, job banks on the Internet, or employment agencies. Watch repairers usually have some job experience before opening their own businesses.

Advancement Possibilities and Employment Outlook

Watch repairers can become supervisors or managers in large repair shops. Many open their own watch repair or jewelry shops. Jewelry businesses require more of an initial investment than watch shops, but loans are available to qualified applicants. Some watch repairers receive further training and move into fields related to watch repair. These fields include electronics and the making and repair of precision instruments used in science and engineering.

Opportunities in this field are expected to decline through the year 2006. Although many watches are being sold, more of them are inexpensive kinds, which people tend to replace rather than have repaired. There will be some job openings to replace watch repairers who leave the field. The best opportunities will be for those with experience and for those who can repair electronic watches. Jobs in jewelry stores and watch repair shops are available in all parts of the country. Jobs in watch factories, however, are more limited.

Working Conditions

Watch repairers who work in repair shops, jewelry stores, and factories generally work in pleasant surroundings. They must be able to sit for long periods and concentrate on the small, detailed parts of a watch. They need patience and must be able to work well with their hands. Watch repairers generally work 40 to 48 hours a week. Those who are self-employed usually work longer than salaried workers. Hours often include some evenings and Saturdays. Some watch repairers belong to unions.

Earnings and Benefits

Beginning watch repairers earn average salaries of $450 to $500 a week. Experienced workers may earn $30,000 to $35,000 a year. In addition, watch repairers working in retail stores sometimes receive a commission on the goods that they sell. Self-employed watch repairers usually earn more than salaried workers. However, those who have their own businesses must provide their own benefits. Many businesses that employ watch repairers are very small, so the benefits that they provide vary widely. Benefits sometimes include paid vacations and holidays, health insurance, and pension plans.

Where to Go for More Information

American Watch Association
P.O. Box 464
Washington, DC 20044-0464
(703) 759-3377

American Watchmakers–Clockmakers
  Institute
701 Enterprise Drive
Harrison, OH 45030
(513) 367-9800

Jewelers of America
1185 Avenue of the Americas, 30th Floor
New York, NY 10036
(212) 768-8777
www.Jewelers.org

Wedding Consultant

Definition and Nature of the Work

Wedding consultants help people to plan weddings. Consultants who work for bridal shops or department stores that have bridal departments may be called bridal consultants. Many wedding consultants are self-employed. They often sell the goods and services that they suggest to the bride and groom.

Wedding consultants seek out possible customers by reading the announcements of engagements in newspapers. They contact the engaged couple and offer their services. Wedding consultants give advice on outfits for the bride and her attendants. They suggest colors, fabrics, and styles for dresses. They help choose suits for the groom and other male members of the wedding party. They also help the bride select her wardrobe for the honeymoon. Sometimes they help with fittings for these clothes.

Wedding consultants may assist the bride and groom as they pick out silver, china, glassware, linens, and other items for their new home. Consultants often keep a gift register, which is a list of the couple's choices and purchases. The register helps people choose a gift that the couple will like and that someone else has not already bought them.

Education and Training
Varies—see profile

Salary Range
Varies—see profile

Employment Outlook
Fair

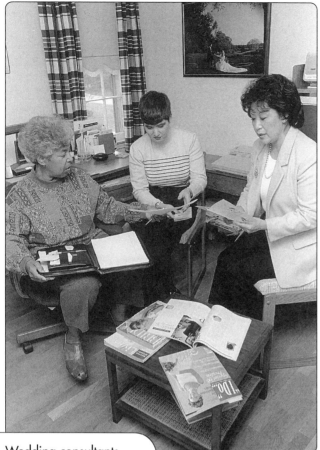

Wedding consultants help plan weddings with families. They provide advice on clothing, invitations, decorations, music, food, and other aspects of the wedding.

Wedding consultants also help to make many of the plans for the wedding itself. For this they need to know about the customs of different religious or ethnic groups. They give advice on the etiquette, or proper manners, for the wedding. They sometimes help to choose, order, address, and mail the invitations. They may suggest and order flower arrangements and other decorations to use. They may hire musicians, photographers, caterers, and bakers. They may also organize the transportation for the wedding party and make travel and lodging arrangements for the bride and groom or for guests. Often they help the members of the wedding party to dress. Wedding consultants may also attend rehearsals and the wedding itself. Sometimes they send information about the wedding to newspapers.

Education and Training Requirements

There are no specific educational requirements to become a wedding consultant. However, you can begin to prepare for the field by taking high school courses in family and consumer science, art, speech and drama, English, psychology, sociology, and business subjects. A college education in liberal arts can also be useful. It should include many of the same courses. Correspondence schools offer courses in bridal and gift consulting. Many wedding consultants learn by working with experienced consultants. You usually need a few years of experience before you can be considered a fully qualified wedding consultant.

Getting the Job

You can get a job as a wedding consultant by applying directly to bridal shops and department stores that have bridal departments. You can also ask self-employed wedding consultants for a job. Some job openings are listed in the classifieds of newspapers or in job banks on the Internet. You might want to check state and private employment agencies as well.

Advancement Possibilities and Employment Outlook

Wedding consultants can advance by becoming consultants for larger or more expensive stores. In large stores they can become supervisors or managers. Some wedding consultants go into business for themselves. They may work from their home or from an office.

Some increase in jobs for wedding consultants is expected to occur through the year 2006. Most job openings will result as experienced workers leave the field.

Working Conditions

Wedding consultants usually work in pleasant, well-decorated stores, shops, or offices. They spend much of the working day outside the store or office. They must check on decorations, shop for clients, and perform other duties. They often need a driver's license. Wedding consultants usually work about 40 hours a week. Working hours are often irregular, however. Consultants must sometimes meet clients in the evenings or on weekends. Spring and summer tend to be the busy seasons for wedding consultants. They must often rush to meet deadlines. Wedding consultants deal directly with a lot of people, including clients and workers in other fields, such as printers and bakers. Therefore, they must have a pleasant, courteous manner. They must be able to coordinate several activities at the same time. They should also have good sales abilities.

Earnings and Benefits

The earnings of wedding consultants vary widely depending on experience, location, and type of business. Currently, experienced sales workers earn between $7 and $10 an hour. In addition, some sales workers receive a commission or a percentage of the value of the goods and services that they sell. Other sales workers earn only a commission. Self-employed wedding consultants generally earn more. They may receive a fee from the customer, but more often they receive a fee from the businesses whose services they recommend. Self-employed wedding consultants must provide their own benefits. Benefits for employed workers may include paid holidays and vacations, health insurance, and pension plans.

Where to Go for More Information

Association of Bridal Consultants
200 Chestnutland Road
New Milford, CT 06776-2521
(860) 355-0464
www.weddingchannel.com

National Bridal Service
3122 West Cary Street
Richmond, VA 23221
(804) 355-6945

Appraiser

Education and Training
Varies—see profile

Salary Range
Varies—see profile

Employment Outlook
Fair

Definition and Nature of the Work

Appraisers examine works of art, jewelry, antiques, and the contents of estates to determine their value and authenticity. This job requires detailed knowledge of the subjects and an understanding of current market values and trends.

A *fine art appraiser*, for example, will study a work of art for style of brush strokes, color values, and other relevant characteristics. This information can establish the period in which it was painted or help identify the artist. If a forgery is suspected, the appraiser may analyze paint samples for their chemical content or examine the painting using sophisticated laser equipment or under X-ray. This judgment requires a knowledge of the materials, style, and techniques employed by different artists in different periods.

Antiques appraisers usually have a specialty, such as silver, jewelry, or furniture of a particular period. They must be familiar with the styles, materials, and markings that help them date and authenticate genuine antiques. They must also assess the condition of an article in relation to others still in existence and determine the rarity of the piece.

Most *jewelry appraisers* have some training in gemology. This training enables them to appraise the value of gemstones according to their color, the clarity of the stones, and the quality of the cut. After examining an article, a jewelry appraiser then determines its wholesale and retail values. This figure is based on the information the appraiser gathers about the piece and how it compares to

After examining a piece of jewelry, an appraiser determines its wholesale and retail value based on information he gathers about the piece and how it compares to similar pieces.

similar pieces. Appraisers also have to know the current market value of an item according to various pricing guidelines and any trends that may affect the price, such as the current price of gold.

Estate appraisers are in great demand today to establish the value of items for purposes of sale, estate planning, insurance, and bankruptcy. Unlike other appraisers, they tend to deal with a group of items rather than individual types of articles. An estate appraiser will visit a house, list and possibly photograph the contents, and take measurements of large pieces of furniture. The appraiser then sets the value of each item by consulting catalogs, comparing retail values, and finding prices for comparable items.

Education and Training Requirements

The educational and training requirements for appraisers vary according to the types of articles they appraise. Generally, training and experience are gained by working as assistants to specialists in retail stores, galleries, and auction houses. For fine art appraisal, galleries and art dealers prefer to hire those with a bachelor's degree in fine art or art history. For those interested in jewelry, the Gemological Institute of America offers a 6-month training program leading to a diploma in diamonds and colored stones. It also offers courses in sales and appraisal. Estate appraisers prefer to hire high school graduates as assistants, whom they will train to appraise certain types of articles.

Getting the Job

Apply directly to retail stores, art galleries, and auction houses for assistant positions. Part-time and summer vacation jobs in these places may help you gain valuable experience. Your high school or college placement office may be able to give you information about job openings. Newspaper classifieds, Internet job banks, and magazines about art and antiques may also list positions for appraisers.

Advancement Possibilities and Employment Outlook

Advancement as an appraiser comes with experience and specialization in a particular area. For example, appraisers become experts in oriental rugs or art from a particular place or period. For those working in retail stores, advancement usually means taking on more types of appraisals and appraising articles of higher value. Experienced appraisers who have a specialty may start their own businesses or work freelance. Some may work as consultants to art galleries and museums. A few become well-known authorities in their field and may be asked to appraise objects around the world.

The employment outlook for appraisers appears to be fair through the year 2006. As more and more people invest in art, jewelry, and antiques, appraisers' services will be in demand. The area of estate appraisal is also expected to grow with appraisals being required for planning, insurance, bankruptcy, and sales. There is currently a shortage of appraisers in this area, and the job prospects for those with experience are very good.

Working Conditions

Working conditions vary widely, depending on whether the appraiser is self-employed and works from a private home or office or is employed by a large jewelry store, museum, or insurance company. Appraisers may be required to do a lot of business travel. Objects can be found both in clean, spacious museums and in dirty, cluttered attics.

Where to Go for More Information

American Association of Certified
  Appraisers
800 Compton Road, Suite 10
Cincinnati, OH 45231
(513) 729-1400

American Society of Appraisers
535 Herndon Parkway, Suite 125
Herndon, VA 22170
(703) 478-2228
www.appraisers.org

Appraisers Association of America
386 Park Avenue South, Suite 2000
New York, NY 10016
(212) 889-5404

Appraisers must be not only skilled in their work but also be able to deal with many different types of people. Occasionally, a client will disagree with the appraised value of an object. In such instances an appraiser must be tactful but firm.

Earnings and Benefits

Currently entry-level salaries for appraisers with a diploma in gemology are about $20,000 a year. Experienced appraisers with a specialty and a good clientele can earn more than $65,000 a year. There is currently a move away from paying appraisers a percentage of the value of the object being appraised and toward basing their fee on the time spent and the expertise required to make the appraisal. Benefits usually include paid holidays and vacations, medical insurance, and pension plans. Self-employed appraisers must provide their own benefits.

Business Family and Consumer Scientist

Education and Training
College

Salary Range
Starting—$17,000
to $35,000

Employment Outlook
Good

Definition and Nature of the Work

Business family and consumer scientists apply their special knowledge of and skills in family and consumer science to the problems of a business firm. They help their companies research and understand what consumers want and need. They also teach consumers about products and services. Business family and consumer scientists help companies in many ways. They may design and market new or improved products, or they may develop goodwill toward the company by conducting consumer information programs. The titles of business family and consumer scientists vary. For example, they may be called marketing specialists or directors of consumer education.

Utility companies and the manufacturers of large household appliances, such as stoves, washers, and dryers, often employ business family and consumer scientists. These family and consumer scientists help people use and care for the appliances they buy. They may give demonstrations on how to operate an appliance and offer tips on saving money by using the machine wisely. For instance, to demonstrate an electric range, business family and consumer scientists may create new recipes that can be made on the range. They also answer consumers' questions. Sometimes they give shows for schools or clubs.

Supermarket chains, food manufacturers, and trade boards also employ business family and consumer scientists to prepare and present information to consumers. These family and consumer scientists may write pamphlets or give demonstrations. They appear on radio or television, teach consumers how to buy meat or prepare potatoes, or suggest menus using canned vegetables. This kind of information increases sales and creates goodwill for the company.

Some business family and consumer scientists work as designers or buyers for clothing, furniture, or textile manufacturers. They help these firms produce attractive and practical articles that consumers will like. Large department stores employ family and consumer scientists to advise them on the buying and displaying of merchandise. Banks, too, sometimes hire family and consumer

These business family and consumer scientists are conducting a dietary study. They may use the information they gather to market new or improved products or to provide consumers with informational programs.

scientists to help their customers plan their family budgets. Most companies that make consumer products or provide services can use the special skills of family and consumer scientists. Some family and consumer scientists have their own consulting firms that advise and help a variety of businesses.

Education and Training Requirements

If you want a career as a business family and consumer scientist, you should take a college preparatory program in high school. You should take courses in family and consumer science, science, English, and speech. A bachelor's degree in family and consumer science is required for most jobs in this field. In addition to family and consumer science courses, you should also try to take courses in marketing, advertising, public relations, economics, and business management. Courses or experience in writing and public speaking are helpful. Any experience you can get in a job related to some phase of business family and consumer science is also useful training.

Getting the Job

The placement office at your college can help you find job openings in business family and consumer science. Also check the classifieds in professional family and consumer science magazines or in the trade magazine of the particular industry that interests you. You can also apply directly to companies for which you would like to work. Your librarian can help you to find the magazines and directories that will give you the names and addresses of the people to contact. You should also check with state or private employment agencies and scan newspaper classifieds and Internet job banks.

Advancement Possibilities and Employment Outlook

Advancement depends on skill, experience, location, and type of industry. After several years of experience a business family and consumer scientist can become the head of a product development department, a manager of customer relations, or a company executive. Business family and consumer scientists who combine their skills in family and consumer science with marketing or management experience will have the best chances of advancement. Some business family and consumer scientists advance by forming their own consulting firms.

There should be many new job openings through the year 2006. Businesses are using more family and consumer scientists to keep them aware of the attitudes, behavior, and needs of their customers. Job opportunities should be available with manufacturers, marketing firms, and the design departments of large department stores.

Working Conditions

Most business family and consumer scientists work in pleasant offices. They may spend some time away from home as they travel from place to place demonstrating products or giving talks. They must often work in unfamiliar surroundings and meet large numbers of people. Those who work for supermarkets or department stores may spend long hours on their feet dealing with customers.

Business family and consumer scientists generally work 40 hours a week. Sometimes they have to work evenings or weekends, depending on the assignment and type of work. Those who are self-employed set their own hours and working conditions. Business family and consumer scientists need to be flexible and creative. Their field is always changing and presenting new challenges. They should have the ability to communicate their ideas to others and deal with a wide variety of people.

Where to Go for More Information

The American Association of Family and
 Consumer Sciences
1555 King Street, Suite 400
Alexandria, VA 22314
(703) 706-4600
www.aafes.org

National Association of Business
 Economists
1233 Twentieth Street, NW, Suite 505
Washington, DC 20036
(202) 463-6223
www.nabe.com

Earnings and Benefits

Earnings vary widely depending on location, experience, and level of responsibility. Many beginning business family and consumer scientists earn annual salaries of about $17,000 to $35,000. Benefits generally include paid holidays and vacations, health insurance, and pension plans. Self-employed family and consumer scientists must provide their own benefits.

Consumer Advocate

Education and Training
Varies—see profile

Salary Range
Varies—see profile

Employment Outlook
Varies—see profile

Definition and Nature of the Work

Consumer advocates support the rights of the consumer to obtain safe goods and services at fair prices. They are employed by government agencies, corporations, consumer protection organizations, and community groups to ensure that the needs of purchasers are met.

Some consumer advocates offer direct assistance through hot lines, seminars, or classes. Others run bureaus for consumers who have specific problems, such as failure to receive mail-order purchases. Some publish magazines or brochures to help people get the most for their money or avoid common buying pitfalls. Many conduct tests on automobiles, clothes, food, toys, office equipment, and other items to ensure that they are not potentially hazardous. Consumer advocates may lobby for legislation to protect the consumer or protest against increases in utility rates. Some advocates specialize in a particular field, such as nutrition or housing.

Education and Training Requirements

People from a variety of backgrounds become consumer advocates. Law, political science, training in research or public information, and community education are all useful backgrounds. Many consumer advocates have degrees in law, government administration, public policy, or political science.

Getting the Job

Public service jobs for consumer advocates are available at all levels of government, from federal to municipal, and these jobs may be listed in civil service bulletins. Volunteer work for a citizens' group or nonprofit consumer organization may provide the experience and visibility necessary to enter the field.

Advancement Opportunities and Employment Outlook

Consumer advocates may become directors of consumer affairs offices in the government or within large companies. They may also run lobbying organizations. Employment forecasts are mixed. Advocate positions in government are vulnerable in times of spending cutbacks. Consumer programs are among the first to be eliminated in times of financial strain. Nevertheless, business is showing increasing support for the consumer movement, and the interest of the general public is intensifying.

Working Conditions

Since consumer advocacy takes many forms, the working conditions are equally varied. Some advocates work a conventional 35- to 40-hour week in offices, while others work weekends. Those who work unusual hours generally include lobbyists and troubleshooters, as well as those whose jobs involve writing or public speaking. The workload may be highly erratic, peaking during seasonal shopping periods, legislative sessions, or other consumer-related events.

Earnings and Benefits

Earnings for consumer advocates vary according to the type of organization for which they work. Many consumer jobs are part-time or volunteer positions. Staff members of consumer advocacy groups usually earn between $16,000 and $28,000 a year, whereas senior lobbyists earn up to $50,000 a year.

Consumer advocates offer direct assistance to consumers. They may be employed by government agencies, corporations, consumer protection organizations, or community groups.

Where to Go for More Information

Consumer Federation of America
1424 Sixteenth Street, NW, Suite 604
Washington, DC 20036
(202) 387-6121

National Consumers League
1701 K Street, NW, Suite 1200
Washington, DC 20006
(202) 835-3323
www.natlconsumersleague.org

Dietitian and Nutritionist

Education and Training
College plus training

Salary Range
Varies—see profile

Employment Outlook
Good

Definition and Nature of the Work

Dietitians and nutritionists are health professionals who study and apply the principles of nutrition and food management. There are several kinds of dietitians and nutritionists. The largest group is made up of administrative dietitians. *Administrative dietitians* manage food services in hospitals, schools, nursing homes, restaurants, industrial plants, military bases, and other institutions. They plan and direct the purchase and preparation of food, as well as supervise other food service workers. Administrative dietitians ensure that the meals served are nutritious, appetizing, and within the institution's budget.

Clinical dietitians plan meals for hospital patients and others who have special dietary needs. They assess patients' nutritional needs, confer with doctors, and may use computers to analyze nutritional intake. Sometimes they teach people who need special diets how to plan and prepare foods at home.

Research dietitians work on projects related to food and nutrition. Projects range from studying the effects of different diets on certain groups of people and the management of food service systems to investigating the dietary needs of older people or space travelers. Research dietitians work in universities, medical centers, food preparation plants, and other institutions. *Teaching dietitians* (or *dietetic educators*) teach medical, nursing, dental, or dietetic students about the role of foods in health care.

Nutritionists study the use of food in the human body. They are not usually involved in feeding people. They deal instead with the broad principles of nutrition. They may teach others about scientific discoveries in the field of nutrition. These discoveries can then be applied to the planning of diets and menus. For example, a nutritionist might develop a course to teach poor families how to eat well on a small budget. Nutritionists are employed in the food industry, schools, hospitals, agriculture, and public health agencies.

Dietitians and nutritionists often combine several of the above functions, especially in small institutions. A few dietitians and nutritionists work as consultants.

A dietitian reviews food plans with other health professionals in a hospital. She is also responsible for directing the purchasing and preparation of the food.

Education and Training Requirements

To be a dietitian or a nutritionist, you need at least a bachelor's degree. You can major in food and nutrition, food service management, or a related field. The American Dietetic Association (ADA) offers training programs that include practical supervised experience. These programs last from 6 months to 2 years. You can take these programs during or after college. You can become a certified registered dietitian (RD) by completing one of these training programs and passing a test given by the ADA. You must continue your education to keep your registration up to date.

To advance in the field of nutrition, you also need a master's degree, which takes about 1 year of advanced study. Many high-level dietitians' jobs in teaching, research, or administration require a master's degree. Some dietitians and nutritionists go on to get a doctoral degree.

Getting the Job

Your college placement office can help you to find a job as a dietitian or nutritionist. Professional journals and the ADA can also provide job information. You can also check job banks on the Internet and newspaper classifieds, or apply directly to the institution or agency for which you want to work.

Advancement Possibilities and Employment Outlook

Dietitians with skill and experience can become directors of food service in a hospital, school, or other institution. With further training they can become nutritionists. Both dietitians and nutritionists can move into teaching or research jobs in colleges if they have the required education. They can also advance to administration and consulting work.

The employment outlook is good through the year 2006. There is a growing public concern about the quality of the American diet. As a result, dietitians and nutritionists are being called on to teach good eating habits and to plan nutritional meals in institutions.

Working Conditions

Dietitians and nutritionists usually work in pleasant surroundings. However, some kitchens may be steamy, and dietitians may be on their feet for extended periods of time. They work in offices, hospital kitchens, or college classrooms. They come into contact with other professional people as well as with kitchen personnel, clerical staff, students, patients, and a wide variety of other people. They should have management ability, an aptitude for science, good health, imagination, and the ability to get along well with others.

Dietitians usually work 40 hours a week. Some dietitians must work on weekends and holidays. Working hours are more flexible for nutritionists.

Earnings and Benefits

Salaries vary widely depending on the field of expertise, education, experience, and place of employment. The average salaries for dieticians in different fields are: clinical—$34,130; food and nutrition—$42,965; community nutrition—$33,900; consulting and business—$43,375; and education and research—$42,785. Experienced dietitians can earn more. Benefits generally include paid holidays and vacations, health insurance, and pension plans.

Where to Go for More Information

American Dietetic Association
216 West Jackson Boulevard, Suite 800
Chicago, IL 60606-6995
(312) 899-0040
www.eatright.org

American Society for Nutritional Sciences
9650 Rockville Pike
Bethesda, MD 20814-3990
(301) 530-7050
www.faseb.org/asns

Consultant Dieticians in Health Care Facilities
216 West Jackson Boulevard, Suite 800
Chicago, IL 60606-6995
(312) 899-0040
www.eatright.org

Divorce Mediator

Education and Training
College

Salary Range
Varies—see profile

Employment Outlook
Good

Definition and Nature of the Work

Divorce mediators have become increasingly popular with couples seeking to negotiate their divorce agreement under the guidance of an impartial professional. While a divorce lawyer counsels only one of the marriage partners, a mediator assists both husband and wife. The mediator's task is to help the couple discuss and agree on division of their property, custody of their children, and other divorce-related issues. These negotiations are designed to avert a costly, stressful, and time-consuming court dispute by settling the terms of the divorce before the case goes to court. Following mediation, the agreement is reviewed by the lawyer for each partner and then filed in court.

Some divorce mediators are employed by mediation centers. Some centers are run by the government, while others are privately owned. Many divorce mediators also maintain private practices.

Education and Training Requirements

Divorce mediators often have a professional background in law, social work, or psychology. In recent years training programs have been developed to instruct prospective mediators in the legal and financial matters related to divorce. However, there is no licensing procedure for divorce mediators.

Getting the Job

You can contact mediation centers for work in this field. Divorce lawyers and family law offices may also need mediators. Many mediators work as lawyers, psychologists, or social workers full-time and do divorce mediation on a freelance basis. As they gain a reputation in the field, they may be requested by lawyers or by the courts to do mediation. Those who work in private practice as mediators may get referrals from satisfied clients.

Advancement Possibilities and Employment Outlook

Divorce mediators who work part-time or who work for mediation centers may decide to open their own consulting firms. Advancement for those in private practice often involves expansion. Those who work in mediation centers may become supervisors. As the need for mediators grows, more social service agencies may start doing this type of work. If so, mediators will be able to move into supervisory positions in those departments.

The employment outlook for divorce mediators is promising because they perform a valued service while providing an alternative to expensive legal assistance. The demand for mediation is increasing on several fronts. More divorcing couples are seeking ways to avoid public court appearances. The judicial and legislative systems are also showing support. The courts frequently appoint mediators to help resolve difficult divorce cases. Several states now require mediation before child custody and financial support disputes are brought to court. Mediators with a background in child psychology or psychiatry will be in demand to mediate child custody issues. In addition, more social service agencies are expected to add divorce mediators to their staffs in the next few years.

As the field expands, however, it is likely to become more regulated. Experts in the field predict that divorce mediators will need to be certified in the future and will be expected to meet standardized training requirements and comply with professional guidelines.

Working Conditions

Divorce mediators work with people who are under a lot of stress. Therefore, they must be calm and reasonable. They must also remain impartial and ethical as they deal with sensitive issues. There is considerable job satisfaction when the mediator is able to arrange an agreement between the divorcing parties with minimal pain.

Earnings and Benefits

The hourly rates of divorce mediators in private practice generally range from $50 to $150. The rates vary with experience and with location. Mediators who are in private practice must provide their own benefits. Those who work part-time as mediators may receive benefits from their full-time jobs.

Where to Go for More Information

American Arbitration Association
140 West 51st Street
New York, NY 10020
(212) 484-4000

Family Service America
11700 West Lake Park Drive
Milwaukee, WI 53224
(414) 359-1040

Embalmer

Definition and Nature of the Work

Embalmers prepare the dead for burial. The embalming process disinfects the body to prevent the spread of disease. It also preserves the body for funeral services. Most embalmers work for funeral homes, hospitals, medical schools, and morgues. Many embalmers also serve as funeral directors. Morgues are places where bodies are held until they can be identified or until the cause of death can be determined.

Embalmers must know and follow the laws that deal with the handling and treatment of dead bodies. When they are given a body to prepare, they wash it with germicidal soap and dry it. They also shave the body if necessary. During the embalming process, embalmers insert tubes into the body to remove the blood and replace it with embalming fluid. Embalmers sometimes also reshape parts of the body using materials such as cotton, plastic, or wax. They may apply cosmetics to give the face a lifelike appearance. They also dress the body and arrange it in a casket. If the body is to be sent to another area for burial, embalmers place it in a special transportation case.

Embalmers who work for small funeral homes also perform other tasks, such as serving as pallbearers or helping during funeral services. Embalmers who work in hospitals, medical schools, or morgues help to prepare bodies for autopsies, which are examinations after death, or for dissection. They may also help at autopsies. Sometimes they have to file police reports or testify at inquests, which are official inquiries into the cause of death.

Education and Training Requirements

You can begin to prepare for a career as an embalmer while in high school. Courses in science and art are useful for the technical and artistic sides of embalming. If you want to work in other areas of funeral service, you will find that psychology, sociology, speech, and business subjects are also helpful. You can get practical experience working part-time or during summers in a funeral home.

Education and Training
High school plus training; license

Salary Range
Average—$590 a week

Employment Outlook
Good

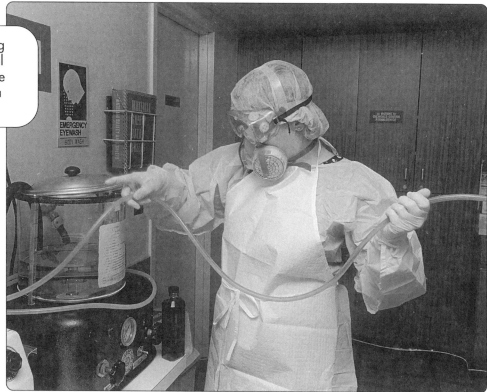

After receiving formal training in mortuary science or funeral service, embalmers must serve an apprenticeship and pass a state board examination.

There are special programs to train embalmers. They are called mortuary science programs and are offered by private vocational schools. They take 9 months to 3 years to complete. A few colleges also offer 4-year programs in funeral service. You will need to serve an apprenticeship of 1 to 3 years during or after formal training.

All states require embalmers to be licensed. Requirements vary, but you must usually be at least 21 years old and a graduate of a high school and a mortuary science school. You also usually need to have completed an apprenticeship and to have passed a state board examination. Most states require you to attend college for a year or more before you start your specialized training. Most embalmers get a license as a funeral director as well.

Getting the Job

You can apply directly to funeral homes or to the other institutions that employ embalmers. Although most funeral homes are family businesses, many employ people who are not members of the family. Embalmers may continue working at funeral homes where they had part-time jobs while still in school or where they served apprenticeships. Most schools of mortuary science have placement services that can help you to find a job. Also check the Yellow Pages of your local phone book, newspaper classifieds, and Internet job banks. You can also contact professional associations. Members of the clergy may be able to introduce you to local funeral directors.

Advancement Possibilities and Employment Outlook

Embalmers who choose to remain strictly in the field of embalming can become a chief embalmer in a large funeral home, hospital, medical school, or morgue. Embalmers on the staff of hospitals or medical schools can be appointed to the boards of professional associations and can write articles for professional and scientific journals. Some embalmers become teachers.

Most embalmers, however, expand their activities and become funeral directors. They can buy an existing funeral home or start a new one. Either venture requires a great deal of money, but loans are available to qualified people.

The employment outlook for embalmers is expected to be good through the year 2006. The number of graduates of mortuary science schools is fewer than the number of jobs available.

Working Conditions

The embalming process is done in clean, well-lighted rooms that must pass state inspections. Embalmers must often lift and carry bodies and other heavy objects during embalming and during funeral services. They must be able to work well with their hands. Because embalmers sometimes meet the family and friends of the deceased, they must have the ability to deal tactfully with people who are under emotional stress.

Embalmers often work more than 40 hours a week. Their hours may be irregular since there may be slow periods followed by a series of funerals within a short period of time. In larger establishments embalmers may work shifts; in smaller ones they may be on call at all times. Sometimes embalmers work for several funeral homes.

Earnings and Benefits

Licensed embalmers currently earn an average salary of $590 a week. Salaries vary, however, depending on their experience and geographical location. Benefits include paid holidays and vacations, health insurance, and pension plans.

Where to Go for More Information

National Funeral Directors Association
11121 West Oklahoma Avenue
Milwaukee, WI 53227-4096
(414) 541-2500
www.nfda.org

National Selected Morticians
5 Revere Drive, Suite 340
Northbrook, IL 60062-8009
(847) 559-9569

Family and Consumer Science Researcher

Definition and Nature of the Work

Family and consumer science researchers plan and carry out studies in various areas related to family and consumer science. For example, they may do research on nutrition or child development or on the preparation and preservation of food, clothing, and furniture. Most family and consumer science researchers work for colleges and universities. Others are employed by hospitals, government agencies, private research groups, and product manufacturers.

In a research study, family and consumer science researchers try to gain new knowledge. First they must define the problem to be solved. They might ask, for example, what effects a certain food preservative has on the human body. Then they read all the available information on the subject. They develop a plan for finding the answers to their question. They may choose a sample of families to study. Or they may decide to do experiments on laboratory animals. They choose or design the equipment that they need to conduct their research study. Then they collect new information. They interpret their findings and write them up in a report that may be published.

The kinds of research studies done by family and consumer science researchers vary widely, depending on their place of employment and area of specialization.

Education and Training
College

Salary Range
Starting—$18,000
Average—$25,000
to $37,000

Employment Outlook
Fair

This family and consumer science researcher is preparing tomato products for a study of the yellow, orange, and red pigments found in fruits and vegetables.

Some, for example, may test a new fabric for a textile manufacturer. Then they try to find out how the public will like the fabric, how well it will wear, and whether it will wrinkle. *Consumer specialists* may do a research study on several brands of laundry detergent. They compare the cost, the effectiveness, and the safety of the detergents. They then suggest which detergents are good buys.

Family and consumer science researchers working for a government agency might study the buying and spending habits of poor families. They might find out how these families feel about keeping a budget. They might suggest ways that poor families could be taught to spend their money wisely. Family and consumer science researchers in a university may study a problem dealing with the development of young children. They may work with psychologists or other specialists to add to our knowledge about child development.

The work of family and consumer science researchers is both varied and important. It forms the basis of advances in family and consumer science and in related areas of knowledge.

Education and Training Requirements

If you want to become a family and consumer science researcher, you should take a college preparatory program in high school. You will need courses in science and communications, as well as family and consumer science. In college you will probably want to major in family and consumer science. You can take family and consumer science courses, such as nutrition, that emphasize research. Courses in other fields, such as chemistry, bacteriology, psychology, and statistics, may also be useful. Any summer or part-time job that involves research would be valuable experience. You will need at least a bachelor's degree to become a family and consumer science researcher. Many jobs require that you have an advanced degree. It takes about a year to earn a master's degree and from 2 to 5 additional years of study to get a doctoral degree.

Getting the Job

Check with your college placement office for job openings for family and consumer science researchers. You can also look at the classifieds in newspapers, Internet job banks, trade magazines, and professional publications. Or you can apply directly to companies or organizations that interest you. Your librarian can help you to find magazines and directories that list the names and addresses of the people to contact. Private or state employment agencies may be able to help you find a job. If you want to work for a government agency, ask your civil service office for information on getting a job.

Advancement Possibilities and Employment Outlook

Advancement depends on education, experience, skill, and the type of research done. Family and consumer science researchers can become the heads of departments or research teams. They may specialize in one or more areas of research, such as new product development or family living. They can become directors or executives in government agencies.

Both government and industry are aware of the value of research done by family and consumer scientists. However, job opportunities for family and consumer science researchers are expected to grow more slowly than the average for all occupations through the year 2006. In addition, there will most likely be a great deal of competition for entry-level jobs. The best jobs will go to those with experience or advanced degrees.

Working Conditions

Family and consumer science researchers generally work in pleasant surroundings. They may have private offices. Much of their time is spent in laboratories, libraries, or test kitchens. They may also need to go out and interview people as part of a research study. They must be able to work well as part of a research team and be able to deal with a wide variety of people. They should also be creative and patient. Family and consumer science researchers generally work 40 hours a week.

Earnings and Benefits

Earnings vary depending on education, experience, and the specific business, agency, or institution. Family and consumer science researchers who work for the federal government start at approximately $18,000 a year. Experienced family and consumer science researchers earn annual salaries of about $25,000 to $37,000 or more. Benefits generally include paid holidays and vacations, health insurance, and pension plans.

Where to Go for More Information

The American Association of Family and
    Consumer Sciences
1555 King Street, Suite 400
Alexandria, VA 22314
(703) 706-4600
www.aafes.org

Family and Consumer Science Teacher

Definition and Nature of the Work

Family and consumer science teachers teach students how to manage a home. They teach topics that include nutrition, menu planning, food preparation, clothing care and construction, money management, grooming, consumer awareness, and child development. Some family and consumer science teachers teach at several educational levels. Others teach only in elementary, junior high, high school, college, or adult education programs. Some teachers specialize in one or more specific subjects, such as clothing or foods.

Most family and consumer science teachers choose and organize their teaching materials and prepare outlines and lesson plans. They plan the best method of teaching the course material. Depending on the subject and the equipment available, they may use lectures, demonstrations, field trips, student projects, or other teaching methods.

Family and consumer science teachers also have many nonteaching duties. They may serve as advisers to student organizations, such as the Future Homemakers of America. Teachers also counsel students and meet with their families to discuss the students' schoolwork and career plans, as well as family relationships and

Education and Training
College

Salary Range
Starting—$20,000
to $22,000

Employment Outlook
Fair

This family and consumer science teacher demonstrates how to prepare granola to elementary school students.

other subjects. Studying for advanced degrees and keeping up with new developments in their field often take up additional time for family and consumer science teachers. Some also write books and articles. Some do research. Others serve as advisers to civic and business organizations. Family and consumer science teachers sometimes serve on education committees and attend faculty meetings. Ordering supplies, teaching materials, and such equipment as sewing machines, stoves, and kitchen utensils may be another part of the job. Family and consumer science teachers also write reports, give and grade tests, read homework papers, and judge student projects.

Education and Training Requirements

If you want to be a family and consumer science teacher, you should take a college preparatory program in high school. You should also be as active as possible in the family and consumer science programs offered. Join the Future Homemakers of America, the 4-H Club, and other organizations. Pay particular attention to courses in chemistry and other sciences, as well as to English and other communications subjects.

The amount of higher education you will need depends on the type of teaching you plan to do. All schools require a teaching certificate. Usually this means that you will need at least a bachelor's degree from an approved 4-year college. You can major in family and consumer science and take the required education courses as well. If you plan to teach at the college level, you will also need a master's or doctoral degree. These degrees normally require from 1 to 5 years of advanced training. Some teachers earn advanced degrees by attending evening classes or summer school.

Getting the Job

To get a teaching job in a public school, you should apply directly to local boards of education. You can also apply to colleges and to private and parochial schools. Newspaper classifieds, Internet job banks, and professional magazines may include openings for family and consumer science teachers. You should also check with state and private employment agencies and with the placement office at your college.

Advancement Possibilities and Employment Outlook

Advancement depends on experience and education. Experienced family and consumer science teachers can become the head of the family and consumer science department in their school. Or they may be made responsible for organizing and overseeing the family and consumer science program of an entire school system. They may hold workshops and seminars to help improve the skills of other teachers. At the college level, family and consumer science teachers can advance by doing research or by writing textbooks or articles for professional magazines. Some teachers move into positions in business or journalism that require a background in family and consumer science.

There will probably be stiff competition for jobs through the year 2006. There will be more qualified family and consumer science teachers than openings. Of course, there will be openings to replace teachers who leave the field each year. The best job opportunities will be for college-level and adult education teachers and for those who specialize in working with the disabled.

Working Conditions

Family and consumer science teachers generally have pleasant working conditions. Class areas are normally clean and well-lighted. Some schools provide individual offices for the teachers.

Family and consumer science teachers must deal with a variety of people—students, parents, administrators, and others. Patience is required, and frustration can be a part of the job. In some cases a teacher may have to make do with old equipment or teach with no equipment at all. Usually, though, most family and consumer science teachers find that these and similar problems are small when compared to the satisfaction the job provides.

Earnings and Benefits

Salaries depend on education, experience, the size and location of the school, and the amount of the work required. The starting salaries for public school teachers with a bachelor's degree range from $20,000 to $22,000 a year. Experienced public school teachers average about $36,000 a year. On the average, college-level family and consumer science teachers earn from $27,700 to $36,800 a year.

Family and consumer science teachers generally work only 10 months a year. But they may need to spend some time studying or doing research during the summer months. Family and consumer science teachers usually work 35 to 40 hours a week. They often have time during the workday to prepare lessons, counsel students, or grade tests and homework. Some evening work may be required. Benefits include paid holidays and vacations, health insurance, and pension plans.

Where to Go for More Information

The American Association of Family and
   Consumer Sciences
1555 King Street, Suite 400
Alexandria, VA 22314
(703) 706-4600
www.aafes.org

Family and Consumer Sciences Education
   Association
Central Washington University
400 East 8th Avenue
Ellensburg, WA 98926-7565
(509) 963-2766

Funeral Director

Education and Training
Voc/tech school; license

Salary Range
Average—$590 a week

Employment Outlook
Excellent

Definition and Nature of the Work

Funeral directors arrange funeral services and burials. They work in funeral homes, where bodies are kept until cremation or burial. Most funeral homes are small and owned by the funeral director. Some, however, have many employees. Funeral directors are sometimes called morticians or undertakers.

When funeral directors are notified of a death, they arrange for the body to be moved to the funeral home. They get the information needed for the death certificate and for the newspaper death notice, or obituary. They meet with the family of the deceased to discuss the details of the funeral service, including the selection of a casket. Funeral directors help the family to set the time and location for burial, arrange for a member of the clergy to conduct any religious services, and choose pallbearers. Once these plans have been made, funeral directors contact cemetery officials, the clergy, and the newspapers.

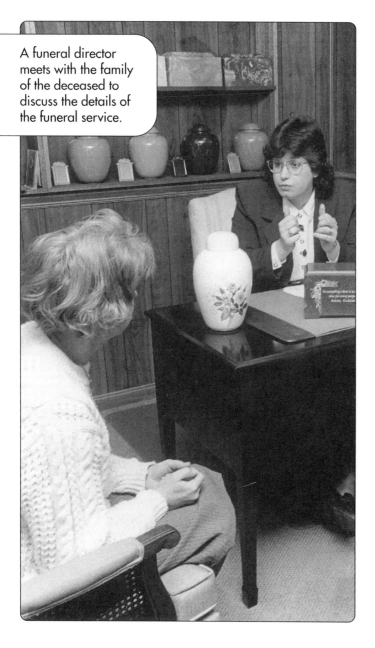

A funeral director meets with the family of the deceased to discuss the details of the funeral service.

Funeral directors need to know about the funeral customs of various religious, ethnic, and fraternal groups. They must also be familiar with the laws dealing with the handling of dead bodies. Since many funeral directors are also licensed embalmers, they may prepare the body for burial. They arrange the casket in a parlor and take care of lighting and flower arrangements. They stay in the parlor to greet and comfort the family and friends of the deceased and to make sure that the services run as planned. They also arrange transportation to the cemetery or crematorium for the family and pallbearers. Funeral directors lead the funeral procession to the church or cemetery, where they may help direct the service. If burial is to be in another area, they oversee the preparation and shipment of the body.

Funeral directors may also help the family of the deceased with insurance claims. They may serve the family for several months until they have taken care of these and other details.

Education and Training Requirements

You can begin to prepare for a career as a funeral director while in high school. Courses in science, biology, bookkeeping, art, sociology, speech, and business subjects are useful. Psychology courses may give you a better understanding of how and why people act as they do under the stress caused by death. A funeral director must be able to stay calm in stressful situations and be willing to handle distasteful tasks, such as the removal of burned or decomposed bodies.

Private vocational schools offer special programs to train funeral directors, called mortuary science programs. They take 9 months to 3 years to complete. A few colleges also offer 4-year programs in funeral service. In addition, you will probably need to serve an apprenticeship of about 1 to 3 years during or after your formal training.

Most states require funeral directors to be licensed. Requirements vary, but you must usually be at least 21 years old and a graduate of a high school as well as of a school of mortuary science or funeral service. You also usually need to have completed an apprenticeship and to have passed a state board examination. Most funeral directors get an embalming license as well.

Getting the Job

You can apply directly to funeral homes for a job. Although most funeral homes are family businesses, many employ people who are not family members. Some funeral directors continue working at the funeral homes where they held part-time jobs while still in school or where they served apprenticeships. Most schools that train funeral directors also have placement services that can help you find a job. Members of the clergy may be able to introduce you to local funeral directors. Also contact professional associations and scan newspaper classifieds and the Yellow Pages of your local phone book for job leads.

Advancement Possibilities and Employment Outlook

Funeral directors can become managers in large funeral homes, buy an existing funeral home, or start a new one. Owning a business requires a great deal of money, but loans are available to qualified funeral directors.

The employment outlook for funeral directors is excellent through the year 2006. The number of graduates of mortuary science programs is fewer than the number of jobs available.

Working Conditions

Funeral homes are usually attractive and well-kept. They range from small frame houses to large, modern buildings. They often serve as the homes of funeral directors and their families. Funeral directors are on call at all times. Evening or weekend funeral services or meetings are not uncommon, and funeral directors often work more than 40 hours a week. Their hours are irregular, since there may be slow periods followed by a series of funerals within a short period of time. In larger funeral homes the directors may work in shifts.

The buyer of funeral services is confronted with some difficult conditions: lack of prior information about costs, time pressures, and a disturbed emotional state. Funeral directors must be tactful, sympathetic to problems, and respectful of the burial customs of all religions. Funeral directors who are also embalmers must be able to work well with their hands.

Earnings and Benefits

Funeral directors earn an average of $590 a week. Their annual salaries range from $21,775 to $106,200 depending on their experience, level of employment, and geographical location. Those who own their own funeral homes and are very successful can earn more. Benefits may include paid holidays and vacations, health insurance, and pension plans.

Where to Go for More Information

Associated Funeral Directors, International
P.O. Box 1382
Largo, FL 34649
(813) 593-0709

National Funeral Directors Association
11121 West Oklahoma Avenue
Milwaukee, WI 53227-4096
(414) 541-2500
www.nfda.org

National Funeral Directors and Morticians
   Association
3951 Snapfinger Parkway
Decatur, GA 30035
(404) 286-6680

Interior Designer

Education and Training
High school plus training

Salary Range
Average—$590 a week

Employment Outlook
Good

Definition and Nature of the Work

Interior designers plan and design the interiors of buildings. They work for interior design firms, architectural firms, retail stores, and the design departments of large industries or institutions. Some have their own businesses. Interior designers often specialize in homes, hospitals, hotels, or banks. Some specialize in stage sets or the interiors of ships or airplanes.

When they plan the interior of a new building or the structural remodeling of an old one, interior designers usually work with architects. The architects consult the interior designers about traffic patterns and may ask them to plan the placement of stairways, windows, and doors, as well as cabinets and other built-in units.

Whether they are involved in the planning of the structure of a building or merely in the decorating of one or more rooms, interior designers give advice on color schemes, window treatments, and hardware and lighting fixtures. They also suggest finishes for walls, ceilings, floors, and cabinets. They choose accessories, such as plants or paintings, that will accent an interior.

Interior designers talk with their clients to establish how much work needs to be done. They also discuss the clients' habits, tastes, and budget requirements. They draw up floor plans or sketches. Interior designers present these plans and sketches to clients along with color charts, fabric swatches, photographs, and sometimes even original designs for furniture. They also submit an estimate of the total cost of the job. They may have to revise their plans several times before the client approves them. Interior designers supervise the actual work of decorating. They order materials and contract for the services of workers. They may shop for those furnishings that will not be custom-made. They make sure that draperies are hung properly and that the furniture is arranged conveniently.

Designers who work for department stores and office or home furnishings stores are expected to help sell the store's merchandise. They also make suggestions to the store's buyers about the wants and needs of customers.

Education and Training Requirements

To become an interior designer, you need several years of formal education after high school. You can take a 3-year program in a professional school of interior design. Or you can study interior design in a 4-year program leading to a bachelor's degree at a college or university. Some students go on to get a master's degree or a doctoral degree.

You must also go through an informal 1- to 3-year apprenticeship before you can become an interior designer. Trainees often act as receptionists, buyers, or clerks while they learn the practical side of the interior design business. Experienced designers assist and advise trainees in such tasks as matching patterns, arranging furniture, and dealing with customers. After completing their training and taking an exam, interior designers may become members of the American Society of Interior Designers or the Institute of Business Designers.

Getting the Job

The placement office of your college or school of interior design may be able to help you find a job as an interior design trainee. You can also ask professional associations or employment agencies for job information. Or you can apply

Interior designers examine material samples before presenting a detailed plan and sketch to a client.

directly to interior design firms, department or furniture stores, architectural firms, or manufacturers of furniture. Some graduates find jobs through newspaper classifieds or Internet job banks. Those who cannot find trainee jobs right away often get job experience selling furniture or accessories until they can find the position they want.

Advancement Possibilities and Employment Outlook

Advancement depends on talent and experience. Interior designers can become supervisors in a design studio or in a department of a large store, manufacturing firm, or design firm. Some interior designers advance by opening their own businesses. Others teach in schools of design or work for magazines that deal with home furnishings and interior design.

There will be an increase in the employment of interior designers through the year 2006. The outlook is good. More businesses and individuals are using their services. However, beginning workers may find heavy competition for jobs. The best jobs will go to those with talent, education, and experience.

Working Conditions

Interior designers work in studios or stores that range from the pleasant to the plush. They are often out consulting with customers, manufacturers, and workers. Some must travel long distances. They may visit expensive homes, buildings under construction, and drafty warehouses. Interior designers often work long and irregular hours. They are sometimes under pressure to meet deadlines.

Interior designers need tact, patience, and flexibility in order to deal with all kinds of customers. They should have artistic and creative talent, as well as good business sense and the ability to solve problems.

Earnings and Benefits

Earnings of interior designers vary widely. The median wages are $590 a week. The top 10 percent earn $1,300 or more a week while the bottom 10 percent of interior designers receive $280 a week. The middle 50 percent receive an average of $380 to $890 a week.

Experienced designers may work for a salary, a commission, or a combination of the two. A few designers with exceptional talent earn well over $85,000 a year. Benefits for salaried interior designers sometimes include paid holidays and vacations, health insurance, and pension plans. Self-employed designers or those who work on commission for small firms must provide their own benefits.

Where to Go for More Information

American Society of Interior Designers
608 Massachusetts Avenue, NE
Washington, DC 20002
(202) 546-3480

International Interior Design Association
341 Merchandise Mart
Chicago, IL 60654-1104
(312) 467-1950
www.iida.com

Personal Exercise Trainer

Education and Training
College

Salary Range
Average—$50
to $200 per session

Employment Outlook
Good

Definition and Nature of the Work

A personal exercise trainer provides one-on-one fitness instruction to people desiring a program tailored to their specific needs. The client may be a business executive or celebrity whose busy schedule or need for privacy rules out aerobics classes. Perhaps the client has suffered an athletic injury that requires a special rehabilitation program. Or the client may travel a lot and want to take along a personal trainer in order to keep up an exercise routine. Trainers may also act as motivators who push clients to their physical limits.

A trainer must develop a program and choose exercises that provide the optimum results. He or she must be able to demonstrate the movements and exercises recommended and must constantly evaluate the client's progress. The trainer provides encouragement and support for the client and recognizes the client's strengths and weaknesses.

Education and Training Requirements

Education, training, and background of trainers vary widely. Most trainers have a formal degree—either a bachelor's degree in physical education or a master's degree in adult fitness. However, some trainers have a background in dance or nursing.

High school courses in physical education, biology, psychology, and business will be useful. A future trainer should enjoy physical activity and understand how certain exercises work certain muscles. An understanding of basic nutrition is also helpful to provide supplementary information to a client. A trainer should also be knowledgeable about the various exercise equipment being used in homes and health clubs, as these are often used in personal training programs. Involvement with running and sporting associations can provide experience and contacts.

The American College of Sports Medicine and the National Athletic Trainers Association provide certification on the completion of accredited college courses. Trainers seeking certification from the American College of Sports Medicine must have completed a bachelor's degree in an allied health field. They must demonstrate knowledge of health appraisal techniques and understanding of motivation, counseling, and teaching in the health and fitness fields. They must also pass practical and written exams.

Getting the Job

Personal exercise trainers usually work for themselves. They develop a clientele largely through personal recommendations, advertising, and contact with health clubs. If you are successful with your first clients, the word will get around. Part-time or summer work as an exercise class instructor will provide valuable knowledge, experience, and contacts.

Advancement Possibilities and Employment Outlook

The employment outlook for personal exercise trainers is good, although the size of the field is inherently limited as not everyone can afford their own personal exercise trainer. However, small groups of individuals will often hire a trainer to direct an exercise program for them.

Personal trainers may start on a part-time basis with just a few private clients and progress to a steady flow of well-paying clients. As the demand for their services increases, personal trainers can open exercise studios and supervise other trainers.

Personal exercise trainers develop fitness programs and choose exercises that provide optimum results for their clients.

Working Conditions

Trainers hold workouts in a variety of places, including clients' homes, offices, and hotels. They may use various types of equipment, including rowing machines, exercise bicycles, and swimming pools. As business builds, a trainer must be able to schedule appointments efficiently and work under pressure. The one-on-one nature of the job calls for an understanding but firm approach to individual clients.

Earnings and Benefits

Currently, personal fitness trainers receive $50 to $200 a visit. Fees increase with a trainer's reputation and experience. When traveling is required, trainers will adjust fees to pay for fares and travel time.

Personal trainers may also offer fitness packages for a set fee. These packages may include in-home consultations, a fitness evaluation, a nutrition program, and an initial training session. Because most trainers are self-employed, they must provide their own insurance and benefits.

Where to Go for More Information

American College of Sports Medicine
ACSM National Center
P.O. Box 1440
Indianapolis, IN 46206-1440
(317) 637-9200

National Athletic Trainers Association
2952 Stemmons Freeway, Suite 200
Dallas, TX 75247-6103
(214) 637-6282

National Strength and Condition
    Association
P.O. Box 38909
Colorado Springs, CO 80937
(719) 632-6722

Resources

General Career Information

Books

Exploring the Working World

The Adams Job Almanac. Holbrook, MA: Adams Media Corp., annual.

American Almanac of Jobs and Salaries, John W. Wright. New York: Avon Books, biennial.

American Salaries and Wages, 4th ed., Helen S. Fisher. Detroit, MI: Gale Research, Inc., 1997.

America's Top Jobs for College Graduates, J. Michael Farr. Indianapolis, IN: JIST Works, 1997.

America's Top Jobs for People Without College Degrees, J. Michael Farr. Indianapolis, IN: JIST Works, 1997.

America's Top Technical and Trade Jobs, J. Michael Farr. Indianapolis, IN: JIST Works, 1997.

The Big Book of Jobs. Lincolnwood, IL: VGM Career Horizons, 1997.

Career Discovery Encyclopedia, Holli Cosgrove, ed., 6 vols. Chicago: Ferguson, 1997.

CareerSmarts: Jobs with a Future, Martin Yate. New York: Ballantine Books, 1997.

The Complete Guide for Occupational Exploration, J. Michael Farr. Indianapolis, IN: JIST Works, 1993.

The Complete Guide to Public Employment, 3rd ed., Ronald Krannich and Caryl Rae Krannich. Manassas Park, VA: Impact Publications, 1995.

The Harvard Guide to Careers, 5th ed., Martha P. Leape and Susan M. Vacca. Cambridge, MA: Harvard University Press, 1995.

Job Hunter's Sourcebook. Detroit, MI: Gale Research, Inc., biennial.

Jobs '98 (title changes annually), Kathryn Petras, Ross Petras, and George Petras. New York: Simon & Schuster, annual.

Jobs Rated Almanac, Les Krantz. New York: World Almanac, 1995.

Joyce Lain Kennedy's Career Book, Joyce Lain Kennedy and Darryl Laramore. Lincolnwood, IL: VGM Career Horizons, 1997.

The National JobBank, 1998 (title changes annually). Holbrook, MA: Adams Media Corp., annual. (The *JobBank* series also includes editions for several major U.S. cities and regions.)

Occupational Outlook series. Washington, DC: United States Government Printing Office. Briefs, separately published.

Occupational Outlook Quarterly. Washington, DC: Occupational Outlook Service, Bureau of Labor Statistics. Quarterly publication.

Recommended

Occupational Outlook Handbook, United States Department of Labor. Washington, DC: United States Government Printing Office, revised biennially. Expands on the *Dictionary of Occupational Titles.* Groups jobs into similar categories. Discusses the nature of the work, the employment outlook, and earnings.

VGM's Careers Encyclopedia, 4th ed. Lincolnwood, IL: VGM Career Horizons, 1997. A one-volume guide to 180 careers.

117

Professional Careers Sourcebook, 4th ed. Detroit, MI: Gale Research, Inc., 1996.

The Quick Internet Guide to Career and College Information, Anne Wolfinger. Indianapolis, IN: JIST Works, 1997.

A Student's Guide to Career Exploration on the Internet, Elizabeth H. Oakes. Chicago: Ferguson, 1998.

Vocational Careers Sourcebook, 2nd ed. Detroit, MI: Gale Research, Inc., 1996.

Education and Training Opportunities

American Universities and Colleges, 15th ed. Hawthorne, NY: De Groyter, 1997.

America's Lowest Cost Colleges, Nicholas A. Roes. Barryville, NY: NAR Publications, biennial.

America's Top Internships, Mark Oldman and Samer Hamadeh. New York: Random House, annual.

Barron's Guide to Graduate Business Schools, Eugene Miller, ed. Hauppauge, NY: Barron's Educational Series, revised regularly.

Barron's Guide to Law Schools. Hauppauge, NY: Barron's Educational Series, revised regularly.

Barron's Guide to Medical and Dental Schools, Saul Wischnitzer and Edith Wischnitzer, eds. Hauppauge, NY: Barron's Educational Series, revised regularly.

Bear's Guide to Earning College Degrees Non-Traditionally, 11th ed., John Bear. Benicia, CA: C&B Publishing, 1994.

Chronicle Vocational School Manual. Moravia, NY: Chronicle Guidance Publications, annual.

Recommended

The following four sources are basic directories of information on colleges and universities. They include general information on each school, its address, a list of the programs offered, the size of the institution, and costs for tuition.

Barron's Top 50: An Inside Look at America's Best Colleges, Tom Fischgrund, ed. Hauppauge, NY: Barron's Educational Series, revised regularly.

The College Blue Book. New York: Macmillan, revised regularly.

Lovejoy's College Guide, Charles T. Straughn II and Barbarasue Lovejoy Straughn, eds. New York: ARCO, revised regularly.

Petersons Guide to Four-Year Colleges. Princeton, NJ: Petersons Guides, revised regularly.

College Applications and Essays, 3rd ed., Susan D. Van Raalte. New York: Macmillan, 1997.

The College Costs and Financial Aid Handbook, The College Board Staff. New York: The College Board, annual.

College Financial Aid for Dummies, Herm Davis and Joyce Lain Kennedy. Foster City, CA: IDG Books Worldwide, 1997.

College Financial Aid Made Easy, Patrick L. Bellatoni. Berkeley, CA: Ten Speed Press, annual.

The College Guide for Parents, 3rd ed., Charles J. Shields. New York: The College Board, 1995.

The College Handbook. New York: The College Board, annual.

College Planning for Gifted Students, 2nd ed., Sandra L. Berger. Reston, VA: Council for Exceptional Children, 1994.

The Complete Book of Colleges. New York: Random House, annual.

Ferguson's Guide to Apprenticeship Programs, 2 vols., C. J. Summerfield and Holli Cosgrove, eds. Chicago: Ferguson, 1994.

Free Money for College: A Guide to More Than 1000 Grants and Scholarships for Undergraduate Study, 4th ed., Laurie Blum. New York: Facts on File, 1996.

Getting into College, Pat Orovensky. Princeton, NJ: Petersons, 1995.

The Gourman Report: A Rating of Undergraduate Programs in American and International Universities, Jack Gourman. Los Angeles, CA: National Education Standards, revised regularly.

Help Yourself: Handbook for College-Bound Students with Learning Disabilities, Erica-Lee Lewis. New York: Random House, 1996.

Index of Majors and Graduate Degrees. New York: The College Board, annual.

Insider's Guide to the Colleges, Yale Daily News Staff, ed. New York: St. Martin's Press, annual.

The Internship Bible. New York: Random House, annual.

Internships for 2-Year College Students. West Hartford, CT: Graduate Group, annual.

Internships Leading to Careers. West Hartford, CT: Graduate Group, annual.

Lovejoy's College Guide for the Learning Disabled, Charles T. Straughn. New York: ARCO, revised regularly.

The National Guide to Educational Credit for Training Programs, American Council on Education. Phoenix, AZ: ACE/Oryx Press, annual.

The 100 Best Colleges for African-American Students, Erlene B. Wilson. New York: Plume, 1998.

Petersons College Money Handbook. Princeton, NJ: Petersons, annual.

Petersons Competitive Colleges. Princeton, NJ: Petersons, annual.

Petersons Guide to Graduate and Professional Programs: An Overview. Princeton, NJ: Petersons, annual.

Petersons Guide to Two-Year Colleges. Princeton, NJ: Petersons, annual.

Petersons Internships. Princeton, NJ: Petersons, annual.

A Student's Guide to College Admissions: Everything Your Guidance Counselor Has No Time to Tell You, 3rd ed., Harlow Unger. New York: Facts on File, 1995.

Vocational Education: Status in 2-Year Colleges and Early Signs of Change. Upland, PA: Diane Publishing Company, 1994.

Career Goals

Adventure Careers, Alex Hiam and Susan Angle. Franklin Lakes, NJ: Career Press, 1995.

Career Anchors: Discovering Your Real Values, Edgar H. Schein. San Diego, CA: Pfeiffer & Co., rev. 1993.

The Career Atlas, Gail Kuenstler. Franklin Lakes, NJ: Career Press, 1996.

The Career Guide for Creative and Unconventional People, Carol Eikleberry. Berkeley, CA: Ten Speed Press, 1995.

Careers for the Year 2000 and Beyond: Everything You Need to Know to Find the Right Career. Piscataway, NJ: Research and Education Association, 1997.

Recommended

What Color Is Your Parachute? Richard N. Bolles. Berkeley, CA: Ten Speed Press, revised annually. One of the best sources for career changers and job hunters. Workbook style with exercises to identify skills and interests. Provides comprehensive list of sources including books, agencies, and associations.

Choices for the High School Graduate: A Survival Guide for the Information Age, Bryna J. Fireside. Chicago: Ferguson, 1997.

Choosing a Career Made Easy, Patty Marler and Jan Bailey Mattia. Lincolnwood, IL: VGM Career Horizons, 1997.

Chronicle Career Index 1994–95, Harriet Scarry, ed. Moravia, NY: Chronicle Guidance Publications, 1994.

The College Board Guide to Jobs and Career Planning, 2nd ed., Joyce Slayton Mitchell. New York: The College Board, 1994.

College Majors and Careers: A Resource Guide for Effective Life Planning, 3rd ed., Phil Phifer. Chicago: Ferguson, 1997.

Dr. Job's Complete Career Guide, Sandra "Dr. Job" Pesmen. Lincolnwood, IL: VGM Career Horizons, 1996.

Finding Your Perfect Work: The New Career Guide to Making a Living, Creating a Life, Paul Edwards and Sarah Edwards. New York: Putnam, 1996.

Graduate to Your Perfect Job in Six Easy Steps, Jason R. Dorsey. Austin, TX: Golden Ladder Productions, 1997.

Green at Work: Finding a Business Career that Works for the Environment, Susan Cohn. Washington, DC: Island Press, 1995.

The Job Seeker's Guide to Socially Responsible Companies, Katherine Jankowski. Detroit, MI: Gale Research, Inc., 1995.

Jobs for People who Love Travel: Opportunities at Home and Abroad, Ronald L. Krannich and Caryl Rae Krannich. Manassas Park, VA: Impact Publications, 1995.

The Off-the-Beaten-Path Job Book: You Can Make a Living and Have a Life!, Sandra Gurvis. Secaucus, NJ: Carol Publishing Group, 1995.

The Parent's Crash Course in Career Planning: Helping Your College Student Succeed, Marcia B. Harris and Sharon L. Jones. Lincolnwood, IL: VGM Career Horizons, 1996.

The PIE Method for Career Success: A Unique Way to Find Your Ideal Job, Daniel Porot. Indianapolis, IN: JIST Works, 1996.

The Right Job for You: An Interactive Career Planning Guide, J. Michael Farr. Indianapolis, IN: JIST Works, 1997.

Success 2000: Moving into the Millennium with Purpose, Power, and Prosperity, Vicki Spina. New York: Wiley, 1997.

Getting the Job and Getting Ahead

The Adams Electronic Job Search Almanac. Holbrook, MA: Adams Media Corp., 1997.

Almanac of American Employers, Jack W. Plunkett. Galveston, TX: Plunkett Research, Ltd., biennial.

CareerXroads: The Directory to Jobs, Resumes, and Career Management on the World Wide Web. Kendall Park, NJ: MMC Group, 1996.

The Complete Idiot's Guide to Getting the Job You Want, Robert Bly. New York: Alpha Books, 1996.

Electronic Job Search Revolution: How to Win with the New Technology that's Re-shaping Today's Job Market, Joyce Lain Kennedy and Thomas J. Morow. New York: Wiley, 1996.

Getting Hired: A Guide for Managers and Professionals, Richard J. Pinsker. Menlo Park, CA: Crisp Publications, 1994.

Getting the Job You Want . . . Now!, David H. Roper. New York: Warner Books, 1994.

Government Job Finder, 1997–2000, Daniel Lauber. River Forest, IL: Planning/Communications, 1997.

Great Jobs Abroad, Arthur H. Bell. New York, McGraw Hill, 1997.

The Guide to Internet Job Searching, Margaret Riley, Frances Roehm, Steve Oserman, and the Public Library Association. Lincolnwood, IL: VGM Career Horizons, 1996.

Hoover's Directory of Human Resources Executives. Austin, TX: The Reference Press, revised regularly.

How to Get a Job in . . . (series for major U.S. cities). Chicago: Surrey Books, Inc., annual.

How to Hit the Ground Running in Your New Job, Lynda Pritchard Clemens and Andrea Trulson Dolph. Lincolnwood, IL: VGM Career Horizons, 1995.

International Job Finder, 1997–2000, Daniel Lauber. River Forest, IL: Planning/Communications, 1997.

Job Hunter's Yellow Pages: The National Directory of Employment Services. Harleysville, PA: Career Communications Inc.

Job Search 101: Getting Started on Your Career Path, Monica R. Fox and Pat Morton, eds. Indianapolis, IN: JIST Works, 1997.

Job Search Organizer, Hal Weatherman. Lincolnwood, IL: VGM Career Horizons, 1997.

Job Seeker's Guide to Private-Public Companies, Charity A. Dorgan, ed. Detroit, MI: Gale Research, Inc., 1995.

Jobsmarts for Twentysomethings, Bradley G. Richardson. New York: Vintage Books, 1995.

National Job Hotline Directory, Sue A. Cubbage. River Forest, IL: Planning/Communications, annual.

Non-Profits & Education Job Finder, 1997–2000, Daniel Lauber. River Forest, IL: Planning/Communications, 1997.

Petersons Hidden Job Market. Princeton, NJ: Petersons, annual.

Professional's Job Finder, 1997–2000, Daniel Lauber. River Forest, IL: Planning/Communications, 1997.

Using the Internet and the World Wide Web in Your Job Search, Fred Edmund Jandt and Mary B. Nemnich. Indianapolis, IN: JIST Works, 1996.

The Very Quick Job Search: Get a Better Job in Half the Time, J. Michael Farr. Indianapolis, IN: JIST Works, 1996.

The Work-At-Home Sourcebook, 6th ed., Lynie Arden. Boulder, CO: Live Oak Publications, 1996.

Recommended

Knock 'Em Dead: The Ultimate Job Seeker's Handbook, Martin J. Yate. Holbrook, MA: Adams Media Corp., 1997. Helps job seekers identify their strengths and improve their interview techniques. Also gives practical advice on networking, handling tough interview questions, and negotiating salaries.

Resumes and Interviews

Better Resumes for Executives and Professionals, 3rd ed., Robert F. Wilson. Hauppauge, NY: Barron's Educational Series, 1996.

The Complete Idiot's Guide to the Perfect Resume, Susan Ireland. New York: Alpha Books, 1996.

The Complete Resume Guide, 5th ed., Marian Faux. New York: Macmillan USA, 1995.

Cover Letters for Dummies, Joyce Lain Kennedy. Foster City, CA: IDG Books Worldwide, 1996.

Cover Letters: Proven Techniques for Writing Letters that Will Help You Get the Job You Want, Taunee Besson and National Business Employment Weekly. New York: Wiley, 1995.

Developing a Professional Vita or Resume, 3rd ed., Carl McDaniels. Chicago: Ferguson, 1997.

Get Hired!: Winning Strategies to Ace the Interview, Paul C. Green. Austin, TX: Bard Books, 1996.

Information Interviewing, 2nd ed., Martha Stoodley. Chicago: Ferguson, 1997.

Interviewing, Arlene S. Hirsch and National Business Employment Weekly. New York: Wiley, 1994.

Job Interviews That Mean Business, 2nd ed., David R. Eyler. New York: Random House, 1996.

The Resume Handbook, 3rd ed., Arthur Rosenberg and David Hizer. Boston: Adams Media Corp., 1996.

The Resume Kit, 3rd ed., Richard H. Beatty. New York: John Wiley & Sons, 1995.

Resume Power: Selling Yourself on Paper, Tom Washington. Bellevue, WA: Mount Vernon Press, 1996.

Recommended

Damn Good Resume Guide, 3rd ed., Yana Parker. Berkeley, CA: Ten Speed Press, 1996. Describes how to write a functional resume.

The New Perfect Resume, Tom Jackson and Ellen Jackson. New York: Doubleday, 1996. A CD-ROM version is also available.

Resume Writing Made Easy, 6th ed., Lola M. Coxford. Scottsdale, AZ: Gorsuch Scarisbrick, 1997.

Resumes for Better Jobs, 7th. ed., Lawrence D. Brennan. New York: ARCO, 1998.

Resumes for Dummies, Joyce Lain Kennedy. Foster City, CA: IDG Books Worldwide, 1996.

Resumes that Knock 'Em Dead, 3rd ed., Martin Yate. Holbrook, MA: Adams Media Corp., 1998.

Your Resume: Key to a Better Job, 6th ed., Leonard Corwen. New York: Macmillan, 1995.

Mid-Career Options

Beat the Odds: Career Buoyancy Tactics for Today's Turbulent Job Market, Martin Yate. New York: Ballantine Books, 1995.

The Career Trap: Breaking Through the 10-Year Barrier to Get the Job You Really Want, Jeffrey G. Allen. New York: AMACOM, 1995.

The Complete Idiot's Guide to Changing Careers, William Charland. New York: Alpha Books, 1998.

The Complete Idiot's Guide to Freelancing, Laurie Rozakis. New York: Alpha Books, 1998.

How to Hold it All Together When You've Lost Your Job, Townsend Albright. Lincolnwood, IL: VGM Career Horizons, 1996.

Kiplinger's Survive and Profit from a Mid-Career Change, Daniel Moreau. Washington, DC: Kiplinger Books, 1994.

Out of Uniform: A Career Transition Guide for Ex-Military Personnel, Harry N. Drier. Lincolnwood, IL: VGM Career Horizons, 1995.

Second Careers: New Ways to Work After 50, Caroline Bird. Boston: Little, Brown, 1992.

Toxic Work: How to Overcome Stress, Overload, and Burnout and Revitalize Your Career, Barbara Bailey Reinhold. New York: Plume, 1997.

Recommended

Career Change: Everything You Need to Know to Meet New Challenges and Take Control of Your Career, David P. Helford. Lincolnwood, IL: VGM Career Horizons, 1995.

Change Your Job, Change Your Life: High Impact Strategies for Finding Great Jobs into the 21st Century, Ronald L. Krannich. Manassas Park, VA: Impact Publications, 1997.

Equality of Opportunity

The Black Resource Guide, 10th ed. Washington, DC: Black Resource Guide, 1992.

Cracking the Corporate Closet, Daniel B. Baker, Sean O'Brien Strub, and Bill Henning. New York: HarperBusiness, 1995.

Equal Opportunity. Hauppauge, NY: Equal Opportunity Publications, published 3 times a year.

Financial Aid for the Disabled and Their Families, 6th ed., Gail A. Schlachter and R. David Weber. San Carlos, CA: Reference Services Press, 1996.

Financial Aid for Minorities. Garrett Park, MD: Garrett Park Press, 1994.

Successful Job Search Strategies for the Disabled: Understanding the ADA, Jeffrey G. Allen. New York: Wiley, 1994.

Women and Work, Susan Bullock. Atlantic Highlands, NJ: Humanities Press, 1994.

Recommended

The Big Book of Minority Opportunities, 6th ed., Willis L. Johnson, ed. Chicago: Ferguson, 1995. Directory of organizations that have special programs to help minorities meet their educational and career goals.

The Big Book of Opportunities for Women, Elizabeth A. Olson, ed. Chicago: Ferguson, 1996. Directory of organizations that have special programs to help women meet their educational and career goals.

Coping with Sexual Harassment, Beryl Black, ed. New York: The Rosen Publishing Group, rev. 1992. Helpful in giving direct ways to respond to and prevent sexual harassment at work.

Lists and Indexes of Career and Vocational Information

The Career Guide: Dun's Employment Opportunities Directory. Parsippany, NJ: Dun and Bradstreet Information Services, annual.

Chronicle Career Index. Moravia, NY: Chronicle Guidance Publications, annual.

Dictionary of Holland Occupational Codes (DHOC), 3rd ed., Gary D. Gottfredson and John L. Holland. Lutz, FL: Psychological Assessment Resources, 1996.

Dictionary of Occupational Titles, 4th ed. United States Department of Labor. Washington, DC: United States Government Printing Office, 1991. Supplemented by *The Classification of Jobs According to Worker Trait Factors* (Elliott & Fitzpatrick, 1992) and *Selected Characteristics of Occupations Defined in the Revised Dictionary of Occupational Titles* (Claitors Pub. Div., 1993).

Where the Jobs Are: A Comprehensive Directory of 1200 Journals Listing Career Opportunities, S. Norman Feingold and Glenda Ann Hansard-Winkler. Garrett Park, MD: Garrett Park Press, 1989.

Internet Sites

Sites with Extensive Links

Career Resource Center
www.careers.org

Catapult
www.jobweb.org/catapult/catapult.htm

JIST Works
www.jist.com

Job Hunt: A Meta-List of On-Line Job-Search Resources and Services
www.job-hunt.org

Job Search and Employment Opportunities: Best Bets
asa.ugl.lib.umich.edu/chdocs/employment/

Online Career Center (OCC)
www.occ.com

The Riley Guide: Employment Opportunities and Job Resources on the Internet
www.dbm.com/jobguide

What Color Is Your Parachute Job Hunting Online
washingtonpost.com/parachute

Career Development Resources

Career Assistance from the Online Career Center
www.occ.com/occ/CareerAssist.html

Career Magazine
www.careermag.com

Kaplan's Career Center
www.kaplan.com/career

Online Information and References

AT&T Toll-Free Internet Directory
www.tollfree.att.net

Beatrice's Web Guide—Careers
www.bguide.com/webguide/careers

The Best Jobs in the USA Today
www.bestjobsusa.com

CareerMart
www.careermart.com

Federal Jobs Digest
www.jobsfed.com

GaleNet
galenet.gale.com

Infoseek Guide—Jobs & Careers
guide-p.infoseek.com/Careers

Job Finders Online
jobfindersonline.com

Occupational Outlook Handbook
stats.bls.gov/ocohome.htm

StudentCenter
www.studentcenter.com

U.S. Bureau of Labor Statistics Home Page
stats.bls.gov/blshome.htm

US News Online Colleges and Career Center
www4.usnews.com/usnews/edu/home.htm

Wall Street Journal Interactive Division
careers.wsj.com

Yahoo! Business and Economy
www.yahoo.com/business

Job Databases and Resume Posting

America's Job Bank
www.ajb.dni.is/index.html

CareerCity
www.careercity.com

CareerMosaic
www.careermosaic.com

CareerPath
www.careerpath.com

Career Site
www.careersite.com

CareerWeb
www.careerweb.com

e-span
www.espan.com

JobBank USA
www.jobbankusa.com

Job Trak
www.jobtrak.com

Job Web
www.jobweb.org

The Monster Board
www.monster.com

World Wide Web Employment Office
www.harbornet.com/biz/office/annex.html

Audiovisual Materials

The following titles include, where possible, the developer's name and location or else the name and location of a distributor. Audiovisual titles may be available through several distributors.

Exploring the Working World

The Career Builders series. Video. New York: Educational Design, Inc.

Career Cluster Decisions. Video; guide. Bloomington, IL: Meridian Education Corp.

Career Exploration: A Job Seeker's Guide to the OOH, DOT, and GOE. Video. Bloomington, IL: Meridian Education Corp.

Career Plan. Video; guide. Bloomington, IL: Meridian Education Corp.

Career Planning: Putting Your Skills to Work. Video; guide. Mt. Kisco, NY: Guidance Associates.

Career Planning Steps. Video. Charleston, WV: Cambridge Educational.

Career S.E.L.F. Assessment: Designing a Self-Directed Job Search. Video. Charleston, WV: Cambridge Educational.

Career Self-Assessment: Where Do You Fit? Video; guide. Mt. Kisco, NY: Guidance Associates.

Careers for the 21st Century series. Video; guide. Bloomington, IL: Meridian Education Corp.

Careers Without College. Video. Charleston, WV: Cambridge Educational.

Connect on the Net: Finding a Job on the Internet. Video. Charleston, WV: Cambridge Educational.

Educational Planning for Your Career. Video. Bloomington, IL: Meridian Education Corp.

The JIST Video Guide for Occupational Exploration series. Video. Indianapolis, IN: JIST Works.

Jobs for the 21st Century. Video; guide. Mt. Kisco, NY: Guidance Associates.

Learning for Earning. Video; guide. Bloomington, IL: Meridian Education Corp.

School-to-Work Transition. Video; guide. Bloomington, IL: Meridian Education Corp.

Skills Identification: Discovering Your Skills. Video. Indianapolis, IN: JIST Works.

Working Towards a Career. Video. Bloomington, IL: Meridian Education Corp.

Your Aptitudes: Related to Learning Job Skills. Video. Bloomington, IL: Meridian Education Corp.

Your First Cruise: A Beginner's Guide to the Internet. Video. Charleston, WV: Cambridge Educational.

Your Future: Planning Through Career Exploration. Video. Bloomington, IL: Meridian Education Corp.

Your Interests: Related to Work Activities. Video. Bloomington, IL: Meridian Education Corp.

Your Life's Work series. Video. Indianapolis, IN: JIST Works.

Your Temperaments: Related to Work Situations. Video. Bloomington, IL: Meridian Education Corp.

Your 21st Century Employability Skills series. Video. Calhoun, KY: NIMCO.

Getting the Job and Getting Ahead

Ace the Interview. Video. Columbus, OH: Career Paths/MarkED.

The Art of Effective Communication. Video; guide. Indianapolis, IN: JIST Works.

Career Change: Meeting the Challenge. Video. Arlington Heights, IL: Library Cable Network.

Common Mistakes People Make in Interviews. Video. Columbus, OH: Career Paths/MarkED.

Dialing for Jobs: Using the Phone in the Job Search. Video. Indianapolis, IN: JIST Works.

Directing Your Successful Job Search. Video; guide. Charleston, WV: Cambridge Educational.

Extraordinary Answers to Common Interview Questions. Video. Charleston, WV: Cambridge Educational.

From Pink Slip to Paycheck: The Road to Reemployment series. Video. Indianapolis, IN: Park Avenue/JIST Works.

Getting a Job series. Video. New York: Educational Design, Inc.

How to Be a Success at Work series. Video. Indianapolis, IN: JIST Works.

Interview Power. Video. Columbus, OH: Career Paths/MarkED.

Interview to Win Your First Job. Video. Indianapolis, IN: Park Avenue/JIST Works.

Job Search and Job Survival series. Video. New York: Educational Design, Inc.

JobSearch: The Right Track. Video. Bountiful, VT: ECLECON.

Job Survival Kit. Video. Charleston, WV: Cambridge Educational.

Job Survival Skills: Working with Others. Video. Mt. Kisco, NY: Guidance Associates.

Kennedy's Career Secrets. Video. Arlington Heights, IL: Library Cable Network.

Making It on Your First Job. Video or laserdisc; guide. Charleston, WV: Cambridge Educational.

Mastering Change: How to Be "Change Skilled" and Thrive in Turbulent Times series. Video; workbook. Harleysville, PA: Career Communications Inc.

Maximizing Your Public Image. Video. Hinesburg, VT: Image Vision.

The Resume Remedy. Video. Indianapolis, IN: JIST Works.

Shhh! I'm Finding a Job: The Library and Your Self-Directed Job Search. Video; workbook. Charleston, WV: Cambridge Educational.

Successful Job Hunting: The Inside Scoop on Finding the Best Jobs. Video. Charleston, WV: Cambridge Educational.

Survival Skills for the World of Work series. Video. New York: Educational Design, Inc.

Take This Job and Love It. Video. Bloomington, IL: Meridian Education Corp.

Ten Ways to Get a Great Job. Video. Charleston, WV: Cambridge Educational.

Tough Times: Finding the Jobs. Video. Bloomington, IL: Meridian Education Corp.

The Very Quick Job Search Video. Indianapolis, IN: JIST Works.

The Video Guide to JIST's Self-Directed Job Search series. Video. Indianapolis, IN: JIST Works.

Your Public Image: Conducting Yourself in the Business World. Video. Hinesburg, VT: Image Vision.

Computer Software

The following titles include, where possible, the developer's name and location or else the name and location of a distributor. Software titles may be available through several distributors.

Ace the Interview: The Multimedia Job Interview Guide. CD-ROM for Macintosh or Windows. Charleston, WV: Cambridge Educational.

Adams JobBank FastResume Suite. CD-ROM for Windows. Holbrook, MA: Adams Media Corp.

Barron's Profiles of American Colleges on CD-ROM. Windows or Macintosh. Hauppauge, NY: Barron's.

The Cambridge Career Counseling System. Diskettes for IBM. Charleston, WV: Cambridge Educational.

Career Area Interest Checklist. Diskettes for IBM or Apple. Bloomington, IL: Meridian Education Corp.

Career Compass. Diskettes for IBM or Apple II. Bloomington, IL: Meridian Education Corp.

Career CompuSearch. Diskettes for IBM or Apple. Bloomington, IL: Meridian Education Corp.

Career Counselor. CD-ROM for Windows. New York: Kaplan Educational Centers.

Career Directions (English and Spanish versions). Diskettes for Apple II. Charleston, WV: Cambridge Educational.

Career Finder. Diskettes for IBM DOS, Windows, or Macintosh. Bloomington, IL: Meridian Education Corp.

Career Match. Diskettes for IBM or Macintosh. Charleston, WV: Cambridge Educational.

Career Moves: The Best of the DOT (Dictionary of Occupational Titles). CD-ROM for Macintosh or Windows. Charleston, WV: Cambridge Educational.

Career Toolbox. CD-ROM for Windows. Orem, UT: Infobusiness, Inc.

CD-ROM Version of the Occupational Outlook Handbook. Charleston, WV: Cambridge Educational.

Create Your Dream Job. CD-ROM for Windows or Macintosh. Columbus, OH: Career Paths/MarkED.

Discovering Careers and Jobs. CD-ROM. Detroit, MI: Gale Research, Inc.

Encyclopedia of Careers and Vocational Guidance. CD-ROM for Windows or Macintosh. Chicago: Ferguson.

Getting into College (U.S. News and World Report). CD-ROM. Portland, OR: Creative Multimedia.

Hoover's Company and Industry Database on CD-ROM. Austin, TX: The Reference Press.

Interview Skills for the Future. CD-ROM for Windows or Macintosh. Charleston, WV: Cambridge Educational.

JIST's Electronic Enhanced Dictionary of Occupational Titles. CD-ROM for Windows. Indianapolis, IN: JIST Works.

JIST's Multimedia Occupational Outlook Handbook. CD-ROM for Windows. Indianapolis, IN: JIST Works.

Job Search Skills for the 21st Century. CD-ROM for Windows or Macintosh. Charleston, WV: Cambridge Educational.

MSPI: Exploring Career Goals and College Courses. Diskettes for IBM or Macintosh. Charleston, WV: Cambridge Educational.

Multimedia Career Center. CD-ROM for Windows or Macintosh. Charleston, WV: Cambridge Educational.

The Multimedia Career Path. CD-ROM for Windows or Macintosh. Charleston, WV: Cambridge Job Search.

The Multimedia Guide to Occupational Exploration. CD-ROM for Windows or Macintosh. Charleston, WV: Cambridge Educational.

Multimedia Take this Job and Love It. CD-ROM for Windows or Macintosh. Charleston, WV: Cambridge Educational.

The Perfect Resume. CD-ROM for Windows. Torrance, CA: Davidson.

Resume Express: The Multimedia Guide. CD-ROM for Windows or Macintosh. Charleston, WV: Cambridge Educational.

Resume Revolution: The Software Solution. Diskettes for Windows or Macintosh. Charleston, WV: Cambridge Educational.

The Ultimate Job Source, 2.0. CD-ROM for Windows. Orem, UT: Infobusiness, Inc.

What Color Is Your Parachute? CD-ROM for Windows. Boston: BumbleBee Technology.

General

Books

The Career Connection for Technical Education: A Guide to Technical Training and Related Career Opportunities, Fred A. Rowe, ed. Indianapolis, IN: JIST Works, 1994.

Careers for Caring People and Other Sensitive Types, Adrian A. Paradis. Lincolnwood, IL: VGM Career Horizons, 1995.

Careers for Crafty People and Other Dextrous Types, Mark Rowh. Lincolnwood, IL: VGM Career Horizons, 1993.

Careers Inside the World of the Trades, Peggy Santamaria. New York: Rosen Publishing Group, 1995.

Careers Serving Families and Consumers, 3rd ed., Elizabeth Kendall Sproles and George B. Sproles. Englewood Cliffs, NJ: Prentice-Hall, 1995.

Choosing a Career in the Helping Professions, Pat Tretout. New York: Rosen Publishing Group, 1997.

Chronicle Home Economics Occupations Guidebook, Paul Downes, ed. Moravia, NY: Chronicle Guidance Publications, 1994.

Great Careers for People Interested in How Things Work, Peter Richardson. Detroit, MI: UXL, 1993.

Great Careers for People Who Like to Work with Their Hands, Julie Czerneda. Detroit, MI: UXL, 1994.

Great Careers for People Who Like Working with People, Helen Mason. Detroit, MI: UXL, 1994.

Internet Sites

American Association of Family and Consumer Sciences
www.aafcs.org

American Massage Therapy Association: Becoming a Massage Therapist
www.amtamassage.org/becometherapist.htm

American Society of Appraisers
www.appraisers.org

AthleticTrainer.com
www.athletictrainer.com

CareGuide (child and elder care)
www.careguide.net

HairNet
www.hairnet.com

Housekeepers, Janitors, Butlers, and Maids
www.housekeeping.com

ISdesigNET: The Online Version of Interiors & Sources Magazine
www.isdesignet.com

The Jewelry Industry WebCenter
polygon.net

National Cosmetology Association
www.nca-now.com

National Funeral Directors Association: Careers and Education
www.nfda.org/careers

Pest Control Technology OnLine
www.pctonline.com

Piano Technicians Guild
www.ptg.org

Security Information Management Online Network (SIMON)
www.simon-net.com

Small and Home Based Business Links
www.bizoffice.com

Small Business Administration
www.sba.gov

Audiovisual Materials

Home Economics (*School to Work* series). Video. Charleston, WV: Cambridge Educational.

Personal Service Cluster (*Vocational Visions* series). Video. Mt. Kisco, NY: Guidance Associates.

Public and Personal Service. Video. Bloomington, IL: Meridian Education Corp.

Success Stories in the World of Work: Multicultural Role Models. Video series with segments on child care teacher, cosmetologist, dietician, interior designer, and janitorial services. Bloomington, IL: Meridian Education Corp.

Consumer Services

Books

Careers for Fashion Plates and Other Trendsetters, Lucia Mauro. Lincolnwood, IL: VGM Career Horizons, 1996.

Careers Without College: Fashion. Princeton, NJ: Petersons Guides, 1992.

Opportunities in Cleaning Services Careers, Adrian A. Paradis. Lincolnwood, IL: VGM Career Horizons, 1992.

Opportunities in Fashion Careers, Roslyn Dolber. Lincolnwood, IL: VGM Career Horizons, 1993.

Opportunities in Installation and Repair Careers, Mark Rowh. Lincolnwood, IL: VGM Career Horizons, 1993.

Audiovisual Materials

Apparel and Textile Careers. Video. Calhoun, KY: NIMCO, Inc.

Careers in Clothing. Video. Bloomington, IL: Meridian Education Corp.

Electronics (*School to Work* series). Video. Charleston, WV: Cambridge Educational.

Florist (*Vocational Visions* series). Video. Mount Kisco, NY: Guidance Associates.

Innerview: Framing. Video. Fresno, CA: Edgepoint Productions.

Innerview: Jewelry. Video. Fresno, CA: Edgepoint Productions.

Innerview: Retail Business. Video. Fresno, CA: Edgepoint Productions.

Innerview: Small Business. Two videos. Fresno, CA: Edgepoint Productions.

Repair Cluster (*Vocational Visions* series). Video. Mt. Kisco, NY: Guidance Associates.

Homemaking, Nutrition, and Child Care Services

Books

Careers in Child Care, Marjorie Eberts. Lincolnwood, IL: VGM Career Horizons, 1994.

Careers Inside the World of Homemaking and Parenting, rev. ed., Maryann Miller. New York: Rosen Publishing Group, 1998.

Child Care. Lincolnwood, IL: VGM Career Horizons, 1995.

Choosing a Career in Nutrition, Sue Hurwitz. New York: The Rosen Publishing Group, 1997.

Opportunities in Child Care Careers, Renee Wittenberg. Lincolnwood, IL: VGM Career Horizons, 1993.

Opportunities in Interior Design Careers, Victoria K. Ball. Lincolnwood, IL: VGM Career Horizons, 1995.

Opportunities in Nutrition Care, Carol C. Caldwell. Lincolnwood, IL: VGM Career Horizons, 1992.

Opportunities in the Nutrition and Food Sciences, Paul R. Thomas and Richard J. Havell, eds. Washington, DC: National Academy Press, 1994.

Audiovisual Materials

Careers in Child Development. Video. Bloomington, IL: Meridian Education Corp.

Careers in the Home Furnishings Industry. Video. Calhoun, KY: NIMCO, Inc.

Careers in Housing. Video. Bloomington, IL: Meridian Education Corp.

Careers in Nutrition. Video. Calhoun, KY: NIMCO, Inc.

Child Care. Video. New York: Educational Design, Inc.

The Food Service Industry: Career Opportunities for You. Video. Mt. Kisco, NY: Guidance Associates.

Innerview: Interior Design. Video. Fresno, CA: Edgepoint Productions.

Innerview: Nutrition. Video. Fresno, CA: Edgepoint Productions.

Interior Design Careers. Video. Calhoun, KY: NIMCO.

Working with Families and Children: Career Opportunities. Video. Calhoun, KY: NIMCO.

Personal Services

Books

Career after Cosmetology School: Step-by-Step Guide to a Lucrative Career and Salon Ownership, Jessica Brooks. Cupertino, CA: Step-by-Step Publications, 1994.

Careers Without College: Fitness. Princeton, NJ: Petersons, 1992.

Choosing a Career in Cosmetology, Jeanne M. Strazzabosco. New York: The Rosen Publishing Group, 1997.

The Hair, Makeup, and Styling Career Guide, 2nd ed., Crystal A. Wright. Los Angeles, CA: Set the Pace Publishing Group, 1997.

Milady's Life Management Skills for Cosmetology, Barber Styling, and Nail Technology, Catherine Lamb. Albany, NY: Milady Publishing Company, 1996.

Opportunities in Beauty Culture Careers, Susan W. Gearhart. Lincolnwood, IL: VGM Career Horizons, 1996.

Opportunities in Funeral Services Careers, Terence J. Sacks. Lincolnwood, IL: VGM Career Horizons, 1997.

Planning Your Cosmetology Career, Mary Murphy-Martin. Englewood Cliffs, NJ: Prentice-Hall, 1994.

Audiovisual Materials

Innerview: Fitness. Video. Fresno, CA: Edgepoint Productions.

Innerview: Funeral Services. Video. Fresno, CA: Edgepoint Productions.

Innerview: Personal Care. Video. Fresno, CA: Edgepoint Productions.

Directory   Institutions Offering Career Training

The information in this directory was generated from the IPEDS (Integrated Postsecondary Education Data System) database of the U.S. Department of Education. It includes only regionally or nationally accredited institutions offering postsecondary occupational training in consumer, homemaking, and personal services. Because college catalogs and directories of colleges and universities are readily available elsewhere, this directory does not include institutions that offer only bachelor's and advanced degrees.

Appliance Repair

CALIFORNIA

American Technical College for Career
   Training
191 South E St.
San Bernardino 92401

California School of Neon
7075 Vineland Ave.
North Hollywood 91605

Computer Learning Center
3130 Wilshire Blvd.
Los Angeles 90010

Computer Learning Center
111 North Market St.
San Jose 95113-1109

Electronics Learning Center
1225 West 17th St.
Santa Ana 92706

Hacienda La Puente Unified School
   District, Valley Vocational Center
15959 East Gale Ave.
La Puente 91749

Santa Fe Technical College, Inc.
9820 Jersey Ave.
Santa Fe Springs 90670

COLORADO

College America, Denver
720 South Colorado Blvd.
Denver 80222

Technical Trades Institute
2315 East Pikes Peak Ave.
Colorado Springs 80909

CONNECTICUT

Data Institute
745 Burnside Ave.
East Hartford 06108

Porter and Chester Institute
670 Lordship Blvd.
Stratford 06497

Porter and Chester Institute
125 Silas Deane Hwy.
Wethersfield 06109

FLORIDA

Automotive Transmission School
453 East Okeechobee Rd.
Hialeah 33010

Florida Programming and Educational
   Center, Inc.
8300 West Flagler St.
Miami 33144

Florida Technical College
4750 East Adamo Dr.
Tampa 33605

Manatee Vocational-Technical Center
5603 34th St. W
Bradenton 34210

Miami Technical College
14701 Northwest Seventh Ave.
North Miami 33168

GEORGIA

Ben Hill-Irwin Technical Institute
P.O. Box 1069
Fitzgerald 31750

ILLINOIS

City College of Chicago,
   Olive-Harvey College
10001 South Woodlawn Ave.
Chicago 60628

City College of Chicago,
   Chicago City-Wide College
226 West Jackson Blvd.
Chicago 60606-6997

National Education Center,
   Bryman Campus
4101 West 95th St.
Oak Lawn 60453-1000

Washburne Trade School
3233 West 31st St.
Chicago 60623

KENTUCKY

Kentucky Advanced Technology Center
1845 Loop Dr.
Bowling Green 42101-9202

LOUISIANA

ITI Technical College
13944 Airline Hwy.
Baton Rouge 70817

MARYLAND

Catonsville Community College
800 South Rolling Rd.
Catonsville 21228

MASSACHUSETTS

Smith & Wesson Academy
2100 Roosevelt Ave.
P.O. Box 2208
Springfield 01102-2208

Woman's Technical Institute
1255 Boylston St.
Boston 02215

MICHIGAN

High-Tech Learning, Inc.
7531 East Eight Mile Rd.
Warren 48091

High-Tech Learning, Inc., Southfield
20755 Greenfield
Southfield 48075

MISSOURI

Concorde Career Institute
3239 Broadway
Kansas City 64111

Electronics Institute
15329 Kensington Ave.
Kansas City 64147

NEVADA

Las Vegas Gaming and Technical School
3030 South Highland Dr.
Las Vegas 89109-1047

NEW JERSEY

Dover Business College
15 East Blackwell St.
Dover 07801

Dover Business College
East 81 Rte. 4 W
Paramus 07652

Lincoln Technical Institute
Rte. 130 N at Haddonfield Rd.
Pennsauken 08110

National Education Center,
   RETS Campus
103 Park Ave.
Nutley 07110

NEW YORK

Mohawk Valley Community College
1101 Sherman Dr.
Utica 13501

Suburban Technical School
2650 Sunrise Hwy.
East Islip 11730

Suburban Technical School
175 Fulton Ave.
Hempstead 11550

NORTH CAROLINA

Catawba Valley Community College
2550 Hwy. 70 SE
Hickory 28602-0699

Central Carolina Community College
1105 Kelly Dr.
Sanford 27330

Central Piedmont Community College
P.O. Box 35009
Charlotte 28235

ECPI Computer Institute,
   Charlotte Center
1121 Wood Ridge Center Dr.
Charlotte 28217

ECPI Computer Institute,
   Greensboro Center
7015 Albert Pick Rd.
Greensboro 2740

ECPI Computer Institute, Raleigh
4509 Creedmoor Rd.
Raleigh 27612

OHIO

Akron Machining Institute, Inc.
2959 Barber Rd.
Barberton 44203

Cincinnati Technical College
3520 Central Pkwy.
Cincinnati 45223

ESI Career Center
1985 North Ridge Rd. E
Lorain 44055

National Education Center,
   National Institute of Technology
1225 Orlen Ave.
Cuyahoga Falls 44221

PENNSYLVANIA

Community College of Allegheny
   County
800 Allegheny Ave.
Pittsburgh 15233-1895

Pennsylvania College of Technology
One College Ave.
Williamsport 17701

SOUTH CAROLINA

Midlands Aviation Corporation
1400 Jim Hamilton Blvd.
Columbia 29205

TENNESSEE

Nashville State Technical Institute
120 White Bridge Rd.
Nashville 37209

TEXAS

American Commercial College
402 Butternut St.
Abilene 79602

American Commercial College
2007 34th St.
Lubbock 79411

American Commercial College
3177 Executive Dr.
San Angelo 76904

Central Texas College
P.O. Box 1800
Killeen 76540-9990

Microcomputer Technology Institute
17164 Blackhawk
Friendswood 77036

Microcomputer Technology Institute
7277 Regency Square Blvd.
Houston 77036

Western Technical Institute
4710 Alabama St., P.O. Box M
El Paso 79951

VIRGINIA

Computer Learning Center
6295 Edsall Rd.
Alexandria 22312

ECPI Computer Institute, Capital Center
4303 West Broad St.
Richmond 23230

ECPI Computer Institute, Main Campus
5555 Greenwich Rd.
Virginia Beach 23462

ECPI Computer Institute,
   Peninsula Center
1919 Commerce Dr.
Hampton 23666

ECPI Computer Institute,
   Roanoke Center
1030 Jefferson St. SE
Roanoke 24016

Falwell Aviation
P.O. Drawer 11409
Lynchburg 24506

WASHINGTON

Edmonds Community College
20000 68th Ave. W
Lynnwood 98036

North Seattle Community College
9600 College Way N
Seattle 98103

WISCONSIN

Blackhawk Technical College
P.O. Box 5009
Janesville 53547

MBTI Business Training Institute
820 North Plankinton Ave.
Milwaukee 53203

Barbering

ALABAMA

Alabama State College of Barber Styling
9480 Parkway E
Birmingham 35215

Atmore State Technical College
P.O. Box 1119
Atmore 36504

Douglas MacArthur Technical College
P.O. Box 649
Opp 36467

Isaac White Barber College
P.O. Box 818
Mobile 36601

J F Ingram State Technical College
P.O. Box 209
Deatsville 36022

Northwest Alabama Community
   College
Rte. 3, P.O. Box 77
Phil Campbell 35581

ALASKA

Anchorage Alaska Barber College
3517 Mountain View Dr.
Anchorage 99508

Fairbanks Beauty School
1255 Airport Rd.
Fairbanks 99701

New Concepts Beauty School
1019 College Rd.
Fairbanks 99701

ARIZONA

Hairstylists Barber College
5620 Hayward Ave.
Glendale 85301

ARKANSAS

Arkadelphia Beauty College
2708 West Pine
Arkadelphia 71923

Arkansas College of Barbering and
   Hair Design
200 East Washington Ave.
North Little Rock 72114

New Tyler Barber College, Inc.
1221 East Seventh St.
North Little Rock 72114

CALIFORNIA

American Barber College
5707 South Vermont Ave.
Los Angeles 90037

Associated Barber College
1045 11th Ave.
San Diego 92101

Educorp Career College
230 East Third St.
Long Beach 90802

Independent Barber College
635 Fifth Ave.
San Diego 92101

Moler Barber and Hairstyling
1880 Tulare St.
Fresno 93708-0287

Moler Barber College
3500 Broadway
Oakland 94611

Moler Barber College
727 J St.
Sacramento 95814

Moler Barber College
2645 El Camino Ave.
Sacramento 95821

Moler Barber College
50 Mason St.
San Francisco 94102

Moler Barber College
410 East Weber Ave.
Stockton 95202

Montebello Beauty College
2201 West Whitier Blvd.
Montebello 90640

Rosston School of Men's Hair Design
673 West Fifth St.
San Bernardino 92410

San Francisco Barber College
64 Sixth St.
   San Francisco 94103

COLORADO

Astral Academy of Hair
1432 North Hancock Ave.
Colorado Springs 80903-2621

Glenwood Beauty Academy
51241 Hwy. 6 and 24
Glenwood Springs 81601

CONNECTICUT

The Leon Institute of Hair Design
111 Wall St.
Bridgeport 06604

National Academy of Hairdressing
117 Main St.
Ansonia 06401

National Academy of Hairdressing
245 Main St.
Bristol 06010

National Academy of Hairdressing
Three Isaac Place
Norwalk 06850

National Academy of Hairdressing
Station House Square, 2505 Main St.
Stratford 06497

Sampieri School of Hair Design
128 Scott Rd.
Waterbury 06705

FLORIDA

Career Training Institute
101 West Main St.
Leesburg 34748

Career Training Institute
2120 West Colonial
Orlando 32804

The Hair Design School
5110 University Blvd.
Jacksonville 32216

Lewis M Lively Area Vocational-
   Technical Center
500 North Appleyard Dr.
Tallahassee 32304

Master School of Bartending
824 Southwest 24th St. & State Rd. 84
Fort Lauderdale 33315

Omni Technical School
2242 West Broward Blvd.
Fort Lauderdale 33312

PHD Hair Academy
27380 U.S. 19 N
Clearwater 34621

Ray-Mar Beauty Academy
3550 South University Dr.
Davie 33328-2003

Sunstate College of Hair Design
1825 Tamiami Trail
Port Charlotte 33948

Sunstate College of Hair Design
4424 Bee Ridge Rd.
Sarasota 34233

GEORGIA

Atlanta Area Technical School
1560 Stewart Ave. SW
Atlanta 30310

Brown's Barber College
283 Ashby St. NW
Atlanta 30314

Roffler Moler Hairstyling College
4033 Jonesboro Rd.
Forest Park 30050

Southeastern Beauty School
1826 Midtown Dr.
Columbus 31906

HAWAII

Hawaii Institute of Hair Design
71 South Hotel St.
Honolulu 96813-3112

IDAHO

Continental College of Beauty and
   Barber Styling
3021 North Cole Rd.
Boise 83704

ILLINOIS

Belleville Barber College
329 North Illinois St.
Belleville 62220

Cain's Barber College, Inc.
365 East 51st St.
Chicago 60615

Lincoln Barber College
653 15th Ave.
East Moline 61244

McCoy Barber College
2059 East 79th St.
Chicago 60649

Moler Hairstyling College, Inc.
5840 West Madison
Chicago 60644

Peoria Barber College
1315 Garden St.
Peoria 61602

INDIANA

Academy of Hair Design
2150 Lafayette Rd.
Indianapolis 46222

Lovell's Barber College
1700 Broadway
Gary 46407

IOWA

Capri Cosmetology College
395 Main St.
Dubuque 52001

Cedar Rapids School of Hairstyling
1531 First Ave. SE
Cedar Rapids 52402

College of Hair Design
810 Laporte Rd.
Waterloo 50702

Davenport Barber College
730 East Kimberly Rd.
Davenport 52807

Iowa School of Barbering and
   Hairstyling
603 East Sixth St.
Des Moines 50309

KANSAS

Advanced Hair Tech
4323 State Ave.
Kansas City 66102

Capitol City Barber College
812 North Kansas Ave.
Topeka 66608

Kansas School of Hair Styling
1207 East Douglas
Wichita 67211

KENTUCKY

Kentucky College of Barbering and
   Hairstyling
1230 South Third St.
Louisville 40203

Tri-City Barber College
2044 South Preston St.
Louisville 40217

LOUISIANA

Baton Rouge Regional Technical
   Institute
3250 North Acadian Hwy. E
Baton Rouge 70805

Katie's School of Beauty Culture
2100 Dryades St.
New Orleans 70113

Louisiana Hair Design College
7909 Airline Hwy.
Metairie 70003

MAINE

Mr. Richard's Hair Styling Academy
41 Broad St.
Auburn 04210

MARYLAND

Academy of Professional Barber-Stylists
2401 Blueridge Ave.
Wheaton 20902

Bladensburg Barber School
4810 Annapolis Rd.
Bladensburg 20711

International Academy of Hair Design
and Technology
1500 West Pratt St.
Baltimore 21223

Progressive Barber School, Inc.
8146 Fort Smallwood Rd.
Baltimore 21226

Ron Thomas School of Cosmetology
5601 Bowleys Ln.
Baltimore 21206

MASSACHUSETTS

Massachusetts School of Barbering and
Men's Hairstyling
152 Parking Way
Quincy 02169

New England Hair Academy
492-500 Main St.
Malden 02148

MICHIGAN

Flint Institute of Barbering
3214 Flushing Rd.
Flint 48504-4395

Michigan Barber School
8990 West Grand River St.
Detroit 48204

MINNESOTA

Minnesota School of Barbering
3615 East Lake St.
Minneapolis 55406

Moler Barber School of Hairstyling
1411 Nicollet Ave.
Minneapolis 55403-2666

MISSISSIPPI

Brocks Hair Design College
116 East Franklin St.
Carthage 39051

Foster's Cosmetology College
1815 Hwy. 15 N
Ripley 38663

Gibson Barber and Beauty College
120 East Main St.
West Point 39773

Jackson Hair Design College
2845 Suncrest Dr.
Jackson 39212

MISSOURI

International Hair Institute
415 South Florissant Rd.
Ferguson 63135

Missouri School of Barbering and
Hairstyling
3740 Noland Rd.
Independence 64055

Missouri School of Barbering &
Hairstyling
1125 North Hwy. 67
Florissant 63031

MONTANA

Big Sky College of Barber Styling, Inc.
750 Kensington Ave.
Missoula 59801

Billings School of Barbering and
Hairstyling
206 North 13th St.
Billings 59101

NEW JERSEY

Parisian Beauty School
362 State St.
Hackensack 07601

NEW MEXICO

Albuquerque Barber College
525 San Pedro NE
Albuquerque 87108

NORTH CAROLINA

Black World College of Hair Design
1550 West Blvd., P.O. Box 669403
Charlotte 28266

Hairstyling Institute of Charlotte
209B South Kings Dr.
Charlotte 28204

Pyramid Institute of Barbering
709 Patterson Ave.
Winston-Salem 27101-3030

Winston-Salem Barber School
1531 Silas Creek Pkwy.
Winston-Salem 27127

OHIO

Akron Barber College
3200 South Arlington Rd.
Akron 44312

Allstate Barber and Hairstyling College
2546 Lorain Ave.
Cleveland 44113

Cincinnati School of Barbering and
Hair Design, Inc.
6500 Colerain Ave.
Cincinnati 45239

Ohio State College of Barber Styling
329 Superior St.
Toledo 43604

Ohio State School of Cosmetology, East
6320 East Livingston Ave.
Reynoldsburg 43068

Pioneer Joint Vocational School District
27 Ryan Rd., P.O. Box 309
Shelby 44875

OKLAHOMA

Enid Barber Styling College
230 West Broadway
Enid 73701

Mid-Del College
3420 South Sunnylane
Del City 73115

State Barber and Hair Design College
2514 South Agnew Ave.
Oklahoma City 73108

Tulsa Barber Styling College
1314 East Third St.
Tulsa 74120

OREGON

Astoria Beauty College
1180 Commercial St.
Astoria 97103

College of Hair Design Careers
3322 Lancaster Dr. NE
Salem 97305-1354

The Dalles Academy of Hair Design
415 East Second St.
The Dalles 97058

Edward Wadsworth Institute for Hair
Design
3301 Northeast Sandy Blvd.
Portland 97232

Magee Brothers Beaverton School of
Beauty
4500 Southwest Watson St.
Beaverton 97005

Pendleton College of Hair Design
326 Main St.
Pendleton 97801

Phagan's Beauty College
142 South Second St.
Corvallis 97333

Phagan's Medford Beauty School
2316 Poplar Dr.
Medford 97504

Phagan's School of Hair Design
16550 Southeast McLoughlin
Portland 97267

Roseburg Beauty College
700 Southeast Stephens St.
Roseburg 97470

Skelton Beauty Academy
495 West Central Ave.
Coos Bay 97420

PENNSYLVANIA

Barber Styling Institute
3447 Simpson Ferry Rd.
Camp Hill 17011

Joseph Donahue International School
of Barbering & Hairstyling
2485 Grant Ave.
Philadelphia 19114

Pittsburgh Beauty Academy
415 Smithfield St.
Pittsburgh 15222

Ralph Amodei International Institute
of Hair Design
4451 Frankford Ave.
Philadelphia 19124

Tri-City Barber School, Inc.
5901 North Broad St.
Philadelphia 19141

SOUTH CAROLINA

Advance Beauty College
180 Hall St.
Spartanburg 29302

Mangums Barber and Hair Styling
College
125 Hampton St.
Rock Hill 29730

Piedmont College of Hair Design
491 Union St., P.O. Drawer 6050
Spartanburg 29304

Professional Hair Design Academy
1540 Wade Hampton Blvd.
Greenville 29609

TENNESSEE

Artiste School of Cosmetology
129 Springbrook Dr.
Johnson City 37601

Chattanooga Barber College
405 Market St.
Chattanooga 37402-1204

The Hair School
3308 Gallatin Pike
Nashville 37216

International Barber and Style College
966 Madison Square
Madison 37115

Jett College of Barbering
3740 North Watkins
Memphis 38127

Knoxville Institute of Hair Design
1221 North Central
Knoxville 37917

Mid State Barber Styling College, Inc.
510 Jefferson St.
Nashville 37208

Mr. Wayne's School of Unisex Hair
Design
170 South Willow Ave.
Cookeville 38501

National School of Hair Design
3641 Brainerd Rd.
Chattanooga 37411

Queen City College
1191 Fort Campbell Blvd.
Clarksville 37042

TEXAS

Careers Unlimited
335 South Bonner
Tyler 75702

Central Texas College
P.O. Box 1800
Killeen 76540-9990

Euro Hair School
2301-A Morgan St.
Corpus Christi 78405

Fairfield Barber College
P.O. Box 1336
Fairfield 75840

Grahams Barber College
3016 Grand Ave.
Dallas 75215

Keith's Metro Hair Academy
3225C Commerce
Amarillo 79109-3275

Larry's Barber and Hairstyling College
6614 South Rte. 1 & Thorton Fwy.
Dallas 75232

Le Hair Design College
1125 East Seminary Dr.
Fort Worth 76115

Mims Classic Beauty College
5121 Blanco Rd.
San Antonio 78216

Modern Barber College
1015 Eagle St.
Houston 77002

RHDC Hair Design College
3209 North Main St.
Fort Worth 76106

RS Institute
7122 Lawndale Ave.
Houston 77023

South Texas Barber College
3917 Ayers
Corpus Christi 78415

Texas Barber College and Hairstyling
School 1
531 West Jefferson St.
Dallas 75208

Texas Barber College and Hairstyling
School 2
2406 Gus Thomasson
Dallas 75228

Texas Barber College and Hairstyling
School 3
525 West Arapaho
Richardson 75080

West Texas Barber Styling College
4001 West Mockingbird Ln.
Amarillo 79109

Williams Barber College
1251 Evans Ave.
Fort Worth 76104

UTAH

Salt Lake Community College
P.O. Box 30808
Salt Lake City 84130

VIRGINIA

Anthony's Barber College
1307 Jefferson Ave.
Newport News 23607-5617

Jan Mar Beauty Academy
411 Jan Mar Dr.
Newport News 23606-3882

Virginia Hair Academy
3312 Williamson Rd. NW
Roanoke 24012

WASHINGTON

Academy of Hair Design
Nine South Wenatchee Ave.
Wenatchee 98801

Bates Technical College
1101 South Yakima Ave.
Tacoma 98405

BJ's Beauty and Barber College
5237 South Tacoma Way
Tacoma 98409

Everett Plaza Beauty School
607 Southeast Everett Mall
Everett 98208

Gene Juarez Academy of Beauty,
    Branch Campus
2222 South 314th St.
Federal Way 98003

The Hair School
3043 Hwy. 101 E
Port Angeles 98362

Ms. BJ's Beauty and Barber College
11510 Meridian S
Puyallup 98373

Paul Mitchell Endorsed Academy of
    Cosmetology
14352 Lake City Way NE
Seattle 98125

WEST VIRGINIA

Charleston School of Beauty Culture
210 Capitol St.
Charleston 25301

Clarksburg Beauty Academy
120 South Third St.
Clarksburg 26301

Wheeling College of Hair Design
1122 Main St.
Wheeling 26003

WISCONSIN

Milwaukee Area Technical College
700 West State St.
Milwaukee 53233

Scientific College of Beauty and
    Barbering
718 Main St.
La Crosse 54601

Wisconsin Area Vocational Training
    and Adult Education System District
    Number Four
3550 Anderson St.
Madison 53704

Care and Guidance of Children

ARIZONA

Glendale Community College
6000 West Olive Ave.
Glendale 85302

ARKANSAS

Crowley's Ridge Technical School
P.O. Box 925
Forrest City 72335

CALIFORNIA

Antelope Valley College
3041 West Ave. K
Lancaster 93534

Cabrillo College
6500 Soquel Dr.
Aptos 95003

Center for Employment Training,
    San Jose-Vine
701 Vine St.
San Jose 95110

Contra Costa College
2600 Mission Bell Dr.
San Pablo 94806

Cuesta College
P.O. Box 8106
San Luis Obispo 93403-8106

El Camino College
16007 Crenshaw Blvd.
Torrance 90506

Glendale Community College
1500 North Verdugo Rd.
Glendale 91208-2894

Grossmont College
8800 Grossmont College Dr.
El Cajon 92020

Imperial Valley College
P.O. Box 158
Imperial 92251-0158

Lassen College
Hwy. 139, P.O. Box 3000
Susanville 96130

Los Angeles Southwest College
1600 West Imperial Hwy.
Los Angeles 90047

Marin Regional Occupational Program
P.O. Box 4925
San Rafael 94913

Merritt College
12500 Campus Dr.
Oakland 94619

Moorpark College
7075 Campus Rd.
Moorpark 93021

Oxnard College
4000 South Rose Ave.
Oxnard 93033

Riverside Community College
4800 Magnolia Ave.
Riverside 92506-1299

Sacramento City College
3835 Freeport Blvd.
Sacramento 95822

Simi Valley Adult School
3192 Los Angeles Ave.
Simi Valley 93065

Solano County Community College
    District
4000 Suisun Valley Rd.
Suisun 94585

Victor Valley College
18422 Bear Valley Rd.
Victorville 92392-9699

COLORADO

Aims Community College
P.O. Box 69
Greeley 80632

Community College of Denver
P.O. Box 173363
Denver 80217

Northeastern Junior College
100 College Dr.
Sterling 80751

CONNECTICUT

Housatonic Community College
510 Barnum Ave.
Bridgeport 06608

South Central Community College
60 Sargent Dr.
New Haven 06511

FLORIDA

Atlantic Vocational Technical Center
4700 Coconut Creek Pkwy.
Coconut Creek 33063

Florida School of Business
2990 Northwest 81st Terrace
Miami 33147

Florida School of Business
405 East Polk St.
Tampa 33602

Garces Commercial College
1301 Southwest First
Miami 33135

Garces Commercial College
5385 Northwest 36th St.
Miami Springs 33166

Martin Technical College
1901 Northwest Seventh St.
Miami 33125

Miami-Dade Community College
300 Northeast Second Ave.
Miami 33132

Pinellas Technical Education Center,
    Clearwater Campus
6100 154th Ave. N
Clearwater 34620

GEORGIA

Albany Technical Institute
1021 Lowe Rd.
Albany 31708

Athens Area Technical Institute
U.S. Hwy. 29 N
Athens 30610-0399

Atlanta Area Technical School
1560 Stewart Ave. SW
Atlanta 30310

Augusta Technical Institute
3116 Deans Bridge Rd.
Augusta 30906

Meadows Junior College
1170 Brown Ave.
Columbus 31906

Valdosta Technical Institute
4089 Valtech Rd.
Valdosta 31602-9796

ILLINOIS

Black Hawk College, Quad-Cities
6600 34th Ave.
Moline 61265

City College of Chicago,
    Olive-Harvey College
10001 South Woodlawn Ave.
Chicago 60628

City College of Chicago, Kennedy-King
6800 South Wentworth Ave.
Chicago 60621

City College of Chicago,
    Truman College
1145 Wilson Ave.
Chicago 60640

College of Du Page
Lambert Rd. and 22nd St.
Glen Ellyn 60137

College of Lake County
19351 West Washington St.
Grays Lake 60030-1198

Illinois Central College
One College Dr.
East Peoria 61635

Illinois Eastern Community Colleges,
    Olney Central College
RR 3
Olney 62450

Lake Land College
5001 Lake Land Blvd.
Mattoon 61938

Lewis and Clark Community College
5800 Godfrey Rd.
Godfrey 62035

Moraine Valley Community College
10900 South 88th Ave.
Palos Hills 60465-0937

Oakton Community College
1600 East Golf Rd.
Des Plaines 60016

Parkland College
2400 West Bradley Ave.
Champaign 61821

Prairie State College
202 Halsted St.
Chicago Heights 60411

Richland Community College
One College Park
Decatur 62521

Triton College
2000 Fifth Ave.
River Grove 60171

Waubonsee Community College
Rte. 47 at Harter Rd.
Sugar Grove 60554-0901

William Rainey Harper College
1200 West Algonquin Rd.
Palatine 60067-7398

INDIANA

Indiana Vocational Technical College,
    Northeast
3800 North Anthony Blvd.
Fort Wayne 46805

IOWA

Des Moines Community College
2006 Ankeny Blvd.
Ankeny 50021

Iowa Valley Community College
P.O. Box 536
Marshalltown 50158

Kirkwood Community College
P.O. Box 2068
Cedar Rapids 52406

KANSAS

Barton County Community College
Rte. 3, P.O. Box 136Z
Great Bend 67530

Butler County Community College
901 South Haverhill Rd.
El Dorado 67042

Wichita Area Vocational Technical
    School
428 South Broadway
Wichita 67202-3910

KENTUCKY

Jefferson Community College
109 East Broadway
Louisville 40202

Kentucky Technical, Daviess County
    Vocational Technical School
1901 Southeastern Pkwy.
Owensboro 42303

Northern Kentucky State Vocational-
    Technical School
1025 Amsterdam Rd.
Covington 41011

Sullivan College
3101 Bardstown Rd.
Louisville 40205

LOUISIANA

Baton Rouge Regional Technical
    Institute
3250 North Acadian Hwy. E
Baton Rouge 70805

Lafayette Regional Technical Institute
1101 Bertrand Dr.
    P.O. Box 4909
Lafayette 70502-4909

New Orleans Regional Technical
    Institute
980 Navarre Ave.
New Orleans 70124

MARYLAND

Charles County Community College
Mitchell Rd., P.O. Box 910
La Plata 20646

Montgomery College of Rockville
51 Mannakee St.
Rockville 20850

Prince Georges Community College
301 Largo Rd.
Largo 23701-1243

Villa Julie College
Green Spring Valley Rd.
Stevenson 21153

MASSACHUSETTS

Becker College, Leicester
Three Paxton St.
Leicester 01524

Holyoke Community College
303 Homestead Ave.
Holyoke 01040

Massachusetts Bay Community College
50 Oakland St.
Wellesley Hills 02181

Mount Ida College
777 Dedham St.
Newton Centre 02159

Quincy College
34 Coddington St.
Quincy 02169

MICHIGAN

Delta College
University Center 48710

Ferris State University
901 South State St.
Big Rapids 49307

Grand Rapids Community College
143 Bostwick Ave. NE
Grand Rapids 49505

Lake Superior State University
Sault Sainte Marie 49783

Lansing Community College
419 North Capitol Ave.
Lansing 48901-7210

Macomb Community College
14500 Twelve Mile Rd.
Warren 48093-3896

Mott Community College
1401 East Court St.
Flint 48503

Oakland Community College
2480 Opdyke Rd.
Bloomfield Hills 48304-2266

Ross Technical Institute
1553 Woodward
Detroit 48226

Siena Heights College
1247 Siena Heights Dr.
Adrian 49221

MINNESOTA

Hennepin Technical College
1820 North Xenium Ln.
Plymouth 55441

Hutchinson-Willmar Technical College,
Hutchinson Campus
Two Century Ave.
Hutchinson 55350

Northeast Metro Technical College
3300 Century Ave. N
White Bear Lake 55110

MISSISSIPPI

Northeast Mississippi Community
College
Cunningham Blvd.
Booneville 38829

Pearl River Community College
Station A
Poplarville 39470

MISSOURI

Macon Area Vocational School
Hwy. 63 N
Macon 63552

Penn Valley Community College
3201 Southwest Trafficway
Kansas City 64111

Saint Louis Community College,
Forest Park
5600 Oakland Ave.
Saint Louis 63110

NEBRASKA

Central Community College,
Grand Island
P.O. Box 4903
Grand Island 68802

Southeast Community College,
Lincoln Campus
8800 O St.
Lincoln 68520

NEW HAMPSHIRE

New Hampshire Technical College at
Claremont
One College Dr.
Claremont 03743

New Hampshire Technical Institute
11 Institute Dr.
Concord 03301

School for Lifelong Learning
25 Concord Rd., Dunlap Center
Durham 03824

NEW JERSEY

Middlesex County College
155 Mill Rd.
P.O. Box 3050
Edison 08818-3050

NEW YORK

Broome Community College
P.O. Box 1017
Binghamton 13902

Cashier Training Institute
500 Eighth Ave.
New York 10018

Cayuga County Community College
Franklin St.
Auburn 13021

Dutchess Community College
Pendell Rd.
Poughkeepsie 12601

Erie Community College, City Campus
121 Ellicott St.
Buffalo 14203

Herkimer County Community College
Reservoir Rd.
Herkimer 13350-1598

Hudson Valley Community College
80 Vandenburgh Ave.
Troy 12180

Maison Sapho School of Dressmaking
and Designing
312 West 83rd St.
New York 10024

Nassau Community College
One Education Dr.
Garden City 11530

Saint Mary's Hospital for Children,
School of Infant and Child Care
29-01 216th St.
Bayside 11360

Suffolk County Community College,
Ammerman Campus
533 College Rd.
Selden 11784

Suffolk County Community College,
Western Campus
Crooked Hill Rd.
Brentwood 11717

Sullivan County Community College
Le Roy Rd., P.O. Box 4002
Loch Sheldrake 12759-4002

SUNY College at Purchase
735 Anderson Hill Rd.
Purchase 10577

SUNY College of Agriculture &
Technology at Cobleskill
Cobleskill 12043

SUNY College of Technology at
Farmingdale
Melville Rd.
Farmingdale 11735

NORTH CAROLINA

Cape Fear Community College
411 North Front St.
Wilmington 28401

Forsyth Technical Community College
2100 Silas Creek Pkwy.
Winston-Salem 27103

Lenoir Community College
P.O. Box 188
Kinston 28502-0188

Rockingham Community College
P.O. Box 38
Wentworth 27375-0038

Rowan-Cabarrus Community College
P.O. Box 1595
Salisbury 28145-1595

OHIO

Jefferson Technical College
4000 Sunset Blvd.
Steubenville 43952-3598

Lakeland Community College
7700 Clocktower Dr.
Mentor 44060-7594

Lima Technical College
4240 Campus Dr.
Lima 45804

Owens Technical College
30335 Oregon Rd., P.O. Box 10000
Toledo 43699-1947

Youngstown State University
410 Wick Ave.
Youngstown 44555

OKLAHOMA

De Marge College
3608 Northwest 58th
Oklahoma City 73112

Kiamichi AVTS SD #7, Hugo Campus
107 South 15th, P.O. Box 699
Hugo 74743

OREGON

Lane Community College
4000 East 30th Ave.
Eugene 97405

PENNSYLVANIA

Clarissa School of Fashion Design
Warner Centre, 332 Fifth Ave.
Pittsburgh 15222-2411

Community College of Philadelphia
1700 Spring Garden St.
Philadelphia 19130

Lehigh County Community College
4525 Education Park Dr.
Schnecksville 18078-2598

Luzerne County Community College
1333 South Prospect St.
Nanticoke 18634

Northampton County Area Community
College
3835 Green Pond Rd.
Bethlehem 18017

Pennsylvania College of Technology
One College Ave.
Williamsport 17701

Pointe Career Institute, Center City
50 North Second St.
Philadelphia 19106

Westmoreland County Community
College
Youngwood 15697-1895

SOUTH CAROLINA

Greenville Technical College
Station B, P.O. Box 5616
Greenville 29606-5616

SOUTH DAKOTA

Lake Area Vocational Technical
Institute
230 11th St. NE
Watertown 57201

Western Dakota Vocational Technical
Institute
1600 Sedivy
Rapid City 57701

TEXAS

San Antonio College
1300 San Pedro Ave.
San Antonio 78284

Tarrant County Junior College District
1500 Houston St.
Fort Worth 76102

UTAH

Salt Lake Community College-Skills
Center, South City Campus
1575 South State St.
Salt Lake City 84115

Southern Utah University
351 West Center
Cedar City 84720

Utah Valley Community College
800 West 1200 S
Orem 84058

WASHINGTON

Lake Washington Technical College
11605 132nd Ave. NE
Kirkland 98034

Olympic College
1600 Chester Ave.
Bremerton 98310-1699

Pierce College
9401 Farwest Dr. SW
Tacoma 98498

Spokane Falls Community College
West 3410 Fort George Wright Dr.
Spokane 99204

WEST VIRGINIA

Ben Franklin Career Center
500 28th St.
Dunbar 25064

WISCONSIN

Blackhawk Technical College
P.O. Box 5009
Janesville 53547

Chippewa Valley Technical College
620 West Clairemont Ave.
Eau Claire 54701

Fox Valley Technical College
1825 North Bluemound Dr.
Appleton 54913-2277

Gateway Technical College
3520 30th Ave.
Kenosha 53144-1690

Lakeshore Vocational Training and
Adult Education System District
1290 North Ave.
Cleveland 53015

Mid-State Technical College,
Main Campus
500 32nd St. N
Wisconsin Rapids 54494

Milwaukee Area Technical College
700 West State St.
Milwaukee 53233

Northeast Wisconsin Technical College
2740 West Mason St.
P.O. Box 19042
Green Bay 54307-9042

Waukesha County Technical College
800 Main St.
Pewaukee 53072

Wisconsin Area Vocational Training
and Adult Education System District
Number Four
3550 Anderson St.
Madison 53704

Wisconsin Indianhead Technical
College
505 Pine Ridge Dr., P.O. Box 10B
Shell Lake 54871

Cosmetology

ALABAMA

Bevill State Community College
P.O. Drawer K
Sumiton 35148

Douglas MacArthur Technical College
P.O. Box 649
Opp 36467

G C Wallace State Community College
P.O. Drawer 1049
Selma 36702-1049

George C Wallace State Community
College, Dothan
Rte. 6, P.O. Box 62
Dothan 36303-9234

Harry M Ayers State Technical College
1801 Coleman Rd.
P.O. Box 1647
Anniston 36202

John M Patterson State Technical
College
3920 Troy Hwy.
Montgomery 36116

Keevil-Curl School of Beauty, Inc.
305 South Fourth St.
Gadsden 35901-5212

Master's Institute of Cosmetology
8215 Stephanie St.
Huntsville 35802

New World College of Beauty
P.O. Box 2287
Anniston 36202

Opelika State Technical College
P.O. Box 2268
Opelika 36803-2268

South Alabama Beauty College
2861 South McKenzie St.
Foley 36535

ALASKA

Ahead of Time
3801 Old Seward Hwy.
Anchorage 99503

Trend Setters School of Beauty
407 East Northern Lights Blvd.
Anchorage 99503

ARIZONA

Allure Career College of Beauty
7730 East McDowell
Scottsdale 85257

Allure Career College of Beauty
3210 East Speedway Blvd.
Tucson 85716

Arizona Academy of Beauty
4046 North Oracle
Tucson 85705

Arizona Academy of Beauty
6015 East Broadway
Tucson 85711

Beebes Academy of Beauty Culture
184 West 25th St.
Yuma 85364

Carlos Valenzuela Academy
7201 East Camelback
Scottsdale 85251

Charles of Italy Beauty College
2350 Miracle Mile Rd.
Bullhead City 86442

Charles of Italy Beauty College
1987 McCulloch Blvd.
Lake Havasu City 86403

Classic Beauty College
2390 North Alma School
Chandler 85224

Classic Beauty College
42 North Stapley Dr.
Mesa 85203

Classic Beauty College
6843 East Main St.
Mesa 85206

Classic Beauty College
1548-A West Montebello
Phoenix 85015

Classic Beauty College
3871 East Thomas
Phoenix 85018

Classic Beauty College
3227 East Bell Rd.
Phoenix 85032

College of Beauty Arts and Science
1229 East Cherry
Cottonwood 86326

College of Beauty Arts and Science
1790 East Santa Fe Ave.
Flagstaff 86004

College of Beauty Arts and Science
410 West Goodwin
Prescott 86303

Cutters Hair Beauty School
4533 West Glendale Ave.
Glendale 85301

Devoe College of Beauty
750 Bartow Dr., P.O. Box 1571
Sierra Vista 85635

Earl's Academy of Beauty
2111 South Alma School Rd.
Mesa 85210

House of Michael Beauty Academy
1946 West Main St.
Mesa 85201

International Academy of Hair Design
4415 North RR 2
Tempe 85282

Maricopa Beauty College
515 West Western Ave.
Avondale 85323

Phoenix Academy of Beauty
10820 North 43rd Ave.
Glendale 85304

Royal College of Beauty, Ltd.
22 North Country Club Dr.
Mesa 85201

United Academy of Beauty
4105 South Central
Phoenix 85040

Yuma School of Beauty
50 West Third St.
Yuma 85364

ARKANSAS

Arkansas Valley Technical Institute
Hwy. 23 N, P.O. Box 506
Ozark 72949

Arthurs Beauty College
2600 John Harden Dr.
Jacksonville 72076

Bee Jay's Academy
1907 Hinson Loop
Little Rock 72212

Bizzell's Beauty School
200 North Moose
Morrilton 72110

Hot Springs Beauty College
634 Malvern Ave.
Hot Springs 71901

Marcel-Royale Beauty Academy
2004 South Eighth St.
Rogers 72756

Paramount Beauty School
426 North Washington St.
El Dorado 71730

Pat Goin's Jonesboro Beauty School
3512 East Nettleton Ave.
Jonesboro 72401

Pat Goin's Pine Bluff Beauty School
3101 West Olive
Pine Bluff 71603-5439

Velvatex Beauty School
1520 High St.
Little Rock 72202

CALIFORNIA

Academy of Hair Design, Poway
14010 Poway Rd.
Poway 92064

Adrian's Beauty College
3701 East 14th St.
Oakland 94601

Adrian's Beauty College of Turlock
2253 Geer Rd.
Turlock 95380

Al Tate Beauty College
2650 East Colorado Blvd.
Pasadena 91107

Alameda Beauty College
2318 Central Ave.
Alameda 94501

Alhambra Beauty College
200 West Main St.
Alhambra 91801

Ambassador Beauty College
2107 North Glenoaks Blvd.
Burbank 91504

American Beauty College
16809 Bellflower Blvd.
Bellflower 90706

Asian American International
Beauty College
7871 Westminster Blvd.
Westminster 92683

Avance Beauty College
750 Beyer Way
San Diego 92154

B Street Beauty College
966 B St.
Hayward 94541

Barstow Academy of Beauty
423 East Main St.
Barstow 92311

Bay Vista College of Beauty
1520 Plaza Blvd.
National 92050

Bjorn's Hairstyling Academy
96 Springstown Center
Vallejo 94591

California Beauty School
1115 15th St.
Modesto 95354

California Cosmetology College
303 South Capitol Ave.
San Jose 95127-3033

California Hair Design Academy
5315 El Cajon Blvd.
San Diego 92115

Camden Beauty College
1824 Hillsdale Ave.
San Jose 95124

Canyon Country Beauty College
18914 Soledad Canyon Rd.
Canyon 91351

Career Academy of Beauty
663 North Euclid
Anaheim 92801

Career Academy of Beauty
12375 Seal Beach Blvd.
Seal Beach 90740

Career College of Cosmetology
407 D St.
Marysville 95901

Career College of Cosmetology
646 Cottonwood Plaza
Woodland 95776

Career College of Cosmetology
100 Carriage Square
Yuba City 95991

Carmichael Beauty College
6243 Fair Oaks Blvd.
Carmichael 95608

Cerritos College
11110 Alondra Blvd.
Norwalk 90650

Chico Beauty College
1356 Longfellow Ave.
Chico 95926

Citrus College
1000 West Foothill Blvd.
Glendora 91741-1899

Citrus Heights Beauty College
7518 Baird Way
Citrus Heights 95610

Colleen O'Haras Beauty Academy
102 North Glassell St.
Orange 92666

College of San Mateo
1700 West Hillsdale Blvd.
San Mateo 94402

Culver Beauty College
3834 Main St.
Culver 90230

Cynthias Beauty Academy
4130 Gage Ave.
Bell 90201

Dean's Westside Beauty College
1581 Meridian Ave.
San Jose 95125

Don's Beauty School
42 North B St.
San Mateo 94401

Elegante Beauty College
17337 East Valley Blvd.
La Puente 91744

Elegante Beauty College
24731 Alicia Pkwy.
Laguna Hills 92653

Elegante Beauty College
31739 Riverside Dr.
Lake Elsinore 92330

Elegante Beauty College
505 Long Beach Blvd.
Long Beach 90802

Elegante Beauty College
33951C Doheni Park Rd.
San Juan Capistrano 92675

Federico Beauty College, Sunnyside
5712 East Kings Canyon Rd.
Fresno 93727

Federico College of Hairstyling
2300 Florin Rd.
Sacramento 95822

Federico College of Hairstyling
2100 Arden Way
Sacramento 95825

Federico's Kern County College of
    Beauty
3203 F St.
Bakersfield 93301

Federico's North Fresno Beauty College
5660 North Blackstone Ave.
Fresno 93710

Federico's Tulare County College of
    Beauty
2544 South Mooney Blvd.
Visalia 93277

Fernando Romero International
    Academy of Beauty
2662 East Florence Ave.
Huntington Park 90255

First California Beauty College
4085 Tweedy Blvd.
South Gate 90280

Flavio Torrance Beauty College
1978 West Carson St.
Torrance 90501

Frederick & Charles Beauty College
831 F St.
Eureka 95501

Ganaye Academy of Cosmetology, Inc.
830 Middlefield Rd.
Redwood 94063

Girard's College of Beauty, Inc.
3021 South Bristol
Santa Ana 92704

Golden West College
15744 Golden West
Huntington Beach 92647

Hacienda La Puente Unified School
    District, Valley Vocational Center
15959 East Gale Ave.
La Puente 91749

Hair Interns School of Cosmetology
1522 Fulton
Fresno 93721

Hair Masters University
208 West Highland Ave.
San Bernardino 92405

Hilltop Beauty School
6317 Mission St.
Daly City 94014

International School of Cosmetology
12004 Hawthorne Blvd.
Hawthorne 90250

J Boutique College of Beauty
1073 East Main St.
El Cajon 92021

Jerrylee Beauty College
100 Eldorado St.
Auburn 95603

Jerrylee Beauty College
200 Whyte Ave.
Roseville 95661

Jerrylee Beauty College
1550 Fulton Ave.
Sacramento 95821

John Peri Beauty College
2418 B Lomita Blvd.
Lomita 90717

Kenneth's College of Hairstyling
3365 Sonoma Blvd.
Vallejo 94590

Kristofers School of Beauty, Inc.
122 West Canon Perdido
Santa Barbara 93101

Lancaster Beauty School
44646 North Tenth St. W
Lancaster 93534

Laurel Beauty Academy
6219 Laurel Canyon Blvd.
North Hollywood 91606

Lola Beauty College
11883 Valley View St.
Garden Grove 92641

Los Angeles Training Technical College
400 West Washington Blvd.
Los Angeles 90015-4181

Lu Ross Academy of Hair Design
97 South Oak
Ventura 93001

Lyles College of Beauty
6735 North First Ave.
Fresno 93710

Lyles Tulare School of Beauty
1400 West Inyo St.
Tulare 93274

Lytles Redwood Empire Beauty
    College, Inc.
186 Wikiup Dr.
Santa Rosa 95403

Madera Beauty College
200 West Olive Ave.
Madera 93637

Manchester Beauty College
3756 North Blackstone Ave.
Fresno 93726

Marin Beauty College
827 Fourth St.
San Rafael 94901

Marin Regional Occupational Program
P.O. Box 4925
San Rafael 94913

Marinello School of Beauty
8374 D on the Mall
Buena Park 90620

Marinello School of Beauty
240 South Market St.
Inglewood 90301

Marinello School of Beauty
5241 Graywood Ave.
Lakewood 90712

Marinello School of Beauty
716 South Broadway
Los Angeles 90014

Marinello School of Beauty
5031 South Plaza Ln.
Montclair 91763

Marinello School of Beauty
12135 Victory Blvd.
North Hollywood 91606

Marinello School of Beauty
18842 Sherman Way
Reseda 91335

Marinello School of Beauty
199 North E St.
San Bernardino 92401

Marinello School of Beauty
1226 University Ave.
San Diego 92103

Marinello School of Beauty
906 North Main St.
Santa Ana 92701

Marinello School of Beauty
891 Fashion Plaza
West Covina 91790

Marinello School of Beauty
6538 Greenleaf Ave.
Whittier 90601

Marinello School of Beauty, Los Angeles
6288 West Third St.
Los Angeles 90036

Marinello Schools of Beauty
13350 East Telegraph Rd.
Santa Fe Springs 90067

Milpitas Beauty School
1350 South Park Victoria Dr.
Milpitas 95035

Miss Marty's School of Beauty
278 Post St.
San Francisco 94108

Modern Beauty Academy
5730 Whittier Blvd.
Los Angeles 90022

Modern Beauty Academy
8610 Van Nuys Blvd.
Panarama City 91402

Monterey Academy of Hair Design
345 East Santa Clara St.
San Jose 95113

Moro Beauty College
124 North Brand Blvd.
Glendale 91203

Nationwide Beauty College
252 Second St.
Pomona 91766

Newberry School of Beauty
9036 Woodman Ave.
Arleta 91331

Newberry School of Beauty
22906 Van Owen St.
West Hills 91307

North Adrian's Beauty College
124 Floyd Ave.
Modesto 95350

North Park College
3956 30th St.
San Diego 92104

Oakland Beauty School
330 13th St.
Oakland 94612

Oceanside College of Beauty
1575 South Hill St.
Oceanside 92054

Oroville Beauty College
2200 Fifth Ave.
Oroville 95965

Pacific Beauty College 3
5345 Crenshaw Blvd.
Los Angeles 90043

Page Antelope Valley Beauty School
601 West Lancaster Blvd.
Lancaster 93534

Palm Springs Beauty College
611 Palm Cyn Dr.
Palm Springs 92264

Palomar Institute of Cosmetology
355 Via Vera Cruz
San Marcos 92069

Pasadena City College
1570 East Colorada Blvd.
Pasadena 91106

Plaza Beauty College
977 East Ave.
Chico 95926

Professional Institute of Beauty
10801 Valley Mall
El Monte 91731

Randy's Beauty College
678 North Market St.
Redding 96001

Richard's Beauty College
16803 Arrow Blvd.
Fontana 92335

Richard's Beauty College
200 North Euclid Ave.
Ontario 91762

Richard's Beauty College
200 East Highland Ave.
San Bernardino 92404

Riverside Community College
4800 Magnolia Ave.
Riverside 92506-1299

Rosemead Beauty College
8531 East Valley Blvd.
Rosemead 91770

Royale College of Beauty
27485 Commerce Center Dr.
Temecula 92590

Salinas Beauty College
916 South Main St.
Salinas 93901

San Fernando Beauty Academy
13714 Foothill Blvd.
Sylmar 91342

San Gorgonio Beauty College
1335 West Ramsey St.
Banning 92220

San Jose Beauty College
1030 the Alameda
San Jose 95126

San Luis Obispo Beauty College
12230 Los Osos Valley Rd.
San Luis Obispo 93405

Santa Barbara Beauty College
4223 State St.
Santa Barbara 93110

Santa Clara Beauty College
2630 El Camino Real
Santa Clara 95051

Santa Maria Beauty College
135 West Carmen Ln.
Santa Maria 93454

Santa Rosa Beauty College
615 Healdsburg Ave.
Santa Rosa 95401

Sierra College of Beauty
1340 West 18th St.
Merced 95340

Simi Valley Adult School
3192 Los Angeles Ave.
Simi Valley 93065

Skyline College
3300 College Dr.
San Bruno 94066

Sonoma Beauty College
714 Petaluma Blvd. N
Petaluma 94952

Tri-City Beauty College,
    Richard Jay's, Inc.
12875 Chapman Ave.
Garden Grove 92640

Ukiah Beauty College
1040 North State St.
Ukiah 95482

United Artist Beauty College
81-695 Hwy. 111
Indio 92201

United Business Beauty College
1021 East Compton Blvd.
Compton 90221

Universal College of Beauty
3419 West 43rd Place
Los Angeles 90008

Universal College of Beauty, Inc.
8619 South Vermont Ave.
Los Angeles 90044

Victor Valley Beauty College
16424 Victor St.
Victorville 92392

Vintage Academy of Hair Design, Inc.
2110 Main St.
Napa 94559

Wayne's College of Beauty
1271 North Main St.
Salinas 93906

Wayne's College of Beauty
189 Walnut Ave.
Santa Cruz 95060

Wayne's College of Beauty, Watsonville
1119 Freedom Blvd.
Watsonville 95076

Western Beauty College
439 South Western Ave.
Los Angeles 90005

Westgate Beauty College
1600 Saratoga Ave.
San Jose 95129

Willow Glen Beauty College
1045 Willow St.
San Jose 95125

Yamano Beauty College
6111 Wilshire Blvd.
Los Angeles 90048

Zenzi's Beauty College, Inc.
677 Portola Dr.
San Francisco 94127

COLORADO

Academy of Beauty Culture
2992 North Ave.
Grand Junction 81501

Colorado Beauty College III
2415 Fremont Dr.
Canon City 81212

Glenwood Beauty Academy
51241 Hwy. 6 and 24
Glenwood Springs 81601

Hair Dynamics Education Center
6464 South College
Fort Collins 80525

Hair Dynamics Education Center II
6572 South Broadway
Littleton 80121

Michael Taylor Institute of
    Hair Design
6520 Wadsworth Blvd.
Arvada 80003

Ultima College of Cosmetology
3049 West 74th Ave.
Westminster 80030

Xenon International School of
    Hair Design III
2231 South Peoria
Aurora 80014

CONNECTICUT

Barbizon School
26 Sixth St.
Stamford 06905

Gal-Mar Academy of Hairdressing
59 Washington Ave.
North Haven 06473

DELAWARE

Brandywine Beauty Academy
2018 Naamans Rd.
Wilmington 19810

Schilling-Douglas School of Hair
    Design
70 Amstel Ave.
Newark 19711

FLORIDA

Academy of Community Education
2911 Jacksonville Rd.
Ocala 34471

Advanced-Basic Hair Design
    Training Center
2088 North Courtenay Pkwy.
Merritt Island 32953

Al Stephens Academy for
    Cosmetology
425 Hollywood Mall
Hollywood 33021-6931

Bradenton Beauty Academy, Inc.
3928C Manatee Ave. W
Bradenton 34205

Brevard Community College
1519 Clearlake Rd.
Cocoa 32922

Central Florida Community College
P.O. Box 1388
Ocala 34478

Daytona Beach Community College
1200 Volusia Ave.
Daytona Beach 32114

Florida Community College at
    Jacksonville
501 West State St.
Jacksonville 32202

Gulf Coast Academy of Cosmetology
1538 West 15th St.
Panama City 32401

Hollywood Institute of Beauty Careers
5981 Funston St.
Hollywood 33023

Indian River Community College
3209 Virginia Ave.
Fort Pierce 34981

International Academy of Hairstyling
1599 Tenth Ave.
Vero Beach 32960

La Belle Beauty School
750D West 49th St.
Hialeah 33012

Labelle Beauty Academy
2960 Southwest Eighth St.
Miami 33184

Lake County Area Vocational-Technical
    Center
2001 Kurt St.
Eustis 32726

Largo Beauty Academy
1156 Jasper St. SE
Largo 33544

Lee County Vocational-Technical
    Center
3800 Michigan Ave.
Fort Myers 33916

Loraine's Hairstyling Academy
1012 58th St. N
Saint Petersburg 33710

Manatee Vocational-Technical Center
5603 34th St. W
Bradenton 34210

Manhattan Beauty School
4315 South Manhattan Ave.
Tampa 33611

Margate International School of Beauty
2515 North State Rd. 7
Margate 33063

Miami Lakes Technical Education
    Center
5780 Northwest 158th St.
Miami Lakes 33169

Mr. Arnold's Excellence Beauty School
1415 Washington Ave.
Miami Beach 33139

Mr. Del's Beauty School
340 Havendale Blvd.
Auburndale 33823

Mr. Del's School of Cosmetology
1712-16 West Chase St.
Lakeland 33801

Normandy Beauty School of
    Jacksonville
5373 Lenox Ave.
Jacksonville 32205

North Technical Education Center
7071 Garden Rd.
Riviera Beach 33404

Nouvelle Institute
3271 Northwest Seventh St.
Miami 33125

Professional School of Electrolysis
12760 West Dixie Hwy.
North Miami 33161

Romar Beauty Academy
1608 South Federal Hwy.
Boynton Beach 33435

Saint Augustine Technical Center
2980 Collins Ave.
Saint Augustine 32095

Santa Fe Community College
3000 Northwest 83rd St.
Gainesville 32601

South Technical Education Center
1300 Southwest 30th Ave.
Boynton Beach 33426-9099

Suwannee-Hamilton Area Vocational
    and Adult Center
415 Southwest Pinewood Dr.
Live Oak 32060

Withlacoochee Technical Institute
1201 West Main St.
Inverness 32650

GEORGIA

Albany Technical Institute
1021 Lowe Rd.
Albany 31708

Atlanta Area Technical School
1560 Stewart Ave. SW
Atlanta 30310

Augusta Technical Institute
3116 Deans Bridge Rd.
Augusta 30906

Beauty College of America
1171 Main St.
Forest Park 30050

Ben Hill-Irwin Technical Institute
P.O. Box 1069
Fitzgerald 31750

Carroll Technical Institute
997 South Hwy. 16
Carrollton 30117

Chattahoochee Technical Institute
980 South Cobb Dr.
Marietta 30060-3398

Coosa Valley Technical Institute
112 Hemlock St.
Rome 30161

De Kalb Beauty College
6254 Memorial Dr.
Stone Mountain 30083

Dekalb Technical Institute
495 North Indian Creek Dr.
Clarkston 30021

Derma Clinic Academy of Makeup
    and Skin Care
5600 Roswell Rd.Prado N
Atlanta 30342

Griffin Technical Institute
501 Varsity Rd.
Griffin 30223

Gwinnett Technical Institute
1250 Atkinson Rd., P.O. Box 1505
Lawrenceville 30246-1505

Ila Garmon Beauty College
4643 Lawrenceville Hwy.
Lilburn 30247

International School of Skin and
    Nailcare
5600 Roswell Rd. NE
Atlanta 30342

Macon Beauty School
630 North Ave.
Macon 31211

Macon Technical Institute
3300 Macon Tech Dr.
Macon 31206

Mar-Jans Beauty School, Inc.
2260 Martin Luther King Blvd.
Augusta 30904

Moultrie Area Technical Institute
P.O. Box 520
Moultrie 31776

North Georgia Technical Institute
Georgia Hwy. 197, P.O. Box 65
Clarkesville 30523

Savannah Technical Institute
5717 White Bluff Rd.
Savannah 31499

West Georgia Technical Institute
303 Fort Dr.
La Grange 30240

HAWAII

Hollywood Beauty College
99-084 Kauhale St.
Aiea 96701

Trendsetters Beauty College, Aiea
99-080 Kauhale St.
Aiea 96701

Trendsetters Beauty College, Hilo
88 Kanoelehua Ave.
Hilo 96720-4615

IDAHO

Career Beauty College
57 College Ave.
Rexburg 83440

Continental College of Beauty and
    Barber Styling
3021 North Cole Rd.
Boise 83704

Excelcis Idaho Falls School of
    Cosmetology
800 Park Ave.
Idaho Falls 83402

Headmasters School of Hair Design
317 Coeur D'Alene Ave.
Coeur D'Alene 83814

Headmasters School of Hair Design
602 Main St.
Lewiston 83501

Idaho State University
741 South Seventh Ave.
Pocatello 83209

Lady Helen's School of Beauty
216 13th Ave. S
Nampa 83651

Lady Sandra's Academy of Beauty
25 South 16th St.
Payette 83661

Meridian School of Beauty
48 East Fairview
Meridian 83642

Mr. Juan's College of Hair Design
577 Lynwood Mall
Twin Falls 83301

Mr. Leon's College of Hair Design
618 South Main St.
Moscow 83843

New Images Academy of Beauty
2757 Broadway
Boise 83706

Razzle Dazzle College of Beauty
214 Holly Shopping Center
Nampa 83651

Sandpoint School of Hair Design
212 North First Ave.
Sandpoint 83864

The School of Hairstyling
257 North Main St.
Pocatello 83204

Superior Western Beauty College
5823 Franklin
Boise 83709

ILLINOIS

Alvareita's College of Cosmetology
333 South Kansas
Edwardsville 62025

Alvareita's College of Cosmetology
5711 Godfrey Rd., Monticello Plaza
    Center
Godfrey 62035

Blue Island School of Cosmetology
1607 West Howard St.
Chicago 60626

Cameo Beauty Academy
9714 South Cicero
Oak Lawn 60453

Cannella School of Hair Design
4269 South Archer Ave.
Chicago 60632

City College of Chicago,
   Truman College
1145 Wilson Ave.
Chicago 60640

Coiffure School of Cosmetology Arts
   and Science, Inc.
402 East Main St.
Belleville 62220

Don Roberts Beauty School
P.O. Box 34
McHenry 60050

Hair Professional Academy of
   Cosmetology
1111 East Lake St.
Streamwood 60103

Hair Professionals Academy
1732 Ogden Ave.
Downers Grove 60515

Hair Professionals Academy of
   Cosmetology
1145 East Butterfield Rd.
Wheaton 60187

Hair Professionals Career College, Inc.
1734 Sycamore Rd.
Dekalb 60115

Hair Professionals School of
   Cosmetology
991 Aurora Ave.
Aurora 60505

Hanover Park College of Beauty Culture
1166 Lake St.
Hanover Park 60103

Haskana Institute of Hair Design
243 West Colfax
Palatine 60067

Hi Fashion Beauty College
201 East College St.
Jacksonville 62650

Illinois Institute of Cosmetology
10321 South Roberts Rd.
Palos Hills 60465

La James College of Hairstyling
485 42nd Ave.
East Moline 61244

Mr. John's School of Cosmetology
304 East Adams St.
Springfield 62701

Mr. John's School of Cosmetology
104 West Main
Urbana 61801

Mr. John's School of Cosmetology and
   Esthetics
1745 East Eldorado
Decatur 62521

Nu-Wave School of Hair Design
14 North McAree Rd.
Waukegan 60085

Pivot Point Beauty School
1791 West Howard St.
Chicago 60626

Pivot Point Beauty School
1530 North Wiley Rd.
Schaumburg 60173-4367

Professionals Choice Hair Design
   Academy
2719 West Jefferson St.
Joliet 60435

Scharfenberg's Beauty Academy
909 North Broadway
Carlinville 62626

Tri-County Beauty Academy
219 North State St.
Litchfield 62056

Virginia's Beauty Academy, Inc.
1429 South Main Village
Jacksonville 62650

INDIANA

Academy Beauty College
113 East Wayne St.
South Bend 46601

Academy of Hair Care, Downtown
1502 East Washington St.
Indianapolis 46201

Academy of Hair Care, Eastgate
7150 East Washington St.
Indianapolis 46219

Academy of Hair Care, Speedway
5734 Crawfordsville Rd.
Indianapolis 46224

Creative Hairstyling Academy, Inc.
2549 Highway Ave.
Highland 46322

A Cut Above Beauty College
437 South Meridian
   Wilgro Shopping Center
Greenwood 46143

Don Roberts Hair Designing Academy
5974 West Ridge Rd.
Gary 46408-1727

Elkhart Beauty College
404 South Main
Elkhart 46514

Evansville Tri-State Beauty College
4920 Tippecanoe
Evansville 47715

Four Winds Academy of Hair Design
121 West Wayne St.
Fort Wayne 46802

Hair Arts Academy
2544 East Third
Bloomington 47401

Hair Fashions By Kaye Beauty College
2605 Shelby St.
Indianapolis 46203

Hair Fashions By Kaye Beauty College
4218 North Post Rd.
Indianapolis 46226

Hair Fashions By Kaye Beauty College
4026 North High School Rd.
Indianapolis 46254

Hair Fashions By Kaye Beauty College
1910 East Conner
Noblesville 46060

House of James, Inc.
6901 East Washington
Indianapolis 46219

House of James, Inc.
831 Main St.
Madison 47250

Huntington Beauty College
442 North Jefferson Park Mall
Huntington 46750

Indiana Cosmetology Academy
3612 West Third
Bloomington 47404

Indiana Cosmetology Academy
1015 Youngstown Shopping Center
Jeffersonville 47130

Indiana Cosmetology Academy, Inc.
115 East Second St.
Seymour 47274

Lafayette Beauty Academy
833 Ferry
Lafayette 47901-1149

Masters of Cosmetology College
1732 Bluffton Rd.
Fort Wayne 46809

Metropolitan Beauty Academy
110 West Washington St.
Lebanon 46052

Michigan City Beauty College
3309 South Franklin St.
Michigan City 46360

PJ's College of Cosmetology
1414 Blackiston Mill Rd.
Clarksville 47129

PJ's College of Cosmetology
113 North Washington St.
Crawfordsville 47933

PJ's College of Cosmetology
1400 West Main St.
Greenfield 46140

PJ's College of Cosmetology
5539 South Madison Ave.
Indianapolis 46227

PJ's College of Cosmetology
3023 South Lafountain
Kokomo 46901

PJ's College of Cosmetology
2006 North Walnut St.
Muncie 47303

PJ's College of Cosmetology
2026 Stafford Rd.
Plainfield 46168

PJ's College of Cosmetology
115 North Ninth St.
Richmond 47374

Tri-State Beauty School
701 Fairway Dr.
Evansville 47710

Vogue School of Beauty Culture
301 Lincoln Way W
Mishawaka 46544

Wright Beauty College
64 West Market
Wabash 46992

IOWA

Bernel College of Cosmetology
114 Fifth St.
Ames 50010

Bill Hill's College of Cosmetology
620 East Kimberly
Davenport 52807

Capri Cosmetology College
315 Second Ave. SE
Cedar Rapids 52401

Capri Cosmetology College
1815 East Kimberly Rd.
Davenport 52807

Dayton's School of Hair Design
315 North Main St.
Burlington 52601

Faust Institute of Cosmetology
502 Erie St., P.O. Box 29
Storm Lake 50588

Hair Tech School of Cosmetology
402 West Montgomery St.
Creston 50801-2206

Institute of Cosmetology Arts
421 North Fourth St.
Burlington 52601-5229

Iowa School Beauty Academy
609 West Second St.
Ottumwa 52501

Iowa School of Beauty
3305 70th St.
Des Moines 50322

Iowa School of Beauty
112 Nicholas Dr.
Marshalltown 50158

La James College of Hairstyling
6222 University Ave.
Cedar Falls 50613

La James College of Hairstyling
211 West 53rd St.
Davenport 52807

La James College of Hairstyling
6336 Hickman Rd.
Des Moines 50322

La James College of Hairstyling
227 East Market-Brewery Square
Iowa City 52240

La James College of Hairstyling
   and Cosmetology
2604 First Ave. S
Fort Dodge 50501

La James College of Hairstyling
   and Cosmetology
24 Second St. NE
Mason City 50401

La James College of Hairstyling
   and Cosmetology
2000 East Ridgeway
Waterloo 50704

Le Mars Beauty College
128 Central Ave. SE
Le Mars 51031

Professional Academy of Sciences
   and Beauty, Ltd.
139-½ Fifth Ave. S
Clinton 52732-4105

Professional Cosmetology Institute
627 Main St.
Ames 50010

Southwest Iowa Cosmetology College
504 West Lowell Ave.
P.O. Box 512
Shenandoah 51601

Stewart School of Hairstyling
2719 East Hwy. 6
Council Bluffs 51503

Stewart School of Hairstyling
710 Pierce St.
Sioux City 51101

KANSAS

Crums Beauty College
512 Poyntz Ave.
Manhattan 66502

Dodge City Community College
2501 North 14th Ave.
Dodge City 67801

Fort Scott Community College
2108 South Horton
Fort Scott 66701

Hays Academy of Hair Design
119 West Tenth St.
Hays 67601

Kansas City Area Vocational Technical
   School
2220 North 59th St.
Kansas City 66104

Kansas School of Hair Styling
1207 East Douglas
Wichita 67211

Liberal Academy of Hair Design
530 South Kansas
Liberal 67901

Mission Hairdressing Academy
5855 Beverly Ave.
Shawnee Mission 66202

KENTUCKY

Academy of Cosmetology
111 West Second St.
Maysville 41056-1201

Ashland School of Beauty Culture
1653 Greenup Ave.
Ashland 41101

Barrett and Company School of Hair
   Design
973 Kimberly Square
Nicholasville 40356

Central Beauty School
Doctors' Building, South First St.
Central City 42330

Collins School of Cosmetology
111 West Chester Ave.
P.O. Box 1370
Middlesboro 40965

Cumberland Beauty College
371 Langdon St.
Somerset 42501

Donta School of Beauty Culture
515 West Oak St.
Louisville 40203

Donta School of Beauty Culture
8314 Preston Hwy.
Louisville 40219

East Kentucky Beauty School
329 Main St.
Pikeville 41501

Eastern School of Hair Design
451 Big Hill Ave.
Richmond 40475

E-Town Beauty School
308 North Miles St.
Elizabethtown 42701

Ezell's Beauty School
306 North Fourth St.
Murray 42071

The Hair Design School
7285 Turfway Rd.
Florence 41042

The Hair Design School
1049 Bardstown Rd.
Louisville 40204

The Hair Design School
3968 Park Dr.
Louisville 40216

The Hair Design School
4160 Bardstown Rd.
Louisville 40218

The Hair Design School
640 Knox Blvd.
Radcliff 40160

Heads Beauty College of Providence
105 East Main St.
Providence 42450

Heads West Kentucky Beauty School
Brairwood Shopping Center
Madisonville 42431

Jenny Lea Academy of Cosmetology
110 Cumberland Ave.
Harlan 40831

Jenny Lea Academy of Cosmetology
Parkway Plaza
Whitesburg 41858

Kaufman's Beauty School
701 East High St.
Lexington 40502

Kentucky Technical, Daviess County
  Vocational Technical School
1901 Southeastern Pkwy.
Owensboro 42303

Lexington Beauty College
1830 East Picadome Park
Lexington 40503

Madisonville Beauty College
55 Union St.
Madisonville 42431

New Image Careers, Inc.
301 South Main
Corbin 40701

Northern Kentucky State Vocational-
  Technical School
1025 Amsterdam Rd.
Covington 41011

Nutek Academy of Beauty, Inc.
Mount Sterling Plaza
Mount Sterling 40353

Paducah Beauty School
124 South Fourth St.
Paducah 42001

Pat Wilson's Beauty School
326 North Main
Henderson 42420

PJ's College of Cosmetology
Western Gateway Shopping Center
Bowling Green 42101

PJ's College of Cosmetology
124 West Washington
Glasgow 42141

Roy's of Louisville Beauty Academy
151 Chenoweth Ln.
Louisville 40207

Roy's of Louisville Beauty Academy
5200 Dixie Hwy.
Louisville 40216

Somerset Beauty College
212 East Mount Vernon
Somerset 42501

Southeast School of Cosmetology
23 Manchester Square
P.O. Box 493
Manchester 40962

State Beauty School
107-109 North Central Ave.
Campbellsville 42718

Trend Setters Academy
7283 Dixie Hwy.
Louisville 40258

Trend Setters Academy of Beauty
  Culture
622B Westport Rd.
Elizabethtown 42701

Tri-State Beauty Academy, Inc.
219 West Main St.
Morehead 40351

Winchester Beauty College
101 South Main
Winchester 40391

LOUISIANA

Academy of Creative Hair Design
4560 Hwy. 1
Raceland 70394

Alexandria Academy of Beauty
321 Cane River Mall
Natchitoches 71457

Alexandria Academy of Beauty Culture
2305 Rapides Ave.
Alexandria 71301

Art of Beauty College
989B Mahlon
De Ridder 70634

The Art of Beauty College
1409 South Fourth St.
Leesville 71446

Cosmetology Training Center
2516 Johnston St.
Lafayette 70503

Dee Jay's School of Beauty
5131 Government St.
Baton Rouge 70806

Denham Springs Beauty School
923 Florida Blvd.
Denham Springs 70726

Jocelyn Daspit Beauty Colleges, Inc.
3204 Independence St.
Metairie 70006

Joclyn Daspit Beauty College
507 South Cypress St.
Hammond 70401

John Jay Beauty College
2844 Tennessee Ave.
Kenner 70062

John Jay Charm and Beauty College
540 Robert E Lee Blvd.
New Orleans 70124

John Jay Charm and Beauty College
3144 Pontchatrain Dr.
Slidell 70458

Larry's Academy of Hairstyling
511 Main St.
Patterson 70392

Moler Beauty College
59 West Bank Expwy.
Gretna 70053

Moler Beauty College
1919 Veterans Hwy.
Kenner 70062

Moler Beauty College
1975 North Causeway Blvd.
Mandeville 70448

Moler Beauty College
2940 Canal St.
New Orleans 70119

Pat Goin's Benton Road Beauty School
1701 Old Minden Rd.
Bossier City 71111

Pat Goin's Minden Beauty School
906 Homer Rd.
Minden 71055

Pat Goin's Monroe Beauty School
3140 Louisville Ave.
Monroe 71201

Pat Goin's Ruston Beauty School
213 West Alabama Ave.
Ruston 71270

Pat Goin's Shreveport Beauty School
6363 Hearne Ave.
Shreveport 71108

Pineville Beauty School
1008 Main St.
Pineville 71360

Ronnie & Dorman's School of Hair
  Design
2002 Johnston St.
Lafayette 70503

Sinclair Career College
3901 Tulane Ave.
New Orleans 70119

Slidell Academy of Creative Hair
  Design
629 Carolla Ave.
Slidell 70458

South Louisiana Beauty College
300 Howard Ave.
Houma 70363

Stage One, The Hair School
3505 Fifth Ave.
Lake Charles 70605

Stevenson's Academy of Hair Design
401 Opelousas St.
New Orleans 70114

Stevenson's Academy of Hair Design
2039 Lapeyrouse St.
New Orleans 70116

MAINE

Headhunter II School of Hair Design
26 Forest Ave.
Portland 04101

Main Street Academy of Hair Design
224 State St.
Brewer 04412

MARYLAND

Aspen Beauty Academy
13639 Georgia Ave.
Silver Spring 20906

Baltimore Studio of Hair Design
18 North Howard St.
Baltimore 21201

Gordon Phillips Beauty School
118 North Liberty St.
Baltimore 21204

Maryland Beauty Academy
10355 Reisterstown Rd.
Owings Mills 21117

Maryland Beauty Academy of Essex
505 Eastern Blvd.
Essex 21221

Northwest Beauty School
6860 Reisterstown Rd.
Baltimore 21215

Rockville Beauty Academy
808 Baltimore Rd.
Rockville 20851

Total Dimension School of Hair Design
2075 Great Mills Rd., P.O. Box 97
Lexington Park 20653-0097

MASSACHUSETTS

Blaine the Hair and Beauty School
314 Moody St.
Waltham 02154

Blue Hills Regional Technical School
800 Randolph St.
Canton 02021

Essex Agricultural-Technical Institute
562 Maple St., P.O. Box 562
Hathorne 01937

Lowell Academy of Hairdressing
136 Central St.
Lowell 01852

New England Hair Academy
492-500 Main St.
Malden 02148

Quincy Beauty Academy
30 Franklin St.
Quincy 02169

Springfield Technical Community
  College
Armory Square
Springfield 01105

MICHIGAN

Alpenas Hollywood School of Beauty
1036 U.S. 23 N
Alpena 49707

American College of Beauty Culture
762 West Main St.
Kalamazoo 49007

Bruno Academy of Beauty
22065 Michigan Ave.
Dearborn 48124

Cadillac Academy of Beauty
205 North Mitchell
Cadillac 49601

Chic University of Cosmetology
1735 Four Mile NE
Grand Rapids 49505

Chic University of Cosmetology
103 West Main Mall
Kalamazoo 49009

Coleman Academy of Beaute
26157 Huron River Dr.
Flat Rock 48134

Douglas J Academy of Cosmetology
701 West Jolly Rd.
Lansing 48910-6610

Edward School of Cosmetology, Inc.
G4439 Clio Rd.
Flint 48504

Excel Academies of Cosmetology
2610 Buchanan SW
Wyoming 49548

Fashion School of Beauty
49648 Van Dyke
Utica 48317

Fenton School of Hair Design
1149 North Leroy St.
Fenton 48430

Ferrari's School of Cosmetology
64 West Michigan Mall
Battle Creek 49017

Grand Sorrento Beauty School
13000 Grand River
Detroit 48227

Hairacy College of Cosmetology
204 East Nepessing St.
Lapeer 48446

Hairacy College of Cosmetology,
  Port Huron
2950 Lapeer Rd.
Port Huron 48060

Hillsdale Beauty College
64 Waldron St.
Hillsdale 49242

Howell College of Cosmetology
2373 West Grand River Ave.
Howell 48843

Kalamazoo Beauty Academy
605 South Burdick
Kalamazoo 49007

La Design Beauty School, Inc.
40716 Hayes Rd.
Clinton Township 48038

Lehmann College of Beauty
673 South Main
Plymouth 48170

M J Murphy Beauty College of Jackson
135 South Mechanic St.
Jackson 49201

M J Murphy Beauty College of Lansing
15557 North East St.
Lansing 48906

M J Murphy Beauty College of Midland
120 East Main
Midland 48640

M J Murphy Beauty College of Mount
    Pleasant
201 West Broadway
Mount Pleasant 48858

M J Murphy Beauty College of Saginaw
2650 McCarty
Saginaw 48603

Mauricio School of Cosmetology
16701 East Warren
Detroit 48224

Michigan College of Beauty
15520 West Warren
Detroit 48228

Michigan College of Beauty
15233-½ South Dixie
Monroe 48161

Michigan College of Beauty
39130 Van Dyke
Sterling Heights 48313

Michigan College of Beauty
3498 Rochester Rd.
Troy 48083

Michigan College of Beauty
5620 Dixie Hwy.
Waterford 48329

Michigan College of Beauty Culture
629 South Saginaw St.
Flint 48502

Mr. Bela's School of Cosmetology, Inc.
29475 John R St.
Madison Heights 48071

Northeast Beauty College
12329 Hayes Ave.
Detroit 48205

Northern Michigan University
1401 Presque Isle
Marquette 49855

Northwest Beauty College
22120 Coolidge
Oak Park 48237

Northwestern Beauty Academy
131 East Eighth St.
Traverse City 49684

Petoskey Beauty Academy
1483 North U.S. 31
Petoskey 49770

Port Huron Cosmetology College
330 Quay
Port Huron 48060

Saginaw Beauty Academy
1720 Janes St.
Saginaw 48601

Saint Mary's Institute, Inc. School of
    Cosmetology
119 Maple
Sault Sainte Marie 49783

Sally Esser Beauty School, Garden City
29901 Ford Rd. W
Garden City 48135

Sharps Academy of Hair Styling
115 Main St.
Flushing 48433

Sharps Academy of Hair Styling
8166 North Holly Rd.
Grand Blanc 48439

Sibyl Beauty School
20783 13 Mile Rd.
Roseville 48066

Sylvias Beauty College
14462 Grand River
Detroit 48227

Taylortown School of Beauty
23015 Ecorse Rd.
Taylor 48180

Virginia Farrell Beauty School
24444 West Seven Mile Rd.
Detroit 48219

Virginia Farrell Beauty School
22925 Woodward Ave.
Ferndale 48220

Virginia Farrell Beauty School
1725 Fort St.
Lincoln Park 48146

Virginia Farrell Beauty School
33425 Five Mile Rd.
Livonia 48154

Virginia Farrell Beauty School
23620 Harper Rd.
Saint Clair Shores 48080

Virginia Farrell Beauty School
3709 Metro Place Mall
Wayne 48184

Wayne Starr School of Cosmetology, Inc.
9220 Lapee Rd.
Davison 48423

MINNESOTA

Avante School of Cosmetology
1650 White Bear Ave.
Saint Paul 55106

Cosmetology Careers Unlimited, Duluth
121 West Superior St.
Duluth 55802

Cosmetology Careers Unlimited,
    Duluth West
4031 Grand Ave.
Duluth 55807

Cosmetology Careers Unlimited,
    Hibbing
110 East Howard St.
Hibbing 55746

Cosmetology Careers Unlimited,
    Virginia
233 Chestnut
Virginia 55792

Cosmetology Training Center
306 Central Ave.
Faribault 55021

Cosmetology Training Center
111 East Hickory St.
Mankato 56001

Cosmetology Training Center
5164 Central Ave. NE
Minneapolis 55421

Cosmetology Training Center
1599 North Broadway, Northbrook
    Shopping Center
Rochester 55904

Hairdressers Educational Center
210 East Third St.
Fairmont 56031

Horst Education Center
400 Central Ave. SE
Minneapolis 55414

Hutchinson-Willmar Technical College,
    Willmar Campus
P.O. Box 1097
Willmar 56201

Minnesota Cosmetology Education
    Center, Inc.
704 Marie Ave. E
South Saint Paul 55075

Model College of Hair Design
201 Eighth Ave. S
Saint Cloud 56301

Northwest Technical College, Wadena
405 Southwest Colfax Ave.
P.O. Box 566
Wadena 56482

Oliver Thein Beauty School
150 Cobblestone Ln.
Burnsville 55337

Regency Beauty Academy
40 Hwy. 10
Blaine 55434

Rita's-Moorhead Beauty College
17 South Fourth St.
Moorhead 56560

Saint Cloud Regency Beauty Academy
912 Saint Germain St. W
Saint Cloud 56301

Saint Paul Technical College
235 Marshall Ave.
Saint Paul 55102

Scot Lewis Beauty School
6406 Bass Lake Rd.
Crystal 55428

Scot Lewis-Florian Scientific School
    of Cosmetology
9801 James Circle
Bloomington 55431

Stewart School of Hairstyling
7831 Brooklyn Blvd.
Brooklyn Park 55445

MISSISSIPPI

Advanced School of Cosmetology, Inc.
6B Morgantown Rd.
Natchez 39120

American Beauty College
15275 Lemoyne Blvd.
Biloxi 39532

American Beauty College
2200 25th Ave.
Gulfport 39501

American Beauty College
703A Hwy. 90
Waveland 39576

Chris Beauty College
1265 Pass Rd.
Gulfport 39501

Creations College of Cosmetology
2419 West Main St.
Tupelo 38803

Final Touch Beauty School
832 Hwy. 19 N
Meridian 39307

Finesse Beauty College, Inc.
57 East Franklin St.
Natchez 39120

Foster's Beauty College
Main St.
Sherman 38869

Foster's Cosmetology College
1815 Hwy. 15 N
Ripley 38663

Geigher's School of Cosmetology
600 North 26th Ave.
Hattiesburg 39401

Gibson Barber and Beauty College
120 East Main St.
West Point 39773

Institute for Cosmetology Sciences
Rte. 6, P.O. Box 46
Corinth 38834

John's Cosmetology School
102 Broad St.
Hattiesburg 39401

Mississippi College of Beauty Culture
732 Sawmill Rd.
Laurel 39440

Nita's Beauty College
100 Bankhead St.
New Albany 38652

Northwest Mississippi Community
    College
Hwy. 51 N
Senatobia 38668

Pascagoula Beauty Academy
3425 Denny Ave.
Pascagoula 39581

The Shirley Little Academy of
    Cosmetology
4725 I-55 N
Jackson 39206

MISSOURI

Abbott Academy of Cosmetology
    Arts and Sciences
191 Mid Rivers Mall Dr. W
Saint Peter's 63376

Adam & Eve College of Cosmetology,
    Inc.
16224 East 24 Hwy.
Independence 64056

Aline Jefferson Beauty Academy
3611 East 27th St.
Kansas City 64127

Artistic School of Hair Design
One Grandview Park Dr.
Arnold 63010

Beauty International Hair Design
9729 Saint Charles Rock Rd.
Saint Louis 63114

Chillicothe Beauty Academy
505 Elm
Chillicothe 64601

Evans Academy of Beauty Arts and
    Sciences
209 East Center St.
Sikeston 63801

Grabber School of Hair Design
14560 Manchester
Ballwin 63011

Grandview Beauty College
1521 Main St.
Grandview 64030

Independence College of Cosmetology
815 West 23rd St.
Independence 64055

Jerry's School of Hairstyling
217 North Ninth St.
Columbia 65201

Kirksville College of Cosmetology
119 North Elson St.
Kirksville 63501

La Plante School of Hairstyling
778 North New Ballas Rd.
Saint Louis 63141

Martinez School of Cosmetology
248-½ East Broadway
Excelsior Springs 64024

Merrell University of Beauty Arts
    and Science
1101R Southwest Blvd.
Jefferson City 65109

Neosho Beauty College
116 North Wood St.
Neosho 64850

Northwest Missouri Community College
4315 Pickett Rd.
Saint Joseph 64503-1635

Patsy and Rob's Academy of Beauty
11977 Saint Charles Rock Rd.
Bridgeton 63044

Saint Louis Institute of Electrology
12166 Old Big Bend
Saint Louis 63122

Sainte Genevieve Beauty College
755 Market St.
Sainte Genevieve 63670

Salem College of Hairstyling
Crossroad Shopping Center
Salem 65560

Sikeston Beauty College
127 Kingswau Mall
Sikeston 63801

Stage One
904 Broadway
Cape Girardeau 63701

Stage One, The Hair School
1304 North Pine St.
Rolla 65401

MONTANA

Academy of Cosmetology
133 West Mendenhall
Bozeman 59715

Butte Academy of Beauty Culture
303 West Park St.
Butte 59701

College of Coiffure Art, Ltd.
603 24th St. W
Billings 59102

Dahl's College of Beauty, Inc.
716 Central Ave.
Great Falls 59401

Maddio's Hairstyling and Cosmetology
College
827 North Main
Helena 59601

Mr. Rich's Beauty College
1805 South Ave. W
Missoula 59801

NEBRASKA

Bahner College of Hairstyling
210 West Fourth St.
Grand Island 68801

Capitol Beauty School, Inc., South
3339 L St.
Omaha 68107

Capitol School of Hairstyling West
2819 South 125th Ave.
Omaha 68144

Columbus Beauty School
2719 13th St.
Columbus 68601

Joseph's College of Beauty
618 Court St.
Beatrice 68310

Joseph's College of Beauty
2250 North Webb Rd.
Grand Island 68803

Joseph's College of Beauty
828 West Second St.
Hastings 68901

Joseph's College of Beauty
2241 O St.
Lincoln 68510

Joseph's College of Beauty
202 Madison Ave.
Norfolk 68701

Joseph's College of Beauty
107 West Sixth St.
North Platte 69101

Joseph's of Kearney School of Hair
Design
2213 Central Ave.
Kearney 68847

McCook Beauty Academy
201 East C St.
McCook 69001

Stewart School of Hairstyling
1849 North 73rd St.
Omaha 68114

Xenon International School of Hair
Design II, Inc.
333 South 78th St.
Omaha 68114

NEVADA

Academy of Hair Design
4445 West Charleston Blvd.
Las Vegas 89102

American Academy for Career
Education
3120 East Desert Inn Rd.
Las Vegas 89121

Carson City Beauty Academy
2531 North Carson St.
Carson 89706

Jerrytone School of Beauty Culture
1110 East Charleston Blvd.
Las Vegas 89104

Marinello Schools of Beauty
953 East Sahara
Las Vegas 89104

Northern Nevada Beauty Academy
816 Holman Way
Sparks 89431

Prater Way College of Beauty
1627 Prater Way
Sparks 89431

Silver State Beauty College, Inc.
588 North McCarran Blvd.
Sparks 89431

Southern Nevada University of
Cosmetology
3430 East Tropicana Ave.
Las Vegas 89121

NEW JERSEY

Capri Institute of Hair Design
527 Rte. 202 N
Raritan 08869

European Academy of Cosmetology
1126 Morris Ave.
Union 07083

Franklin School of Cosmetology
1210 East Grand St.
Elizabeth 07201

Gordon Phillips School of Beauty
Culture
729 Haddon Ave.
Collingswood 08108

New Horizon Institute of Cosmetology,
Inc.
5518 Bergenline Ave.
West New York 07093

Vineland Academy of Beauty Culture
525 North Delsea Dr.
Vineland 08360

NEW MEXICO

Aladdin Beauty College 22
108 South Union Ave.
Roswell 88201

De Wolff College Hair Styling and
Cosmetology
6405 Lomas NE
Albuquerque 87110

Eddy County Beauty College
1115 West Mermod St.
Carlsbad 88220

Heights Beauty College
3804 Central Ave. SE
Albuquerque 87108

Heights Beauty College, South
3044 Isleta Blvd. SW
Albuquerque 87105

Hollywood Beauty School
7915 Menaul Blvd. NE
Albuquerque 87110

Monte's Academy of Cosmetology 1
1515 Florida
Alamagordo 88310

Monte's Academy of Cosmetology 2
1306 Schofield Ln.
Farmington 87401

Montrose Beauty College, Inc.
4020 Peggy Rd.
Rio Rancho 87124

Mr. John's Academy of Beauty College
626 East Main St.
Farmington 87401

Olympian University of Cosmetology
1810 East Tenth St.
Alamogordo 88310

NEW YORK

Berkowits School of Electrolysis
107-25 Metrop Ave.
Forest Hills 11375

Continental School of Beauty Culture
515 North Union St.
Olean 14760

Gloria Francis School of Makeup
Artistry, Ltd.
Two Nelson Ave.
Hicksville 11801

Headpeople School of Hair Design
27 South Middletown Rd.
Nanuet 10954

Triple Cities School of Beauty Culture
Five Court St.
Binghamton 13901

Troy School of Beauty Culture
86 Congress St.
Troy 12180

NORTH CAROLINA

Alpha Beauty School, Asheville
85 Tunnel Rd., Innsbruck Mall
Asheville 28805

Brand's College of Beauty Culture
4900B Old Pineville Rd.
Charlotte 28217

Carolina Beauty College 2
801 English Rd.
High Point 27260

Carolina Beauty College 4
North Park Mall, 5430-0 North Tryon St.
Charlotte 28213

Carolina Beauty College 5
244 Front St.
Burlington 27215

Carolina Beauty College 6
501 South St.
Mount Airy 27030

Carolina Beauty College 7
123 Berry St.
Statesville 28677

Carolina Beauty College 8
2001 East Wendover Ave.
Greensboro 27405

Carolina Beauty College 9
810 East Winston Rd.
Lexington 27292

Carolina Beauty College 10
1483B East Franklin Blvd.
Gastonia 28053

Carolina Beauty College 13
338 North Main St.
Kennersville 27284

Carolina Beauty College 14
930 Floyd St.
Kannapolis 28081

Carolina Beauty College 15
1902 South Main St.
Salisbury 28144-6714

Carolina Beauty College 16
231 North Lafayette St.
Shelby 28150

Carolina Beauty College 17
1201 Stafford St.
Monroe 28110

Carolina Beauty College 20
1253-24 Corporation Pkwy.
Winston-Salem 27127

Mitchell's Hairstyling Academy
222 Tallywood Shopping Center
Fayetteville 28303

Mr. David's School of Hair Design
4348 Market St.
Wilmington 28403

Plaza School of Beauty Culture
1419-½ Central Ave.
Charlotte 28205

Robeson Community College
P.O. Box 1420
Lumberton 28359

Rowan-Cabarrus Community College
P.O. Box 1595
Salisbury 28145-1595

Vance-Granville Community College
State Rd. 1126, P.O. Box 917
Henderson 27536

Wilson Technical Community College
902 Herring Ave.
Wilson 27893

NORTH DAKOTA

Hairdesigners Academy
2011 South Washington St.
Grand Forks 58201

Headquarters Academy of Hair Design
108 South Main St.
Minot 58701

Josef's School of Hair Design
202 East Broadway
Bismarck 58501

Josef's School of Hair Design
627 North P Ave.
Fargo 58102

Josef's School of Hair Design
21 East Central Ave.
Minot 58701

Road Hairstyling College
124 North Fourth St.
Bismarck 58501

Town and Country Beauty College
312 Second Ave. SW
P.O. Box 350
Jamestown 58402-0350

OHIO

3-B School of Beauty
11 South Third St.
Newark 43055

Academy of Hair Design
1440 Whipple Ave.
Canton 44708

Alliance Beauty College
1917 South Union Ave.
P.O. Box 3215
Alliance 44601

Boardman Beauty School
7110 Market St.
Youngstown 44512

Carousel Beauty College
125 East Second St.
Dayton 45402

Carousel Beauty College
1220 Main St.
Hamilton 45013

Carousel Beauty College
633 South Breiel Blvd.
Middletown 45042

Carousel of Miami Valley Beauty
College
7809 Waynetowne Blvd.
Huber Heights 45424

Continental Beauty School
417 North Wayne St., P.O. Box 309
Piqua 45356

Fredericks Beauty College
226 North Main St.
Lima 45801

Gerber's Akron Beauty School
1686 West Market St.
Akron 44313

Grace College of Cosmetology
6807 Pearl Rd.
Middleburg Heights 44130

Hair Academy
6000 Mahoning Ave.
Youngstown 44515

Inner State Beauty School
5150 Mayfield Rd.
Lyndhurst 44124

International Academy of Hair Design
8419 Colerain Ave.
Cincinnati 45239

International Beauty School
1285 Som Center Rd.
Mayfield Heights 44124

Lewis Weinberger and Hill Beauty
    School
128 East Fourth St.
East Liverpool 43920

M Lords Lakewood School of
    Cosmetology
15616 Detroit Rd.
Lakewood 44107

Ma Chere Hair Style Academy, Inc.
1010 West Sylvania Ave.
Toledo 43612

Moler Hollywood Beauty College
985 Lila Ave.
Milford 45150

Moler Pichens Beauty College
6121B Dixie Hwy.
Fairfield 45014

Moore University of Hair Design
6011 Montgomery Rd.
Cincinnati 45213

Nationwide Beauty Academies, Inc.
898 South Hamilton Rd.
Columbus 43213

Nationwide Beauty Academy
3120 Olentangy River Rd.
Columbus 43202

Nationwide Beauty Academy
88 Wilson Rd.
Columbus 43204

Nationwide Beauty Academy
5050 North High St.
Columbus 43214

Ohio State School of Cosmetology
3717 South High St.
Columbus 43207

Ohio State School of Cosmetology
1416 West Broad St.
Columbus 43222

Ohio State School of Cosmetology
5970 Westerville Rd.
Westerville 43081

Ohio State School of Cosmetology &
    Experts Barber School
4390 Karl Rd.
Columbus 43224

Ohio State School of Cosmetology, East
6320 East Livingston Ave.
Reynoldsburg 43068

Paramount Beauty Academy
917 Gallia St.
Portsmouth 45662

Raphael's School of Beauty Culture
5555 Youngstown Warren Rd.
Niles 44446

Raphael's School of Beauty Culture
330 East State St.
Salem 44460

Raphael's School of Beauty Culture, Inc.
2668 Mahoning Ave.
Warren 44483

Raphael's School of Beauty Culture, Inc.
3107-½ Belmont Ave.
Youngstown 44505

Riggs Lemar Beauty College
3464 Hudson Dr.
Cuyahoga Falls 44221

Rocco's School of Hair Skin and Nails
36212 Euclid Ave.
Willoughby 44094

Skelly Beauty Academy
5585 Pearl Rd.
Parma 44129

State Beauty Academy
137 East Center St.
Marion 43302

Tiffin Academy of Hair Design
104 East Market St.
Tiffin 44883

Toledo Academy of Beauty Culture, East
2592 Woodville Rd.
Northwood 43619

Toledo Academy of Beauty Culture,
    North
5020 Lewis Ave.
Toledo 43612

Toledo Academy of Beauty Culture,
    South
1554 South Byrne Rd., Glenbyrne
    Center
Toledo 43614

Tusco Beauty School
814 Blvd.
Dover 44622

Western Hills School of Beauty and
    Hair Design
6490 Glenway
Cincinnati 45211

OKLAHOMA

Aladdin Beauty College 11
1312 West Lee
Lawton 73501

Alva Beauty Academy
503 Oklahoma Blvd.
Alva 73717

American Beauty Institute
123 West Main
Ardmore 73401

Bartlesville Beauty College
622 East Frank Phillips Blvd.
Bartlesville 74003

Beauty Technical College, Inc.
1600 Downing, P.O. Box 1506
Tahlequah 74465

Broken Arrow Beauty College
400 South Elm Place
Broken Arrow 74012

Central Oklahoma Area Vocational
    Technical School
Three Court Circle
Drumright 74030

Central State Beauty Academy
8442 Northwest Expwy.
Oklahoma City 73162

Claremore Beauty College
200 North Cherokee
Claremore 74017

Enid Beauty College
1601 East Broadway
Enid 73701

Francis Tuttle Area Vocational-
    Technical Center
12777 North Rockwell Ave.
Oklahoma City 73142-2789

Hollywood Cosmetology Center
1708 West Lindsey
Norman 73069

Metro Tech Vocational Technical Center
1900 Springlake Dr.
Oklahoma City 73111

Sand Springs Beauty College
P.O. Box 504
Sand Springs 74063

Shampoo Academy of Hair
2630 West Britton Rd.
Oklahoma City 73120

Shawnee School of Cosmetology
400 East Highland
Shawnee 74801

Southern School of Beauty
140 West Main St.
Durant 74701

Virgil's Beauty College
111 South Ninth St.
Muskogee 74401-6802

Woodward Beauty College
502 Texas
Woodward 73801

OREGON

A'Arts College of Beauty
2101 Bailey Hill Rd.
Eugene 97405

Academy of Hair Design, Inc.
305 Court NE
Salem 97301

Artistic School of Hair Design
130 Southeast K St., City Center Plaza
Grants Pass 97526

Artistic School of Hair Design
2370 Jacksonville Hwy.
Medford 97501

Astoria Beauty College
1180 Commercial St.
Astoria 97103

Beaumonde College of Beauty and Hair
    Design
1026 Southwest Salmon
Portland 97204

College of Cosmetology
357 East Main St.
Klamath Falls 97601

College of Hair Design Careers
3322 Lancaster Dr. NE
Salem 97305-1354

The Dalles Academy of Hair Design
415 East Second St.
The Dalles 97058

Edward Wadsworth Institute for Hair
    Design
3301 Northeast Sandy Blvd.
Portland 97232

Lady Helen's School of Beauty
1482 West Park Plaza
Ontario 97914

Milwaukie Beauty School
6128 Southeast King Rd.
Milwaukie 97222

Pendleton College of Hair Design
326 Main St.
Pendleton 97801

Phagan's Central Oregon Beauty
    College
355 Northeast Second
Bend 97701

Phagan's Gateway College of Beauty
11131 Northeast Halsey
Portland 97220

Phagan's Medford Beauty School
2316 Poplar Dr.
Medford 97504

Phagan's School of Beauty
622 Lancaster NE
Salem 97301

Phagan's School of Hair Design
16550 Southeast McLoughlin
Portland 97267

Phagan's Tigard Beauty School
8820 Southwest Center
Tigard 97223

Roseburg Beauty College
700 Southeast Stephens St.
Roseburg 97470

Springfield College of Beauty
727 Main St.
Springfield 97477

PENNSYLVANIA

Academy of Creative Hair Design
Narrows Shopping Center
Edwardsville 18704

Academy of Hair Design, Inc.
Five East Third St.
Bloomsburg 17815

Allentown School of Cosmetology
1921 Union Blvd.
Allentown 18103-1629

Ambler Beauty Academy
50 East Butler Pike
Ambler 19002

Berean Institute
1901 West Girard Ave.
Philadelphia 19130

Bucks County School of Beauty Culture
1761 Bustleton Pike
Feasterville 19047

Clearfield Beauty Academy
22 North Third St.
Clearfield 16830

Empire Beauty School
544 Hamilton St.
Allentown 18101

Empire Beauty School
60 Centre Square
Easton 18042

Empire Beauty School
3941 Jonestown Rd.
Harrisburg 17101

Empire Beauty School
124 West Broad St.
Hazleton 18201

Empire Beauty School
1801 Columbia Ave.
Lancaster 17604

Empire Beauty School
38 South Eighth St.
Lebanon 17042

Empire Beauty School
101 East Market St.
Lewistown 17044

Empire Beauty School
5103 Carlisle Pike
Mechanicsburg 17055

Empire Beauty School
141 High St.
Pottstown 19464

Empire Beauty School
302 North Centre St.
Pottsville 17901

Empire Beauty School
219 Lackawanna Ave.
Scranton 18503

Empire Beauty School
208 West Hamilton St.
State College 16801

Empire Beauty School
448 Market St.
Sunbury 17801

Empire Beauty School
117 South Main St.
Wilkes-Barre 18701

Empire Beauty School
344 West Fourth St.
Williamsport 17701

Empire Beauty School
500 North York Rd.
Willow Grove 19090

Empire Beauty School
132 West Market St.
York 17401

Empire Beauty School
2302 North Fifth St.
Reading 19601

Gordon Phillips School of Beauty
Culture
2838 Street Rd.
Bensalem 19055

Gordon Phillips School of Beauty
Culture
Union Blvd. and Penn Station
Bethlehem 18018

Gordon Phillips School of Beauty
Culture
Seven Downing Center
Downington 19335

Gordon Phillips School of Beauty
Culture
108 West Germantown Pke Hillcrest
Plaza
Norristown 19401

Gordon Phillips School of Beauty
Culture
1101 Chestnut St.
Philadelphia 19107

Gordon Phillips School of Beauty
Culture
7203 Frankford Ave.
Philadelphia 19135

Gordon Phillips School of Beauty
Culture
910 Penn St.
Reading 19602

Gordon Phillips School of Beauty
Culture
37 Garrett Rd.
Upper Darby 19082

Hanover School of Beauty
408B Baltimore St.
Hanover 17331

Lancaster School of Cosmetology
50 Ranck Ave.
Lancaster 17602

Lansdale School of Cosmetology, Inc.
215 West Main St.
Lansdale 19446

New Castle School of Beauty Culture
314 Washington St.
New Castle 16101

Pittsburgh Beauty Academy
313 Fifth Ave.
Charleroi 15022

Pittsburgh Beauty Academy
851 Fifth Ave.
New Kensington 15068

Pittsburgh Beauty Academy
415 Smithfield St.
Pittsburgh 15222

Pruonto's Hair Design Institute
705 12th St.
Altoona 16602

Punxy Beauty School
222-224 North Findley St.
Punxsutawney 15767

Randy Rick Beauty Academy
450 Penn St.
Reading 19602

Signature Beauty Academy
129 Charles Ln.
Red Lion 17356

South Hills Beauty Academy
3269 Liberty Ave.
Pittsburgh 15216

Star Beauty Academy
38 West Broad St.
Bethlehem 18018

Stroudsburg School of Cosmetology
100 North Eighth St.
Stroudsburg 18360-1720

Uniontown Beauty Academy
31 Pittsburgh St.
Uniontown 15401

Uniontown Beauty Academy of
Washington
Two South Main St.
Washington 15301

Venus Beauty School
1033 Chester Pike
Sharon Hill 19079

RHODE ISLAND

Arthur Angelo School of Cosmetology
& Hair Design
151 Broadway
Providence 02903

Loretta's School of Cosmetology
1925 Pawtucket Ave.
East Providence 02914

Warwick Academy of Beauty Culture
1800 Post Rd.
Warwick 28860

SOUTH CAROLINA

Alpha Beauty School
Ten Liberty Ln.
Greenville 29607

Alpha Beauty School, Anderson
2619 South Main St.
Anderson 29624

Alpha Beauty School, Seneca
112 East North Second St.
Seneca 29678

Alpha Beauty School, Spartanburg
653 North Church St.
Spartanburg 29301

Betty Stevens Cosmetology Institute
301 Rainbow Dr., P.O. Box 3827
Florence 29501

Chris Logan Career College
P.O. Box 261
Myrtle Beach 29578-0261

Chris Logan Career College
Martintown Plaza
North Augusta 29841

Chris Logan Career College
256 South Pike Rd.
Sumter 29150

SOUTH DAKOTA

Black Hills Beauty College
623 Saint Joe
Rapid City 57701

Headlines Academy of Cosmetology
520 Main St., P.O. Box 8184
Rapid City 57709

Stewart School of Hairstyling
201 South Main St.
Aberdeen 57401

Stewart School of Hairstyling
225 East 11th St.
Sioux Falls 57101

TENNESSEE

Arnold's Beauty School
1179 South Second St.
Milan 38358

Fayetteville Beauty School
201 South Main
Fayetteville 37334-0135

Hair Academy
120 Center Park Dr.
Knoxville 37922

Jon Nave University of Unisex
Cosmetology
5128 Charlotte Ave.
Nashville 37209

Knoxville Institute of Hair Design
1221 North Central
Knoxville 37917

Knoxville State Area Vocational-
Technical School
1100 Liberty St.
Knoxville 37919

McCollum & Ross, The Hair School
1433 Hollywood
Jackson 38301

Memphis Area Vocational-Technical
School
550 Alabama Ave.
Memphis 38105-3799

Mid South School of Beauty
3974 Elvis Presley Blvd.
Memphis 38116

Nashville State Area Vocational
Technical School
100 White Bridge Rd.
Nashville 37209

Nu Wave Hair Academy
140-141 South Dupree
Brownsville 38012

Pazazz Hair School
623 Old Hickory Blvd.
Jackson 38303

Pazazz Hair School
1270 Getwell Rd.
Memphis 38111

Plaza Beauty School
4682 Spottswood
Memphis 38117

Queen City College
1191 Fort Campbell Blvd.
Clarksville 37042

Tennessee School of Beauty
343 Sanderson St.
Alcoa 37701

Tennessee School of Beauty, Inc.
168 Randolph Rd.
Oak Ridge 37830

Tennessee School of Beauty of
Knoxville, Inc.
4551 Kingston Park
Knoxville 37919

Volunteer Beauty School
117 East Court St.
Dyersburg 38024

TEXAS

Aladdin Beauty College 13
203 East Henderson St.
Cleburne 76031

Aladdin Beauty College 17
1720 West Houston
Sherman 75090

Aladdin Beauty College 18
6560 Montana
El Paso 79915

Aladdin Beauty College 2
4011 Rhea Rd.
Wichita Falls 76301

Aladdin Beauty College 21
407 Sunset Dr.
Denton 76201

Aladdin Beauty College 26
1801 Galloway Ave.
Mesquite 75149

Aladdin Beauty College 27
8702 Spring Valley
Dallas 75240

Aladdin Beauty College 29
3044 Clarsville
Paris 75460

Aladdin Beauty College 30
1103 South Josey
Carrollton 75006

Aladdin Beauty College 4
506 West University
Odessa 79760

Aladdin Beauty College 5
793 East Park Row
Arlington 76010

Aladdin Beauty College 8
2940 North First
Abilene 79603

Amarillo College of Hairdressing
East Campus, 2400 Southeast 27th Ave.
Amarillo 79103

American Beauty Academy
354 West Little York Rd.
Houston 77076

American Beauty Academy
304 East Southmore
Pasadena 77502

The Art of Beauty College
138 West Houston St.
Jasper 75951

Baldwin Beauty School 5
3005 South Lamar
Austin 78704

Barrow Beauty School
520 East Front St.
Tyler 75702

Bee County College
3800 Charco Rd.
Beeville 78102

Central Texas College
P.O. Box 1800
Killeen 76540-9990

Charles and Sue's School of Hair Design
1711 Briarcrest Dr.
Bryan 77801

Circle J Beauty School
1611 Spencer Hwy.
South Houston 77587

Classic Beauty Academy
1212D South Frazier St.
Conroe 77301

Conlee College of Cosmetology
402 Quinlan
Kerrville 78028

Cosmetology Career Center
8030 Spring Valley Rd.
Dallas 75240

Dempsey's Beauty College
4661 Concord
Beaumont 77703

Espanolas Beauty College, Inc.
2129 Lockwood Dr.
Houston 77020

Exposito School of Hair Design, Inc.
3710 Mockingbird
Amarillo 79109

Grayson County College
6101 Grayson Dr.
Denison 75020

Greenville Beauty School
2310 Stonewall St.
Greenville 75401

Houston Community College System
22 Waugh Dr.
P.O. Box 7849
Houston 77270-7849

Houston Training School, Woodridge
6969 Gulf Fwy.
Houston 77087

Institute of Cosmetology
434 West Parker at I-45
Houston 77091

International Beauty College
2413 West Airport Fwy.
Irving 75062

Jackson Beauty School
3931 Spencer Hwy.
Pasadena 77504

Jackson Beauty School 2
223 West Main
League City 77573

John Robert Powers School
13601 Preston Rd.
Dallas 75240

John's Beauty College
2120 Texas Ave.
Texas City 77590

Marshall College of Beauty
2100 East End Blvd. N
Marshall 75670

McLennan Community College
1400 College Dr.
Waco 76708

Metroplex Beauty School
519 North Galloway
Mesquite 75149-3405

Metroplex Beauty School 2
113 North Gun Barrel Ln.
Gun Barrel City 75147

National Beauty School
1864 Ave. K
Plano 75074

Neilson Beauty College
416 West Jefferson Blvd.
Dallas 75208

North Harris Montgomery Community
College District
250 North Sam Houston Pkwy. E
Houston 77060

Panola College
West Panola St.
Carthage 75633

San Antonio Beauty College 3
4021 Naco Perrin
San Antonio 78217

San Antonio Beauty College 4
2423 Jamar
San Antonio 78226

Star College of Cosmetology
700 East Whaley
Longview 75601

Star College of Cosmetology 2
3502B South Broadway
Tyler 75701

Texas University of Cosmetology
117 Sayles St.
Abilene 79605

Tri-State Beauty School 1
6800 Gateway E
El Paso 79915

Tri-State Beauty School 2
Two and Three Rushfair Center
El Paso 79924

Tri-State Beauty School 3
5300 Doniphan
El Paso 79932

Trinity Valley Community College
500 South Prairieville
Athens 75751

University of Cosmetology Arts and
Sciences
913 North 13th St.
Harlingen 78550

University of Cosmetology Arts and
Sciences
8401 North Tenth St., P.O. Box 720391
McAllen 78504

USA Hair Academy
2525 North Laurent St.
Victoria 77901

Waco Beauty College
1208 DIH 35 N
Round Rock 78664

Waco Beauty College
2010 South 57th St.
Temple 76504

UTAH

Beau La Reine College of Beauty
1093-½ North Main St.
Logan 84321

Bonn Losse Academy of Hair Artistry
2230 North University Pkwy.
Provo 84604

Continental College of Beauty
2230 South 700 E
Salt Lake City 84106

Evans Hairstyling College
90 West Hoover
Cedar City 84720

Evans Hairstyling College
50 West Center St.
Orem 84057

Evans Hairstyling College
955 East Tabernacle
Saint George 84770

Fran Brown College of Beauty
521 West 600 N
Layton 84041

Fran Brown College of Beauty
460 Second St.
Ogden 84404

Hairitage College of Beauty
5414 South 900 E
Salt Lake City 84117

International Institute of Hair Design
5712 South Redwood Rd.
Taylorsville 84123

Mary Kawakami College of Beauty
336 West Center St.
Provo 84601

Odgen-Weber Applied Technology
Center
559 East AVC Ln.
Ogden 84404-6704

Stacey's Hands of Champions
3733 South 250 W
Ogden 84405

Universal Academy of Hair Design
2344 East 70th S
Salt Lake City 84121

Von Curtis Academy of Hair Design
480 North 900 E
Provo 84606

Von Curtis Academy of Hair Design
3330 South 700 E
Salt Lake City 84106

VERMONT

O'Brien's Training Center
1475 Shelburne Rd.
South Burlington 05403

Whitman's Academy of Hair Design
Landmark Hill, RR 5
P.O. Box 109
Brattleboro 05301

VIRGINIA

ATI Hollywood
3024 Trinkle Ave. NW
Roanoke 24012

ATI Hollywood
1108 Brandon Ave. SW
Roanoke 24015

ATI Hollywood
109 East Main St.
Salem 24153

Graham Webb International Academy
of Hair
2625 Wilson Blvd.
Arlington 22201

Potomac Academy of Hair Design
101 West Broad St.
Falls Church 22046-4202

Ralph's Virginia School of Cosmetology
Forest Plaza West Shopping Center
Lynchburg 24501

Staunton School of Cosmetology
128 East Beverly St.
Staunton 24401

Summit School of Cosmetology
140 South First St.
Wytheville 24382

Victor Beauty Academy
7732D Richmond Hwy.
Alexandria 22306

Virginia School of Hair Design
101 West Queensway
Hampton 23669

Ward's Corner Beauty Academy
216 East Little Creek Rd.
Norfolk 23505

WASHINGTON

Academy of Hair Design
Nine South Wenatchee Ave.
Wenatchee 98801

American Pacific School of Hair Design
North 6414 Division St.
Spokane 99208

Bellingham Technical College
3028 Lindbergh Ave.
Bellingham 98225

BJ's Beauty and Barber College
5237 South Tacoma Way
Tacoma 98409

Christine's Institute of Hair Design
West Ten Mission
Spokane 99205

Cinderella Beauty School
620 Callow Ave. N
Bremerton 98312

Clare's Beauty College
104 North Fourth Ave.
Pasco 99301

Dewitt Beauty School
209 East Wishkah St.
Aberdeen 98520

Everett Plaza Beauty School
607 Southeast Everett Mall
Everett 98208

Gene Juarez Academy of Beauty
10715 Eighth Ave. NE
Seattle 98125

Gene Juarez Academy of Beauty,
Branch Campus
2222 South 314th St.
Federal Way 98003

Gerri's Style Trend Beauty Academy
529 East Broadway
Moses Lake 98837

Glen Dow Academy of Hair Design
West 309 Riverside Ave.
Spokane 99201

Govan Beauty School
314 West Kennewick Ave.
Kennewick 99336

Greenwood Beauty School
8501 Greenwood N
Seattle 98103

The Hair School
3043 Hwy. 101 E
Port Angeles 98362

Kent Beauty School
25725 101st Ave. SE
Kent 98031

Lacey Beauty College
909 Sleater Kinney Rd. 2
Lacey 98503

Magee Brothers Beauty School
8078 East Mill Plain Blvd.
Vancouver 98664

Mount Vernon Beauty School
615 South First St.
Mount Vernon 98273

Ms. BJ's Beauty and Barber College
11510 Meridian S
Puyallup 98373

Paul Mitchell Endorsed Academy of
Cosmetology
14352 Lake City Way NE
Seattle 98125

Phagan's Orchards Beauty School
10411 Northeast Fourth Plain Blvd.
Vancouver 98662

Professional Beauty School
214 South Sixth St.
Sunnyside 98944

Professional Beauty School
112 West Third St., P.O. Box 856
Wapato 98951-0856

Renton Beauty School
2828 Sunset Ln. NE
Renton 98056

Sakie International College of
Cosmetology
221 West Yakima Ave.
Yakima 98902

Stylemaster College of Hair Design
1224 Commerce
Longview 98632

Vancouver School of Beauty
114 West Sixth
Vancouver 98662

Wenatche College of Beauty
16 South Wenatchee Ave.
Wenatchee 98801

West Olympia Beauty College
2703 Capitol Mall Dr. Southwest
Olympia 98502-5095

Whatcom School of Cosmetology
208 West Holly
Bellingham 98225

WEST VIRGINIA

Appalachian Beauty School
U.S. Hwy. 119, P.O. Box 2485
Williamson 25661

Beckley Beauty Academy
109 South Fayette St.
Beckley 25801

Capital City Beauty College
225 Hale St.
Charleston 25301

Charleston School of Beauty Culture
210 Capitol St.
Charleston 25301

Huntington School of Beauty Culture,
Branch Campus
5181 Rte. 60, East Hills Mall
Huntington 25705

International Beauty School 4
329 South Queen St.
Martinsburg 25401

Little French Beauty Academy
3230 Cumberland Rd.
Bluefield 24701

Morgantown Beauty College, Inc.
276 Walnut St.
Morgantown 26505

Weirton Beauty Academy
3105 Main St.
Weirton 26062

Wheeling College of Hair Design
1122 Main St.
Wheeling 26003

WISCONSIN

Advanced Institute of Hair Design
5655 South 27th St.
Milwakee 53221

Advanced Institute of Hair Design
11010 West Hampton Ave.
Milwaukee 53225

Capri College
6414 Odana Rd.
Madison 53719

Geneva Academy of Barber Styling &
Beauty Culture
520 Broad St.
Lake Geneva 53147

Gill Technical Academy of Hair Design
West College Ave.
Appleton 54911

JGM Cosmetology Institute
322 State St.
Beloit 53511

John Robert Powers School
700 North Water St.
Milwaukee 53202

Martin's School of Hair Design
2310 West College Ave.
Appleton 54914

Martin's School of Hair Design
2575 West Mason
Green Bay 54304

Martin's School of Hair Design
620 West Murdock St.
Oshkosh 54901

Martin's School of Hair Design of
  Manitowoc
1034 South 18th St.
Manitowoc 54220

Scot Lewis School
320 Pearl St.
La Crosse 54601

State College of Beauty Culture
7430 Harwood Ave.
Wauwatosa 53213

State College of Beauty Culture, Inc.
527-' Washington St.
Wausau 54403

Wisconsin College of Cosmetology, Inc.
417 Pine St.
Green Bay 54301

WYOMING

Classic School of Hair Design
2133 Garfield St.
Laramie 82070

College of Cosmetology
1211 Douglas Hwy.
Gillette 82716

Cosmetic Arts and Sciences
P.O. Box 1933
Casper 82602

Modern Trend Beauty School
1620 Thomes
Cheyenne 82001

Wright Beauty Academy
207 West 18th St.
Cheyenne 82001

Dog Grooming

ARIZONA

Pedigree Career Institute, Phoenix
  Campus
3037 West Clarendon
Phoenix 85017

Pedigree Professional School for Dog
  Grooming
3781 East Technical Dr.
Tucson 85713

CALIFORNIA

Clipper Ship Grooming School
208372 Roscoe Blvd.
Canoga Park 91306

International Grooming School
3211 West Lincoln Ave.
Anaheim 92801

San Francisco SPCA Dog Grooming
  School
2500 16th St.
San Francisco 94103

FLORIDA

Florida School of Dog Grooming, Inc.
2315 North A St.
Tampa 33609

ILLINOIS

The Academy of Dog Grooming Arts,
  Ltd.
1790 West Algonquin Rd.
Arlington Heights 60005

Midwest School of Dog Grooming
6125-27 North Northwest Hwy.
Chicago 60631

MARYLAND

Maryland School of Dog Grooming, Inc.
8025 13th St.
Silver Spring 20910

MASSACHUSETTS

Pedigree Career Institute
Harbor Mall, Rte. 1A Lynnway
Lynn 01901

MICHIGAN

American School of Dog Grooming
11004 East Nine Mile Rd.
Warren 48089

Master School of Dog Grooming
24335 Plymouth Rd.
Redford 48239

MISSOURI

Central Academy of Dog Grooming
1437 South Morley
Moberly 65270

NEVADA

Nevada Dog Grooming School
1233 East Sahara Ave.
Las Vegas 89104

NEW JERSEY

North Jersey School of Dog Grooming
11A Roosevelt Ave.
Chatham 07928

NEW YORK

M and M School of Dog Grooming
3679 Delaware Ave.
Kenmore 14217

Rochester Institute of Dog Grooming,
  Inc.
2070 East Henrietta Rd.
Rochester 14623

OREGON

Tara Lara Academy of K-9 Hair Design
16037 Southeast McLoughlin Blvd.
Portland 97267

WISCONSIN

Wisconsin School of Professional Pet
  Grooming
34917 Wisconsin Ave.
P.O. Box 175
Okauchee 53069

Electronics and Machine Repair

ALABAMA

Southeast College of Technology
828 Downtowner Loop W
Mobile 36609

ALASKA

University of Alaska, Anchorage
3211 Providence Dr.
Anchorage 99508

ARIZONA

Roberto-Venn School of Luthiery
4011 South 16th St.
Phoenix 85040

ARKANSAS

Northwest Technical Institute
P.O. Box A
Springdale 72765

Quapaw Technical Institute
201 Vo-Tech Dr.
Hot Springs 71913

CALIFORNIA

Antelope Valley College
3041 West Ave. K
Lancaster 93534

California Institute of Locksmithing,
  Inc.
14721 Oxnard St.
Van Nuys 91411

Cerritos College
11110 Alondra Blvd.
Norwalk 90650

College of the Canyons
26455 North Rockwell Canyon Rd.
Santa Clarita 91355

Golden State School
1690 Universe Circle
Oxnard 93033-2441

Los Angeles Training Technical College
400 West Washington Blvd.
Los Angeles 90015-4181

Los Angeles Valley College
5800 Fulton Ave.
Van Nuys 91401

Mission College
3000 Mission College Blvd.
Santa Clara 95054-1897

Practical Schools
900 East Ball Rd.
Anaheim 92805

Purple Heart Veterans Rehabilitation
  Training Center
615 South St.
Sacramento 95814

Riverside Community College
4800 Magnolia Ave.
Riverside 92506-1299

Sacramento City College
3835 Freeport Blvd.
Sacramento 95822

San Joaquin Delta College
5151 Pacific Ave.
Stockton 95207

Santa Barbara City College
721 Cliff Dr.
Santa Barbara 93109-2394

Santa Fe Technical College, Inc.
9820 Jersey Ave.
Santa Fe Springs 90670

Sierra Hi-Tech
7200 Fair Oaks Blvd.
Carmichael 95608

Solano County Community College
  District
4000 Suisun Valley Rd.
Suisun 94585

Southwestern College
900 Otay Lakes Rd.
Chula Vista 92010

Valley Technical Institute
5408 North Blackstone Ave.
Fresno 93710

COLORADO

Colorado Locksmith College, Inc.
4991 West 80th Ave.
Westminster 80030

CONNECTICUT

Baran Institute of Technology
611 Day Hill Rd.
Windsor 06095

Baran Institute of Technology
605 Day Hill Rd.
Windsor 06095

New England Technical Institute of
  Connecticut, Inc.
200 John Downey Dr.
New Britain 06051

FLORIDA

Automotive Transmission School
453 East Okeechobee Rd.
Hialeah 33010

Saint Augustine Technical Center
2980 Collins Ave.
Saint Augustine 32095

Taylor Technical Institute
3233 Hwy. 19 S
Perry 32347

GEORGIA

Albany Technical Institute
1021 Lowe Rd.
Albany 31708

Chattahoochee Technical Institute
980 South Cobb Dr.
Marietta 30060-3398

Gwinnett Technical Institute
1250 Atkinson Rd.
P.O. Box 1505
Lawrenceville 30246-1505

Macon Technical Institute
3300 Macon Tech Dr.
Macon 31206

Middle Georgia Technical Institute
1311 Corder Rd.
Warner Robins 31088

North Georgia Technical Institute
Georgia Hwy. 197
P.O. Box 65
Clarkesville 30523

Okefenokee Technical Institute
1701 Carswell Ave.
Waycross 31501

Swainsboro Technical Institute
201 Kite Rd.
Swainsboro 30401

ILLINOIS

Consumer Electronics Training Center
6239-41 South Western Ave.
Chicago 60636

Coyne American Institute, Inc.
1235 West Fullerton Ave.
Chicago 60614

IOWA

Indian Hills Community College
525 Grandview
Ottumwa 52501

Western Iowa Technical Community
  College
4647 Stone Ave.
P.O. Box 265
Sioux City 51102-0265

KANSAS

Amtech Institute
4011 East 31st St.
Wichita 67210

Butler County Community College
901 South Haverhill Rd.
El Dorado 67042

Kansas City Area Vocational Technical
  School
2220 North 59th St.
Kansas City 66104

Kaw Area Vocational-Technical School
5724 Huntoon
Topeka 66604

Liberal Area Vocational Technical
School
P.O. Box 1599
Liberal 67905-1599

Manhattan Area Technical Center
3136 Dickens Ave.
Manhattan 66502

Northwest Kansas Area Vocational
Technical School
P.O. Box 668
Goodland 67735

Salina Area Vocational Technical
School
2562 Scanlan Ave.
Salina 67401

Southeast Kansas Area Vocational
Technical School
Sixth and Roosevelt
Coffeyville 67337

KENTUCKY

Lockmasters, Inc.
5085 Danville Rd.
Nicholasville 40356

Northern Kentucky State Vocational-
Technical School
1025 Amsterdam Rd.
Covington 41011

LOUISIANA

Baton Rouge Regional Technical
Institute
3250 North Acadian Hwy. E
Baton Rouge 70805

Sullivan Technical Institute
1710 Sullivan Dr.
Bogalusa 70427

MARYLAND

National Education Center, Temple
School Campus
3601 O'Donnell St.
Baltimore 21224

MASSACHUSETTS

Bay State School of Appliances
225 Turnpike St.
Canton 02021

Computer Processing Institute
615 Massachusetts Ave.
Cambridge 02139

Smith & Wesson Academy
2100 Roosevelt Ave.
P.O. Box 2208
Springfield 01102-2208

Woman's Technical Institute
1255 Boylston St.
Boston 02215

MICHIGAN

National Education Center,
National Institute of Technology
2620 Remico St. SW
Wyoming 49509

MINNESOTA

Brainerd-Staples Technical College,
Brainerd Campus
300 Quince St.
Brainerd 56401

Red Wing-Winona Technical College,
Red Wing Campus
Hwy. 58 at Pioneer Rd.
Red Wing 55066

MISSOURI

Gibson Technical Center
P.O. Box 169
Reeds Spring 65737

Rolla Area Vocational-Technical School
1304 East Tenth St.
Rolla 65401

Waynesville Area Vocational School
810 Roosevelt
Waynesville 65583

MONTANA

Billings Vocational Technical Center
3803 Central Ave.
Billings 59102

NEBRASKA

Central Community College, Grand
Island
P.O. Box 4903
Grand Island 68802

Mid Plains Community College
416 North Jeffers
North Platte 69101

NEVADA

All Rite Trade School
93 West Lake Mead Dr.
Henderson 89015

NEW JERSEY

Lincoln Technical Institute
Rte. 130 North at Haddonfield Rd.
Pennsauken 08110

NEW YORK

Fegs Trades and Business School
199 Jay St.
Brooklyn 11201

NORTH DAKOTA

Bismarck State College
1500 Edwards Ave.
Bismarck 58501

OHIO

Akron Machining Institute, Inc.
2959 Barber Rd.
Barberton 44203

Vocational Guidance Services
2239 East 55th St.
Cleveland 44103

OKLAHOMA

Kiamichi AVTS SD #7, Hugo Campus
107 South 15th, P.O. Box 699
Hugo 74743

Oklahoma State University, Okmulgee
1801 East Fourth St.
Okmulgee 74447-3901

PENNSYLVANIA

Gateway Technical Institute
100 Seventh St.
Pittsburgh 15222

ICS-International Correspondence
Schools
Oak St. and Pawnee Ave.
Scranton 18515

Triangle Technical, Erie
2000 Liberty St.
Erie 16502

SOUTH CAROLINA

Technical College of the Low Country
100 South Ribaut Rd.
Beaufort 29902

SOUTH DAKOTA

Western Dakota Vocational Technical
Institute
1600 Sedivy
Rapid City 57701

TENNESSEE

McMinnville State Area Vocational
Technical School
Vo Tech Dr.
McMinnville 37110

Memphis Area Vocational-Technical
School
550 Alabama Ave.
Memphis 38105-3799

Morristown State Area Vocational-
Technical School
821 West Louise Ave.
Morristown 37813

Shelbyville State Area Vocational
Technical School
1405 Madison St.
Shelbyville 37160

State Technical Institute of Memphis
5983 Macon Cove
Memphis 38134

TEXAS

ATI Computer Training Center
2351 West Northwest Hwy.
Dallas 75220

Laredo Junior College
West End Washington St.
Laredo 78040

National Education Center,
Bryman Campus
16416 North Chase Dr.
Houston 77060

Odessa College
201 West University
Odessa 79764

San Antonio Training Division
9350 South Presa
San Antonio 78223-4799

Tarrant County Junior College District
1500 Houston St.
Fort Worth 76102

Texas State Technical College,
Harlingen Campus
2424 Boxwood
Harlingen 78550-3697

Texas State Technical College, Waco
Campus
3801 Campus Dr.
Waco 76705

Tyler School of Business, Trade and
Technical
Hwy. 64 E & Rte. 14
P.O. Box 176
Tyler 75707

WASHINGTON

Bellingham Technical College
3028 Lindbergh Ave.
Bellingham 98225

ITT Technical Institute
North 1050 Argonne Rd.
Spokane 99212

Lake Washington Technical College
11605 132nd Ave. NE
Kirkland 98034

WEST VIRGINIA

Marion County Vocational-Technical
Center
Rte. 1, P.O. Box 100A
Farmington 26571

WISCONSIN

Chippewa Valley Technical College
620 West Clairemont Ave.
Eau Claire 54701

Home Economics Technology

ALABAMA

Gadsden State Community College
P.O. Box 227
Gadsden 35902-0227

ARIZONA

Central Arizona College
8470 North Overfield Rd.
Coolidge 85228-9778

Pima Community College
2202 West Anklam Rd.
Tucson 85709-0001

ARKANSAS

Quapaw Technical Institute
201 Vo-Tech Dr.
Hot Springs 71913

CALIFORNIA

Allan Hancock College
800 South College Dr.
Santa Maria 93454

American River College
4700 College Oak Dr.
Sacramento 95841

Antelope Valley College
3041 West Ave. K
Lancaster 93534

Bakersfield College
1801 Panorama Dr.
Bakersfield 93305-1299

Butte College
3536 Butte Campus Dr.
Oroville 95965

Canada College
4200 Farm Hill Blvd.
Redwood City 94061

Chaffey Community College
5885 Haven Ave.
Rancho Cucamonga 91737-3002

College of the Canyons
26455 North Rockwell Canyon Rd.
Santa Clarita 91355

College of the Sequoias
915 South Mooney Blvd.
Visalia 93277

Compton Community College
1111 East Artesia Blvd.
Compton 90221

Cosumnes River College
8401 Center Pkwy.
Sacramento 95823-5799

Cuesta College
P.O. Box 8106
San Luis Obispo 93403-8106

Diablo Valley College
321 Golf Club Rd.
Pleasant Hill 94523

El Camino College
16007 Crenshaw Blvd.
Torrance 90506

Fresno City College
1101 East University Ave.
Fresno 93741

Fullerton College
321 East Chapman Ave.
Fullerton 92632-2095

Glendale Community College
1500 North Verdugo Rd.
Glendale 91208-2894

Grossmont College
8800 Grossmont College Dr.
El Cajon 92020

Long Beach City College
4901 East Carson St.
Long Beach 90808

Los Angeles City College
855 North Vermont Ave.
Los Angeles 90029

Los Angeles Mission College
1310 San Fernando Rd.
San Fernando 91340

Marin Regional Occupational Program
P.O. Box 4925
San Rafael 94913

Merced College
3600 M St.
Merced 95348-2898

Mission College
3000 Mission College Blvd.
Santa Clara 95054-1897

Modesto Junior College
435 College Ave.
Modesto 95350-9977

Moorpark College
7075 Campus Rd.
Moorpark 93021

Ohlone College
43600 Mission Blvd.
Fremont 94539

Orange Coast College
2701 Fairview Rd.
Costa Mesa 92626

Palomar College
1140 West Mission
San Marcos 92069-1487

Sacramento City College
3835 Freeport Blvd.
Sacramento 95822

San Joaquin Delta College
5151 Pacific Ave.
Stockton 95207

Santa Monica College
1900 Pico Blvd.
Santa Monica 90405-1628

Santa Rosa Junior College
1501 Mendocino Ave.
Santa Rosa 95401-4395

Shasta College
P.O. Box 496006
Redding 96049

Sierra College
5000 Rocklin Rd.
Rocklin 95677

Simi Valley Adult School
3192 Los Angeles Ave.
Simi Valley 93065

Solano County Community College
District
4000 Suisun Valley Rd.
Suisun 94585

Ventura College
4667 Telegraph Rd.
Ventura 93003

Yuba College
2088 North Beale Rd.
Marysville 95901

COLORADO

Front Range Community College
3645 West 112th Ave.
Westminster 80030

National Institute of Nutritional
Education
1010 South Joliet
Aurora 80012

CONNECTICUT

South Central Community College
60 Sargent Dr.
New Haven 06511

FLORIDA

Broward Community College
225 East Las Olas Blvd.
Fort Lauderdale 33301

Florida Community College at
Jacksonville
501 West State St.
Jacksonville 32202

Lindsey Hopkins Technical Education
Center
750 Northwest 20th St.
Miami 33127

Manatee Vocational-Technical Center
5603 34th St. W
Bradenton 34210

Miami-Dade Community College
300 Northeast Second Ave.
Miami 33132

Palm Beach Community College
4200 Congress Ave.
Lake Worth 33461

Pensacola Junior College
1000 College Blvd.
Pensacola 32504

Valencia Community College
P.O. Box 3028
Orlando 32802

HAWAII

Brigham Young University, Hawaii
Campus
55-220 Kulanui St.
Laie 96762

IDAHO

Northwest Nazarene College
623 Holly
Nampa 83686-5897

ILLINOIS

City College of Chicago, Malcolm X
College
1900 West Van Buren
Chicago 60612

Illinois Central College
One College Dr.
East Peoria 61635

William Rainey Harper College
1200 West Algonquin Rd.
Palatine 60067-7398

INDIANA

Ball State University
2000 University Ave.
Muncie 47306

Marian College
3200 Cold Spring Rd.
Indianapolis 46222-1997

Vincennes University
1002 North First St.
Vincennes 47591

KANSAS

Barton County Community College
Rte. 3, P.O. Box 136Z
Great Bend 67530

Cloud County Community College
2221 Campus Dr., P.O. Box 1002
Concordia 66901-1002

Colby Community College
1255 South Range
Colby 67701

Garden City Community College
801 Campus Dr.
Garden City 67846

Hutchinson Community College
1300 North Plum St.
Hutchinson 67501

Independence Community College
Brookside Dr. and College Ave.
Independence 67301

Johnson County Area Vocational-
Technical School
311 East Park
Olathe 66061

Liberal Area Vocational Technical
School
P.O. Box 1599
Liberal 67905-1599

Salina Area Vocational Technical
School
2562 Scanlan Ave.
Salina 67401

Wichita Area Vocational Technical
School
428 South Broadway
Wichita 67202-3910

KENTUCKY

Eastern Kentucky University
Lancaster Ave.
Richmond 40475

MAINE

Southern Maine Technical College
Fort Rd.
South Portland 04106

University of Maine
Office of Institutional Studies
Orono 04469

University of Maine at Farmington
86 Main St.
Farmington 04938

MARYLAND

Baltimore City Community College
2901 Liberty Heights Ave.
Baltimore 21215

International Fabricare Institute
12251 Tech Rd., Montgomery Industrial
Park
Silver Spring 20904

MASSACHUSETTS

Catherine Laboure College
2120 Dorchester Ave.
Boston 02124

MICHIGAN

Detroit Health Department, Nutrition
Division
1151 Taylor
Detroit 48202

Grand Rapids Community College
143 Bostwick Ave. NE
Grand Rapids 49505

Michigan Christian College
800 West Avon Rd.
Rochester Hills 48307

Wayne County Community College
801 West Fort St.
Detroit 48226

MINNESOTA

Albert Lea-Mankato Technical College
2200 Tech Dr.
Albert Lea 56007

Alexandria Technical College
1601 Jefferson St.
Alexandria 56308

Lakewood Community College
3401 Century Ave. N
White Bear Lake 55110

Minnesota Multi-Housing Association
4250 Park Glen Rd.
Minneapolis 55416

Normandale Community College
9700 France Ave. S
Bloomington 55431

Northeast Metro Technical College
3300 Century Ave. N
White Bear Lake 55110

Southwestern Technical College,
Granite Falls Campus
1593 11th Ave.
Granite Falls 56241

University of Minnesota, Crookston
105 Selvig Hall
Crookston 56716

MISSOURI

Penn Valley Community College
3201 Southwest Trafficway
Kansas City 64111

Saint Louis Community College,
Forest Park
5600 Oakland Ave.
Saint Louis 63110

MONTANA

Little Big Horn College
P.O. Box 370
Crow Agency 59022

NEBRASKA

Central Community College,
Grand Island
P.O. Box 4903
Grand Island 68802

NEW JERSEY

Middlesex County College
155 Mill Rd., P.O. Box 3050
Edison 08818-3050

NEW YORK

Dutchess Community College
Pendell Rd.
Poughkeepsie 12601

Erie Community College, North Campus
Main St. and Youngs Rd.
Williamsville 14221

Fashion Institute of Technology
227 West 27th St.
New York 10001

New York School of Dry Cleaning
252 West 29th St.
New York 10001

Rockland Community College
145 College Rd.
Suffern 10901

Suffolk County Community College,
Eastern Campus
Speonk Riverhead Rd.
Riverhead 11901

SUNY College of Technology &
Agriculture at Morrisville
Morrisville 13408

SUNY Westchester Commmunity
College
75 Grasslands Rd.
Valhalla 10595

OHIO

Bowling Green State University,
Firelands
901 Rye Beach Rd.
Huron 44839

Cincinnati Technical College
3520 Central Pkwy.
Cincinnati 45223

Cuyahoga Community College District
700 Carnegie Ave.
Cleveland 44115-2878

Hocking Technical College
3301 Hocking Pkwy.
Nelsonville 45764

Lima Technical College
4240 Campus Dr.
Lima 45804

Mount Vernon Nazarene College
Martinsburg Rd.
Mount Vernon 43050-9500

Owens Technical College
30335 Oregon Rd., P.O. Box 10000
Toledo 43699-1947

Scioto County Joint Vocational
School District
Rte. 2 & Houston Hollow Rd.
Lucasville 45648

Sinclair Community College
444 West Third St.
Dayton 45402

Youngstown State University
410 Wick Ave.
Youngstown 44555

OKLAHOMA

Connors State College
Rte. 1, P.O. Box 1000
Warner 74469

Francis Tuttle Area Vocational-
Technical Center
12777 North Rockwell Ave.
Oklahoma City 73142-2789

Northeastern Oklahoma Agricultural
and Mechanical College
200 Eye St. NE
Miami 74354

Northern Oklahoma College
P.O. Box 310
Tonkawa 74653

Oklahoma City Community College
7777 South May Ave.
Oklahoma City 73159

Oklahoma Northwest Area Vocational-
Technical School
1801 South 11th St.
Alva 73717

Redland Community College
1300 South Country Club Rd.
P.O. Box 370
El Reno 73036

Rose State College
6420 Southeast 15th
Midwest City 73110

Western Oklahoma State College
2801 North Main St.
Altus 73521-1397

OREGON

Montessori Institute Northwest
P.O. Box 771
Oregon City 97045

Portland Community College
P.O. Box 19000
Portland 97280-0990

PENNSYLVANIA

Community College of Allegheny
County
800 Allegheny Ave.
Pittsburgh 15233-1895

Community College of Philadelphia
1700 Spring Garden St.
Philadelphia 19130

Harrisburg Area Community College,
Harrisburg Campus
One HACC Dr.
Harrisburg 17110

Luzerne County Community College
1333 South Prospect St.
Nanticoke 18634

Pennsylvania State University,
Du Bois Campus
College Place
Du Bois 15801

Pennsylvania State University,
Main Campus
201 Old Main
University Park 16802

Pennsylvania State University,
Schuylkill Campus
200 University Dr.
Schuylkill Haven 17972

TENNESSEE

Shelby State Community College
P.O. Box 40568
Memphis 38174-0568

Tennessee Temple University
1815 Union Ave.
Chattanooga 37404

TEXAS

Amarillo College
P.O. Box 447
Amarillo 79178

Hill College
P.O. Box 619
Hillsboro 76645

Houston Montessori Center
9601 Katy Fwy.
Houston 77024-1330

North Harris Montgomery Community
College District
250 North Sam Houston Pkwy. E
Houston 77060

Saint Philip's College
2111 Nevada St.
San Antonio 78203

South Plains College
1401 College Ave.
Levelland 79336

Tarrant County Junior College District
1500 Houston St.
Fort Worth 76102

Texas Southmost College
80 Fort Brown
Brownsville 78520

Trinity Valley Community College
500 South Prairieville
Athens 75751

Tyler Junior College
P.O. Box 9020
Tyler 75711

UTAH

Dixie College
225 South, 700 East
Saint George 84770

VIRGINIA

Northern Virginia Community College
4001 Wakefield Chapel Rd.
Annandale 22003

Tidewater Community College
Rte. 135
Portsmouth 23703

WASHINGTON

Edmonds Community College
20000 68th Ave. W
Lynnwood 98036

Highline Community College
P.O. Box 98000
Des Moines 98198-9800

Shoreline Community College
16101 Greenwood Ave. N
Seattle 98133

Spokane Community College
North 1810 Greene Ave.
Spokane 99207

Yakima Valley Community College
P.O. Box 1647
Yakima 98907

WISCONSIN

Milwaukee Area Technical College
700 West State St.
Milwaukee 53233

Southwest Wisconsin Technical College
Hwy. 18 E
Fennimore 53809

Wisconsin Area Vocational Training
and Adult Education System,
Moraine Park
235 North National Ave.
P.O. Box 1940
Fond Du Lac 54936-1940

Wisconsin Area Vocational Training
and Adult Education System District
Number Four
3550 Anderson St.
Madison 53704

WYOMING

Casper College
125 College Dr.
Casper 82601

Northwest Community College
231 West Sixth St.
Powell 82435

Interior Design

ARKANSAS

Northwest Technical Institute
P.O. Box A
Springdale 72765

CALIFORNIA

Fresno City College
1101 East University Ave.
Fresno 93741

Fullerton College
321 East Chapman Ave.
Fullerton 92632-2095

Southern California School of Floral
Design
2964 East Yorba Linda Blvd.
Fullerton 92631

COLORADO

Columbine College
5801 West 44th Ave.
Denver 80212

FLORIDA

Florida Community College at
Jacksonville
501 West State St.
Jacksonville 32202

GEORGIA

American School of Paperhanging
Little and Oak Sts.
Commerce 30529

ILLINOIS

American Floral Art School
529 South Wabash Ave.
Chicago 60605-1679

College of Du Page
Lambert Rd. and 22nd St.
Glen Ellyn 60137

William Rainey Harper College
1200 West Algonquin Rd.
Palatine 60067-7398

INDIANA

Academy of Professional Floral
360 Market Plaza
Greenwood 46142

KANSAS

Kansas City Area Vocational Technical
School
2220 North 59th St.
Kansas City 66104

Kansas School of Floral Design
826 Iowa St.
Lawrence 66044-1783

MASSACHUSETTS

New England School of Floral Design
88 West Main St.
Norton 02766

Rittners School of Floral Design
345 Marlborough St.
Boston 02115

MINNESOTA

Dakota County Technical College
1300 East 145th St.
Rosemount 55068

NEW JERSEY

Creative Designs Institute
4530 Hwy. 9 S
Howell 07731

NEW YORK

Fashion Institute of Technology
227 West 27th St.
New York 10001

Suffolk County Community College,
Eastern Campus
Speonk Riverhead Rd.
Riverhead 11901

OHIO

Alexander's School of Floral Design
25780 Miles Rd.
Bedford Heights 44146

OKLAHOMA

Kiamichi AVTS SD #7, Hugo Campus
107 South 15th, P.O. Box 699
Hugo 74743

PENNSYLVANIA

American Institute of Design
1616 Orthodox St.
Philadelphia 19124

Pittsburgh Floral Academy
922 Western Ave.
Pittsburgh 15233

TEXAS

Art Institute of Dallas
8080 Park Ln., Two Northpark E
Dallas 75231

The Art Institute of Houston
1900 Yorktown
Houston 77056-4115

WASHINGTON

Career Floral Design Institute
13200 Northup Way
Bellevue 98005

Lake Washington Technical College
11605 132nd Ave. NE
Kirkland 98034

Mortuary Science

ALABAMA

Jefferson State Community College
2601 Carson Rd.
Birmingham 35215-3098

CALIFORNIA

Cypress College
9200 Valley View
Cypress 90630

FLORIDA

Miami-Dade Community College
300 Northeast Second Ave.
Miami 33132

GEORGIA

Gupton Jones College of Funeral
Services
5141 Snapfinger Woods Dr.
Decatur 30035-4022

ILLINOIS

Southern Illinois University,
Carbondale
Carbondale 62901

Worsham College
495 Northgate Pkwy.
Wheeling 60090-2646

INDIANA

Mid-America College of Funeral
Services
3111 Hamburg Pike
Jeffersonville 47130

KANSAS

Kansas City Kansas Community College
7250 State Ave.
Kansas City 66112

LOUISIANA

Delgado Community College
615 City Park Ave.
New Orleans 70119

MARYLAND

Catonsville Community College
800 South Rolling Rd.
Catonsville 21228

MASSACHUSETTS

Mount Ida College
777 Dedham St.
Newton Centre 02159

MICHIGAN

Wayne State University
656 West Kirby
Detroit 48202

NEW JERSEY

Mercer County Community College
1200 Old Trenton Rd.
Trenton 08690

NEW YORK

American Academy McAlister Institute
of Funeral Services
450 West 56th St.
New York 10019

Hudson Valley Community College
80 Vandenburgh Ave.
Troy 12180

Simmons Institute of Funeral Service,
Inc.
1828 South Ave.
Syracuse 13207

SUNY College of Technology at Canton
Canton 13617

SUNY College of Technology at
Farmingdale
Melville Rd.
Farmingdale 11735

OHIO

Cincinnati College of Mortuary Science
3860 Pacific Ave.
Cincinnati 45207-1033

OREGON

Mount Hood Community College
26000 Southeast Stark St.
Gresham 97030

PENNSYLVANIA

Northampton County Area Community
College
3835 Green Pond Rd.
Bethlehem 18017

Pittsburgh Institute of Mortuary
Science
5808 Baum Blvd.
Pittsburgh 15206-3706

TENNESSEE

John A Gupton College
1616 Church St.
Nashville 37203

TEXAS

Commonwealth Institute of Funeral
Services
415 Barren Springs Dr.
Houston 77090

Dallas Institute of Funeral Services
3909 South Buckner Blvd.
Dallas 75227

VIRGINIA

John Tyler Community College
13101 Jefferson Davis Hwy.
Chester 23831-5399

WISCONSIN

Milwaukee Area Technical College
700 West State St.
Milwaukee 53233

Personal Service Technology

ALABAMA

Baldwin County School of Cosmetology
27339 A1 U.S. Hwy. 98
Daphne 36526

Holland School for Jewelers
1034 Dawson Ave., P.O. Box 882
Selma 36701

ARIZONA

Allure Career College of Beauty
3210 East Speedway Blvd.
Tucson 85716

Charles of Italy Beauty College
2350 Miracle Mile Rd.
Bullhead City 86442

Charles of Italy Beauty College
1987 McCulloch Blvd.
Lake Havasu City 86403

Desert Institute of the Healing Arts
639 North Sixth Ave.
Tucson 85705

Phoenix Therapeutic Massage College
2720 East Thomas Rd.
Phoenix 85016

ARKANSAS

Arkadelphia Beauty College
2708 West Pine
Arkadelphia 71923

Arkansas Valley Technical Institute
Hwy. 23 N, P.O. Box 506
Ozark 72949

Bee Jay's Academy
1907 Hinson Loop
Little Rock 72212

Bizzell's Beauty School
1007 Oak
Conway 72032

Fayetteville Beauty College
1200 North College Ave.
Fayetteville 72703

Northwest Technical Institute
P.O. Box A
Springdale 72765

Paramount Beauty School
426 North Washington St.
El Dorado 71730

CALIFORNIA

Alhambra Beauty College
200 West Main St.
Alhambra 91801

Amma Institute of Skilled Touch
1881 Post St.
San Francisco 94115

Body Therapy Center
368 California Ave.
Palo Alto 94306

California College of Physical Arts, Inc.
18582 Beach Blvd.
Huntington Beach 92648

California Medical School of Shiatsu
4635 North First St.
Fresno 93726

Calistoga Massage Therapy School
5959 Commerce Blvd.
Rohnert Park 94928

Career Academy of Beauty
12375 Seal Beach Blvd.
Seal Beach 90740

Career College of Cosmetology
407 D St.
Marysville 95901

Career College of Cosmetology
646 Cottonwood Plaza
Woodland 95776

Frederick & Charles Beauty College
831 F St.
Eureka 95501

Hair Interns School of Cosmetology
1522 Fulton
Fresno 93721

Institute of Psycho-Structural Balancing
1131 Olympic Blvd.
Santa Monica 90404

Institute of Psychostructural Balancing
1366 Hornblend St.
San Diego 92109

Jerrylee Beauty College
100 Eldorado St.
Auburn 95603

Jerrylee Beauty College
1550 Fulton Ave.
Sacramento 95821

Manchester Beauty College
3756 North Blackstone Ave.
Fresno 93726

Moler Barber and Hairstyling
1880 Tulare St.
Fresno 93708-0287

Moler Barber College
727 J St.
Sacramento 95814

Monterey Institute of Touch
27820 Dorris Dr.
Carmel 93923

Pacific School of Massage and Healing
Arts
44800 Fish Rock Rd.
Gualala 95445

Palomar Institute of Cosmetology
355 Via Vera Cruz
San Marcos 92069

Paramount School of Beauty
16260 Paramount Blvd.
Paramount 90723

Phillips School of Massage
10281 Tillicum Way
Nevada 95959

Randy's Beauty College
678 North Market St.
Redding 96001

Richard's Beauty College
200 East Highland Ave.
San Bernardino 92404

San Francisco Barber College
64 Sixth St.
San Francisco 94103

San Francisco School of Massage
2209 Van Ness Ave.
San Francisco 94109

School of Healing Arts
975 Hornblend E
Pacific Beach 92109

Shiatsu Massage School of California
2309 Main St.
Santa Monica 90405

Southern California School of Floral
Design
2964 East Yorba Linda Blvd.
Fullerton 92631

Therapeutic Learning Center
3636 North First St.
Fresno 93726

Victor Valley Beauty College
16424 Victor St.
Victorville 92392

Western Beauty College
439 South Western Ave.
Los Angeles 90005

Western College of Massage
2002 White Oaks Rd.
Campbell 95008

COLORADO

Boulder School of Massage Therapy
3285 30th St.
Boulder 80301-1451

Cheeks International Academy of
Beauty Culture
4025 South Mason St.
Fort Collins 80525

Cheeks International Academy of
Beauty Culture
2547B 11th Ave.
Greeley 80631

Colorado School of Healing Arts
7655 West Mississippi
Lakewood 80226

Columbine Beauty School I
1225 Wadsworth Blvd.
Lakewood 80215

Columbine Beauty School II
5801 West 44th
Denver 80212

Columbine College
5801 West 44th Ave.
Denver 80212

Denver Institute of Taxidermy Training
126 Acoma St.
Denver 80223

International Beauty Academy
1185 North Circle Dr.
Colorado Springs 80909

Massage Therapy Institute of Colorado
1441 York St.
Denver 80206

Xenon International School of Hair
Design III
2231 South Peoria
Aurora 80014

CONNECTICUT

Connecticut Center for Massage
Therapy, Inc.
75 Kitts Ln.
Newington 06111

Connecticut Center for Massage
Therapy, Westport
25 Sylvan Rd. S
Westport 06880

DELAWARE

Brandywine Beauty Academy
2018 Naamans Rd.
Wilmington 19810

FLORIDA

Academy of Cosmetology
1900 Evans
Melbourne 32901

ASM Beauty World Academy
2510 North 60th Ave.
Hollywood 33021

Atlantic Vocational Technical Center
4700 Coconut Creek Pkwy.
Coconut Creek 33063

Boca Raton Institute, Inc.
5499 North Federal Hwy.
Boca Raton 33487

Charlotte Vocational-Technical Center
18300 Toledo Blade Blvd.
Port Charlotte 33948-3399

Florida Institute of Massage Therapy
5453 North University Dr.
Lauderhill 33351

Florida School of Massage
6421 Southwest 13th St.
Gainesville 32608-5419

Hollywood Institute of Beauty Careers
5981 Funston St.
Hollywood 33023

Humanities Center Institute of Allied
Health School of Massage
4045 Park Blvd.
Pinellas Park 34665

La Baron Hairdressing Academy
5215 Ramsey Way
Fort Myers 33907

Lindsey Hopkins Technical Education
Center
750 Northwest 20th St.
Miami 33127

Mr. Arnold's Excellence Beauty School
1415 Washington Ave.
Miami Beach 33139

Nouvelle Institute
3271 Northwest Seventh St.
Miami 33125

Orlando Academy of Beauty Culture
902 Lee Rd.
Orlando 32810

Ramsay's Career Institute
2201 West Sample Rd.
Pompano Beach 33073

Reese Institute, Inc. School of Massage
Therapy
425 Geneva Dr.
Oviedo 32765

Seminar Network International, Inc.
518 North Federal Hwy.
Lake Worth 33460

Sheridan Vocational Center
5400 West Sheridan St.
Hollywood 33021

Suncoast School
4910 West Cypress St.
Tampa 33607

GEORGIA

Arnold-Padricks University of
Cosmetology
4971 Courtney Dr.
Forest Park 30050

Mar-Jans Beauty School, Inc.
2260 Martin Luther King Blvd.
Augusta 30904

Minosa School of Beauty and Hair
Design
1365 Mayson Turner Rd.
Atlanta 30314

Southeastern Beauty School
3448 North Lumpkin Rd.
Columbus 31903

Southeastern Beauty School
1826 Midtown Dr.
Columbus 31906

HAWAII

Honolulu School of Massage, Inc.
1123 11th Ave.
Honolulu 96816

IDAHO

Headmasters School of Hair Design
317 Coeur D'Alene Ave.
Coeur D'Alene 83814

Idaho School of Massage Therapy
5353 Franklin Rd.
Boise 83705

Meridian School of Beauty
48 East Fairview
Meridian 83642

Mr. Juan's College of Hair Design
577 Lynwood Mall
Twin Falls 83301

Sandpoint School of Hair Design
212 North First Ave.
Sandpoint 83864

ILLINOIS

Alvareita's College of Cosmetology
333 South Kansas
Edwardsville 62025

American Floral Art School
529 South Wabash Ave.
Chicago 60605-1679

Bloomington Academy of Beauty
Culture
218-220 North Center St.
Bloomington 61701

Blue Island School of Cosmetology
1607 West Howard St.
Chicago 60626

Cannella School of Hair Design
3442 South Halsted St.
Chicago 60608

Cannella School of Hair Design
6614 South Halsted St.
Chicago 60620

Cannella School of Hair Design
2874 West Cermak
Chicago 60623

Cannella School of Hair Design
113 East Jefferson
Joliet 60432

Capri Garfield Ridge School of Beauty
Culture
6388 West Archer Ave.
Chicago 60638

Capri School of Beauty Culture
2653 West 63rd St.
Chicago 60629

Don Roberts Beauty School
P.O. Box 34
McHenry 60050

Du Quoin Beauty College
202 South Washington St.
Du Quoin 62832

Educators of Beauty
122 Wright St.
La Salle 61301

Educators of Beauty
211 East Third St.
Sterling 61081

Granite City School of Beauty Culture
1815 Edison Ave.
Granite City 62040

Hair Professionals Academy of
Cosmetology
1145 East Butterfield Rd.
Wheaton 60187

Hair Professionals School of
Cosmetology
5460 Rte. 34
Oswego 60543

Kankakee Academy of Hair Design
100 East 115th St.
Chicago 60628

Mr. John's School of Cosmetology
304 East Adams St.
Springfield 62701

Mr. John's School of Cosmetology
104 West Main
Urbana 61801

Mr. John's School of Cosmetology and
Esthetics
1745 East Eldorado
Decatur 62521

Niles School of Beauty Culture
8057 North Milwaukee
Niles 60714

Pal's International School Beauty
Culture
3442 West 26th St.
Chicago 60623

Pivot Point Beauty School
1791 West Howard St.
Chicago 60626

Trend Beauty College
Six East Gate Plaza
East Alton 62024

Universe Beauty School
4738 North Kedzie Ave.
Chicago 60625

Waukegan School of Hair Design
3150 North Lincoln Ave.
Chicago 60657

INDIANA

Academy of Hair Care, Eastgate
7150 East Washington St.
Indianapolis 46219

Academy of Professional Floral
360 Market Plaza
Greenwood 46142

Alexandria School of Scientific
Therapeutics
809 South Harrison St., P.O. Box 287
Alexandria 46001

Artistic Beauty College
6101 North Keystone
Indianapolis 46220

A Cut Above Beauty College
437 South Meridian, Wilgro Shopping
Center
Greenwood 46143

Don Roberts Hair Designing Academy
5974 West Ridge Rd.
Gary 46408-1727

Don Roberts School of Hair Design
7975 Calumet Ave.
Munster 46321

Doree School of Beauty Culture
3816 Grant St.
Gary 46408

Hair Fashions By Kaye Beauty College
2605 Shelby St.
Indianapolis 46203

Hair Fashions By Kaye Beauty College
Ten East Washington St.
Indianapolis 46204

Hair Fashions By Kaye Beauty College
4218 North Post Rd.
Indianapolis 46226

Hair Fashions By Kaye Beauty College
4026 North High School Rd.
Indianapolis 46254

Hair Fashions By Kaye Beauty College
1910 East Conner
Noblesville 46060

Merrillville Beauty College
48 West 67th Place
Merrillville 46410

Metropolitan Beauty Academy
110 West Washington St.
Lebanon 46052

New Concepts Beauty College
3830 Meadows Dr.
Indianapolis 46205

PJ's College of Cosmetology
2026 Stafford Rd.
Plainfield 46168

IOWA

Bernel College of Cosmetology
114 Fifth St.
Ames 50010

Capri Cosmetology College
1815 East Kimberly Rd.
Davenport 52807

Capri Cosmetology College
395 Main St.
Dubuque 52001

Iowa School Beauty Academy
609 West Second St.
Ottumwa 52501

Iowa School of Beauty
3305 70th St.
Des Moines 50322

Iowa School of Beauty
112 Nicholas Dr.
Marshalltown 50158

La James College of Hairstyling and
Cosmetology
24 Second St. NE
Mason City 50401

KANSAS

Kansas City Area Vocational Technical
School
2220 North 59th St.
Kansas City 66104

Kansas School of Floral Design
826 Iowa St.
Lawrence 66044-1783

La Baron Hairdressing Academy
8119 Robinson
Overland Park 66204

KENTUCKY

Ashland School of Beauty Culture
1653 Greenup Ave.
Ashland 41101

Barrett and Company School of Hair
   Design
973 Kimberly Square
Nicholasville 40356

College of Cosmetology and Hair
   Design
1100 U.S. 127 S
Frankfort 40601

Cumberland Beauty College
371 Langdon St.
Somerset 42501

Donta School of Beauty Culture
515 West Oak St.
Louisville 40203

Donta School of Beauty Culture
8314 Preston Hwy.
Louisville 40219

The Hair Design School
3968 Park Dr.
Louisville 40216

The Hair Design School
640 Knox Blvd.
Radcliff 40160

Heads West Kentucky Beauty School
Brairwood Shopping Center
Madisonville 42431

Jenny Lea Academy of Cosmetology
Parkway Plaza
Whitesburg 41858

Kaufman's Beauty School
701 East High St.
Lexington 40502

New Image Careers, Inc.
301 South Main
Corbin 40701

Nutek Academy of Beauty, Inc.
Mount Sterling Plaza
Mount Sterling 40353

Pat Wilson's Beauty School
326 North Main
Henderson 42420

Southeast School of Cosmetology
23 Manchester Square, P.O. Box 493
Manchester 40962

Trend Setters Academy
7283 Dixie Hwy.
Louisville 40258

Tri-State Beauty Academy, Inc.
219 West Main St.
Morehead 40351

LOUISIANA

Academy of Creative Hair Design
4560 Hwy. 1
Raceland 70394

Academy of Hair Technology
105 Leonie St.
Lafayette 70506

Blalocks Professional Beauty College
3553 Greenwood Rd.
Shreveport 71109

Cloyd's Beauty School 2
1311 Winnsboro Rd.
Monroe 71202

Cloyd's Beauty School 3
2514 Ferrand St.
Monroe 71201

Cosmetology Training Center
2516 Johnston St.
Lafayette 70503

Dee Jay's School of Beauty
5131 Government St.
Baton Rouge 70806

Demmon School of Beauty
1222 Ryan St.
Lake Charles 70601

Geneva's Beauty College
926 Benton Rd.
Bossier City 71111

Jocelyn Daspit Beauty College
507 South Cypress St.
Hammond 70401

Jocelyn Daspit Beauty College
3204 Independence St.
Metairie 70006

Lockworks Academie Hairdressing
4950 Government St.
Baton Rouge 70806

Moler Beauty College
59 West Bank Expwy.
Gretna 70053

Moler Beauty College
2940 Canal St.
New Orleans 70119

Opelousas School of Cosmetology
556 East Vine St.
Opelousas 70570

Peterson's Institute of Hair and Skin
   Technology
9037 West Judge Perez Dr.
Chalmette 70043

Pineville Beauty School, Jonesville
1112 First St.
Jonesville 71343

Ronnie & Dorman's School of Hair
   Design
2002 Johnston St.
Lafayette 70503

Southland School of Taxidermy
2603 Osceola St.
Baton Rouge 70805

Stage One, The Hair School
3505 Fifth Ave.
Lake Charles 70605

Stefan's Beauty College
7384 Highland Rd., Kenilworth Plaza
Baton Rouge 70808

Stevenson's Academy of Hair Design
2039 Lapeyrouse St.
New Orleans 70116

MAINE

Main Street Academy of Hair Design
224 State St.
Brewer 04412

MARYLAND

Baltimore Studio of Hair Design
18 North Howard St.
Baltimore 21201

Maryland Beauty Academy of Essex
505 Eastern Blvd.
Essex 21221

MASSACHUSETTS

Catherine Hind's Institute of Esthetics
65 Riverside Place
Medford 02155

Elizabeth Grady School of Esthetics
Ten Cabot Rd.
Medford 02155

Essex Agricultural-Technical Institute
562 Maple St.
P.O. Box 562
Hathorne 01937

Muscular Therapy Institute
122 Rindge Ave.
Cambridge 02140

New England School of Floral Design
88 West Main St.
Norton 02766

North Bennet Street School
39 North Bennet St.
Boston 02113

Rob Roy Academy
150 Pleasant St.
Worcester 01609

MICHIGAN

Alpenas Hollywood School of Beauty
1036 U.S. 23 N
Alpena 49707

David Pressley School of Cosmetology
1127 South Washington St.
Royal Oak 48067-3219

Mauricio School of Cosmetology
16701 East Warren
Detroit 48224

Mid Michigan Community College
1375 South Clare Ave.
Harrison 48625

Sylvias Beauty College
14462 Grand River
Detroit 48227

Twin City Beauty College
1889 South M-139
Benton Harbor 49022

Wright Beauty Academy
492 Capital SW
Battle Creek 49015

MINNESOTA

Cosmetology Careers Unlimited,
   Duluth
121 West Superior St.
Duluth 55802

Cosmetology Careers Unlimited,
   Duluth West
4031 Grand Ave.
Duluth 55807

Cosmetology Careers Unlimited,
   Hibbing
110 East Howard St.
Hibbing 55746

Cosmetology Careers Unlimited,
   Virginia
233 Chestnut
Virginia 55792

Horst Education Center
400 Central Ave. SE
Minneapolis 55414

North America Institute of Taxidermy
5781 Queens Ave. NE
Elk River 55330-6457

Scot Lewis-Florian Scientific School
   of Cosmetology
9801 James Circle
Bloomington 55431

MISSISSIPPI

Advanced School of Cosmetology, Inc.
6B Morgantown Rd.
Natchez 39120

American Beauty College
2200 25th Ave.
Gulfport 39501

American Beauty College
703A Hwy. 90
Waveland 39576

Chris Beauty College
1265 Pass Rd.
Gulfport 39501

Creations College of Cosmetology
2419 West Main St.
Tupelo 38803

Final Touch Beauty School
832 Hwy. 19 N
Meridian 39307

KC's School of Hair Design
37 Lafayette St.
Pontotoc 38863

The Shirley Little Academy of
   Cosmetology
4725 I-55 N
Jackson 39206

MISSOURI

Academy of Beauty Culture
401 First St.
Kennett 63857

Career Beauty School
1821 Dunn Rd.
Florissant 63033-6116

Chillicothe Beauty Academy
505 Elm
Chillicothe 64601

Columbia College of Hairstyling
1729 West Broadway
Columbia 65201

Elaine Steven Beauty School
2208 Chambers Rd.
Saint Louis 63136

Jerry's School of Hairstyling
217 North Ninth St.
Columbia 65201

Missouri Beauty Academy
201 South Washington St.
Farmington 63640

New Dimensions Beauty School
1905 Vine St.
Kansas City 64108

Sainte Genevieve Beauty College
755 Market St.
Sainte Genevieve 63670

Sikeston Beauty College
127 Kingswau Mall
Sikeston 63801

NEBRASKA

Bahner College of Hairstyling
1660 North Grant
Fremont 68025

Capitol Beauty School, Inc., South
3339 L St.
Omaha 68107

Capitol School of Hairstyling West
2819 South 125th Ave.
Omaha 68144

Dr. Welbes College of Massage Therapy
2602 J St.
Omaha 68107

Omaha School of Massage Therapy
7905 L St.
Omaha 68127

NEVADA

Nevada Jewelry Manufacturing School
953 East Sahara B27
Las Vegas 89104

NEW HAMPSHIRE

Michael's School of Hair Design
533 Elm St.
Manchester 03101

New England School of Hair Design,
   Inc.
Interchange Dr.
West Lebanon 03784

NEW JERSEY

Capri Institute of Hair Design
268 Brick Blvd.
Brick 08723

Capri Institute of Hair Design
1595 Main Ave.
Clifton 07011

Capri Institute of Hair Design
660 North Michigan Ave.
Kenilworth 07033

Capri Institute of Hair Design
475 High Mountain Rd.
North Haledon 07508

Capri Institute of Hair Design
615 Winter Ave.
Paramus 07652

Concorde School of Hair Design,
Wanamassa
Rte. 35 and Sunset Ave.
Wanamassa 07712

Creative Designs Institute
4530 Hwy. 9 S
Howell 07731

PB School of Beauty Culture, Inc.
110 Monmouth St.
Gloucester 08030

NEW MEXICO

Aladdin Beauty College 22
108 South Union Ave.
Roswell 88201

Eddy County Beauty College
1115 West Mermod St.
Carlsbad 88220

Hollywood Beauty School
7915 Menaul Blvd. NE
Albuquerque 87110

Monte's Academy of Cosmetology 1
1515 Florida
Alamagordo 88310

Monte's Academy of Cosmetology 2
1306 Schofield Ln.
Farmington 87401

Montrose Beauty College, Inc.
4020 Peggy Rd.
Rio Rancho 87124

Olympian University of Cosmetology
1810 East Tenth St.
Alamogordo 88310

NEW YORK

Fashion Institute of Technology
227 West 27th St.
New York 10001

Gloria Francis School of Makeup
Artistry, Ltd.
Two Nelson Ave.
Hicksville 11801

NORTH CAROLINA

Brand's College of Beauty Culture
4900B Old Pineville Rd.
Charlotte 28217

Fayetteville Beauty College
2018 Fort Bragg Rd.
Fayetteville 28303

Hair Stylist Academy of Cosmetology
807 Corporation Pkwy.
Winston-Salem 27127

South Eastern College of Beauty Culture
1535 Elizabeth Ave.
Charlotte 28204

NORTH DAKOTA

Hairdesigners Academy
2011 South Washington St.
Grand Forks 58201

OHIO

Alexander's School of Floral Design
25780 Miles Rd.
Bedford Heights 44146

Fairview Beauty Academy
22610 Lorain Rd.
Fairview Park 44126

Gerber's Akron Beauty School
1686 West Market St.
Akron 44313

Grace College of Cosmetology
6807 Pearl Rd.
Middleburg Heights 44130

International Beauty School
1285 Som Center Rd.
Mayfield Heights 44124

Ohio College of Massotherapy, Inc.
1018 Kenmore Blvd.
Akron 44314

Ohio State Beauty Academy
57 Town Square
Lima 45801

Paramount Beauty Academy
917 Gallia St.
Portsmouth 45662

Rocco's School of Hair Skin and Nails
36212 Euclid Ave.
Willoughby 44094

OKLAHOMA

Alva Beauty Academy
503 Oklahoma Blvd.
Alva 73717

American Beauty College, Inc.
7337 South Western
Oklahoma City 73139

American Beauty Institute
123 West Main
Ardmore 73401

Central State Beauty Academy
8442 Northwest Expwy.
Oklahoma City 73162

Claremore Beauty College
200 North Cherokee
Claremore 74017

Owasso Beauty College, Inc.
108 West First Ave.
Owasso 74055

Paul's Beauty College
5912 Northwest 38th
Oklahoma City 73122

Sand Springs Beauty College
P.O. Box 504
Sand Springs 74063

Shampoo Academy of Hair
2630 West Britton Rd.
Oklahoma City 73120

OREGON

Academy of Hair Design, Inc.
305 Court NE
Salem 97301

Astoria Beauty College
1180 Commercial St.
Astoria 97103

College of Hair Design Careers
3322 Lancaster Dr. NE
Salem 97305-1354

East West College of the Healing Arts
812 Southwest 10
Portland 97205

Pendleton College of Hair Design
326 Main St.
Pendleton 97801

Phagan's Beauty College
142 South Second St.
Corvallis 97333

Phagan's Central Oregon Beauty College
355 Northeast Second
Bend 97701

Phagan's Medford Beauty School
2316 Poplar Dr.
Medford 97504

Phagan's School of Beauty
622 Lancaster NE
Salem 97301

Phagan's School of Hair Design
16550 Southeast McLoughlin
Portland 97267

Phagan's Tigard Beauty School
8820 Southwest Center
Tigard 97223

PENNSYLVANIA

Bucks County School of Beauty Culture
1761 Bustleton Pike
Feasterville 19047

Butler Beauty School
233 South Main St.
Butler 16001

Community College of Beaver County
One Campus Dr.
Monaca 15061

Empire Beauty School, Inc.
2302 North Fifth St.
Reading 19601

Hanover School of Beauty
408B Baltimore St.
Hanover 17331

JH Thompson Academies
2910 State St.
Erie 16508

Kittanning Beauty School
120 Market St.
Kittanning 16201

Levittown Beauty Academy
4257 Newportville Rd.
Levittown 19056

Pennsylvania School of Muscle
Therapy, Ltd.
651 South Gulph Rd.
King of Prussia 19406-3704

Pittsburgh Floral Academy
922 Western Ave.
Pittsburgh 15233

Signature Beauty Academy
129 Charles Ln.
Red Lion 17356

South Hills Beauty Academy
3269 Liberty Ave.
Pittsburgh 15216

Star Beauty Academy
1600 Nay Aug Ave., Greenridge
Shopping Center
Scranton 18509

Star Beauty Academy
34 South Main St.
Wilkes Barre 18701

RHODE ISLAND

Arthur Angelo School of Cosmetology
& Hair Design
151 Broadway
Providence 02903

SOUTH CAROLINA

Academy of Hair Technology
1530 Wade Hampton Blvd.
Greenville 29609

Avant Garde College of Cosmetology
104 George Bishop Pkwy.
Myrtle Beach 29577

Charleston Cosmetology Institute
8484 Dorchester Rd.
Charleston 29420

Chris Logan Career College
P.O. Box 261
Myrtle Beach 29578-0261

Chris Logan Career College
256 South Pike Rd.
Sumter 29150

TENNESSEE

Chattanooga Barber College
405 Market St.
Chattanooga 37402-1204

Fayetteville Beauty School
201 South Main
Fayetteville 37334-0135

The Hair Design School
3515 Ramil Rd.
Memphis 38128

Jon Nave University of Unisex
Cosmetology
5128 Charlotte Ave.
Nashville 37209

Memphis Area Vocational-Technical
School
550 Alabama Ave.
Memphis 38105-3799

Pro Way Hair School
3099 South Perkins
Memphis 38115

TEXAS

Aladdin Beauty College 30
1103 South Josey
Carrollton 75006

Amarillo College of Hairdressing, East
Campus
2400 Southeast 27th Ave.
Amarillo 79103

American Beauty College
96 Lanark St.
San Antonio 78218

The Art of Beauty College
138 West Houston St.
Jasper 75951

Barrow Beauty School
520 East Front St.
Tyler 75702

Careers Unlimited
335 South Bonner
Tyler 75702

Christine Valmy International School
7800 Harwin
Houston 77036

Circle J Beauty School
1611 Spencer Hwy.
South Houston 77587

Classic Beauty Academy
1212D South Frazier St.
Conroe 77301

Espanolas Beauty College, Inc.
2129 Lockwood Dr.
Houston 77020

Houston Training School, Woodridge
6969 Gulf Fwy.
Houston 77087

Institute of Cosmetology
434 West Parker at I-45
Houston 77091

International Beauty College
2413 West Airport Fwy.
Irving 75062

Jackson Beauty School
3931 Spencer Hwy.
Pasadena 77504

Jackson Beauty School 2
223 West Main
League City 77573

John's Beauty College
2120 Texas Ave.
Texas City 77590

Keith's Metro Hair Academy
3225C Commerce
Amarillo 79109-3275

Marshall College of Beauty
2100 East End Blvd. N
Marshall 75670

Microcomputer Technology Institute
7277 Regency Square Blvd.
Houston 77036

Sebring Career Schools
6715 Bissonnet St.
Houston 77055

Sebring Career Schools
6672 Hwy. 6 S
Houston 77083

Southwest School of Business &
Technical Careers, Cosmetology
505 East Travis
San Antonio 78205

Taylors Institute of Cosmetology
842c West Seventh Ave.
Corsicana 75110

Temple Academy of Cosmetology
Five South First St.
Temple 76501

Texas University of Cosmetology
117 Sayles St.
Abilene 79605

Tri-State Beauty School 1
6800 Gateway E
El Paso 79915

Tri-State Beauty School 2
Two and Three Rushfair Center
El Paso 79924

Tri-State Beauty School 3
5300 Doniphan
El Paso 79932

USA Hair Academy
2525 North Laurent St.
Victoria 77901

Visible Changes University
7075 Southwest Fwy.
Houston 77074

UTAH

Fran Brown College of Beauty
521 West 600 N
Layton 84041

Fran Brown College of Beauty
460 Second St.
Ogden 84404

Mary Kawakami College of Beauty
336 West Center St.
Provo 84601

Utah College of Massage Therapy
25 South 300 E
Salt Lake City 84111

VIRGINIA

Potomac Academy of Hair Design
101 West Broad St.
Falls Church 22046-4202

Virginia School of Hair Design
101 West Queensway
Hampton 23669

WASHINGTON

Academy of Hair Design
Nine South Wenatchee Ave.
Wenatchee 98801

Bellevue Beauty School
14045 Northeast 20th St.
Bellevue 98007

Christine's Institute of Hair Design
West Ten Mission
Spokane 99205

Greenwood Beauty School
8501 Greenwood N
Seattle 98103

The Hair School
3043 Hwy. 101 E
Port Angeles 98362

Lake Washington Technical College
11605 132nd Ave. NE
Kirkland 98034

Mount Vernon Beauty School
615 South First St.
Mount Vernon 98273

Paul Mitchell Endorsed Academy of
Cosmetology
14352 Lake City Way NE
Seattle 98125

Professional Beauty School
112 West Third St., P.O. Box 856
Wapato 98951-0856

Seattle Massage School-High Tide, Inc.
7120 Woodlawn Ave. NE
Seattle 98115

Stylemaster College of Hair Design
1224 Commerce
Longview 98632

WISCONSIN

Capri College
6414 Odana Rd.
Madison 53719

John Robert Powers School
700 North Water St.
Milwaukee 53202

Steven's Point Central Beauty Academy
3017 Church St.
Steven's Point 54481

WYOMING

College of Cosmetology
1211 Douglas Hwy.
Gillette 82716

Cosmetic Arts and Sciences
P.O. Box 1933
Casper 82602

Modern Trend Beauty School
1620 Thomes
Cheyenne 82001

Wright Beauty Academy
207 West 18th St.
Cheyenne 82001

Small Engine Repair

CALIFORNIA

California School of Neon
7075 Vineland Ave.
North Hollywood 91605

Electronics Learning Center
1225 West 17th St.
Santa Ana 92706

Santa Fe Technical College, Inc.
9820 Jersey Ave.
Santa Fe Springs 90670

COLORADO

Technical Trades Institute
2315 East Pikes Peak Ave.
Colorado Springs 80909

FLORIDA

Manatee Vocational-Technical Center
5603 34th St. W
Bradenton 34210

GEORGIA

Ben Hill-Irwin Technical Institute
P.O. Box 1069
Fitzgerald 31750

ILLINOIS

City College of Chicago, Chicago
City-Wide College
226 West Jackson Blvd.
Chicago 60606-6997

National Education Center, Bryman
Campus
4101 West 95th St.
Oak Lawn 60453-1000

Washburne Trade School
3233 West 31st St.
Chicago 60623

LOUISIANA

ITI Technical College
13944 Airline Hwy.
Baton Rouge 70817

MASSACHUSETTS

Woman's Technical Institute
1255 Boylston St.
Boston 02215

NEVADA

Las Vegas Gaming and Technical School
3030 South Highland Dr.
Las Vegas 89109-1047

NEW JERSEY

Metropolitan Technical Institute
11 Daniel Rd.
Fairfield 07004

NEW YORK

Mohawk Valley Community College
1101 Sherman Dr.
Utica 13501

Suburban Technical School
2650 Sunrise Hwy.
East Islip 11730

NORTH CAROLINA

Catawba Valley Community College
2550 Hwy. 70 SE
Hickory 28602-0699

Central Carolina Community College
1105 Kelly Dr.
Sanford 27330

OHIO

ESI Career Center
1985 North Ridge Rd. E
Lorain 44055

SOUTH CAROLINA

Midlands Aviation Corporation
1400 Jim Hamilton Blvd.
Columbia 29205

UTAH

Salt Lake Community College-Skills
Center, South City Campus
1575 South State St.
Salt Lake City 84115

VIRGINIA

Falwell Aviation
P.O. Drawer 11409
Lynchburg 24506

WISCONSIN

Blackhawk Technical College
P.O. Box 5009
Janesville 53547

Upholstering

ARIZONA

Central Arizona College
8470 North Overfield Rd.
Coolidge 85228-9778

ARKANSAS

Northwest Technical Institute
P.O. Box A
Springdale 72765

CALIFORNIA

Southern California School of Floral
Design
2964 East Yorba Linda Blvd.
Fullerton 92631

COLORADO

Columbine College
5801 West 44th Ave.
Denver 80212

GEORGIA

American School of Paperhanging
Little and Oak Sts.
Commerce 30529

ILLINOIS

American Floral Art School
529 South Wabash Ave.
Chicago 60605-1679

Washburne Trade School
3233 West 31st St.
Chicago 60623

INDIANA

Academy of Professional Floral
360 Market Plaza
Greenwood 46142

KANSAS

Kansas School of Floral Design
826 Iowa St.
Lawrence 66044-1783

Liberal Area Vocational Technical
School
P.O. Box 1599
Liberal 67905-1599

LOUISIANA

Delta School of Business and
Technology
517 Broad St.
Lake Charles 70601

MASSACHUSETTS

New England School of Floral Design
88 West Main St.
Norton 02766

Rittners School of Floral Design
345 Marlborough St.
Boston 02115

NEVADA

Ikendeo Floral Arts
2162 North Lamb Blvd.
Las Vegas 89110

NEW JERSEY

Creative Designs Institute
4530 Hwy. 9 S
Howell 07731

NORTH CAROLINA

Catawba Valley Community College
2550 Hwy. 70 SE
Hickory 28602-0699

OHIO

Alexander's School of Floral Design
25780 Miles Rd.
Bedford Heights 44146

PENNSYLVANIA

Pittsburgh Floral Academy
922 Western Ave.
Pittsburgh 15233

TENNESSEE

Memphis Area Vocational-Technical
School
550 Alabama Ave.
Memphis 38105-3799

TEXAS

Lee College
511 South Whiting St.
Baytown 77520-4703

WASHINGTON

Career Floral Design Institute
13200 Northup Way
Bellevue 98005

Lake Washington Technical College
11605 132nd Ave. NE
Kirkland 98034

Index

All jobs mentioned in this volume are listed and cross-referenced in the index. Entries that appear in all capital letters have separate occupational profiles. For example, APPLIANCE SERVICE WORKER, APPRAISER, BARBER AND HAIRSTYLIST, and so on are profiles in this volume. Entries that are not capitalized refer to jobs that do not have a separate profile but for which information is given.

Under some capitalized entries there is a section entitled "Profile includes." This lists all jobs that are mentioned in the profile. For example, in the case of PET CARE WORKER, two jobs that are described in the profile are: Animal breeder and Handler.

Some entries are followed by a job title in parentheses after the page number on which it can be found. This job title is the occupational profile in which the entry is discussed. For instance, the Animal breeder entry is followed by the profile title (Pet care worker).

Photographic Credits

Earl Dotter 29, 58, 75, 88; Tom Dunham 82; Robert Matthews 51, 53; Sara Matthews 49, 61; Martha Tabor 1, 3, 7, 32, 34, 47, 56, 69, 77, 79, 84, 86, 92, 99, 100, 104, 108, 110, 113; The Terry Wild Studio 31, 37, 43, 45; USDA-ARS 72, 97, 106; Visual Education Corporation 55, 67; Shirley Zeiberg 8, 40, 65, 94, 115